Education for Intercultural Citizenship

LANGUAGES FOR INTERCULTURAL COMMUNICATION AND EDUCATION
Editors: Michael Byram, *University of Durham, UK*
Alison Phipps, *University of Glasgow, UK*

The overall aim of this series is to publish books which will ultimately inform learning and teaching, but whose primary focus is on the analysis of intercultural relationships, whether in textual form or in people's experience. There will also be books which deal directly with pedagogy, with the relationships between language learning and cultural learning, between processes inside the classroom and beyond. They will all have in common a concern with the relationship between language and culture, and the development of intercultural communicative competence.

Other Books in the Series
Developing Intercultural Competence in Practice
    Michael Byram, Adam Nichols and David Stevens (eds)
Intercultural Experience and Education
    Geof Alred, Michael Byram and Mike Fleming (eds)
Critical Citizens for an Intercultural World: Foreign Language Education as Cultural Politics
    Manuela Guilherme
How Different Are We? Spoken Discourse in Intercultural Communication
    Helen Fitzgerald
Audible Difference: ESL and Social Identity in Schools
    Jennifer Miller
Context and Culture in Language Teaching and Learning
    Michael Byram and Peter Grundy (eds)
An Intercultural Approach to English language Teaching
    John Corbett
Critical Pedagogy: Political Approaches to Language and Intercultural Communication
    Alison Phipps and Manuela Guilherme (eds)
Vernacular Palaver: Imaginations of the Local and Non-native Languages in West Africa
    Moradewun Adejunmobi
Foreign Language Teachers and Intercultural Competence: An International Investigation
    Lies Sercu with Ewa Bandura, Paloma Castro, Leah Davcheva, Chryssa Laskaridou, Ulla Lundgren, María del Carmen Méndez García and Phyllis Ryan
Language and Culture: Global Flows and Local Complexity
    Karen Risager
Living and Studying Abroad: Research and Practice
    Michael Byram and Anwei Feng (eds)

Other Books of Interest
Age, Accent and Experience in Second Language Acquisition
    Alene Moyer
Language Teachers, Politics and Cultures
    Michael Byram and Karen Risager

For more details of these or any other of our publications, please contact:
Multilingual Matters, Frankfurt Lodge, Clevedon Hall,
Victoria Road, Clevedon, BS21 7HH, England
http://www.multilingual-matters.com

LANGUAGES FOR INTERCULTURAL COMMUNICATION AND EDUCATION 13
Series Editors: Michael Byram and Alison Phipps

Education for Intercultural Citizenship

Concepts and Comparisons

Edited by

Geof Alred, Mike Byram and Mike Fleming

MULTILINGUAL MATTERS LTD
Clevedon • Buffalo • Toronto

Library of Congress Cataloging in Publication Data
Education for Intercultural Citizenship: Concepts and Comparisons/Edited by Geof
Alred, Mike Byram and Mike Fleming.
Languages for Intercultural Communication and Education: 13
Includes bibliographical references and index.
1. Citizenship–Study and teaching–Cross-cultural studies. 2. Multicultural
education–Cross-cultural studies. I. Alred, Geof. II. Byram, Michael. III. Fleming,
Michael (Michael P.) IV. Series.
LC1091.E464 2006
370.11' 5–dc22   2006014471

British Library Cataloguing in Publication Data
A catalogue entry for this book is available from the British Library.

ISBN 1-85359-919-0 / EAN 978-1-85359-919-4 (hbk)
ISBN 1-85359-918-2 / EAN 978-1-85359-918-7 (pbk)

Multilingual Matters Ltd
UK: Frankfurt Lodge, Clevedon Hall, Victoria Road, Clevedon BS21 7HH.
USA: UTP, 2250 Military Road, Tonawanda, NY 14150, USA.
Canada: UTP, 5201 Dufferin Street, North York, Ontario M3H 5T8, Canada.

Typeset by Datapage Ltd.
Printed and bound in Great Britain by the Cromwell Press Ltd.

Contents

The Contributors

Geof Alred is a BPS Chartered Psychologist, counsellor trainer, counsellor in the UK National Health Service and in private practice, and former university student counsellor. His research interests include metaphorical understanding, language in therapy, mentoring and intercultural experience, in particular the experience and long-term significance of student residence abroad.

Michael Byram is Professor of Education at Durham University. He first taught French and German at secondary-school level and in adult education in an English comprehensive community school. Since being appointed to a post in teacher education at the University of Durham in 1980, he has carried out research into the education of linguistic minorities, foreign language education and student residence abroad. His publications include *Teaching and Assessing Intercultural Communicative Competence, Language Teachers, Politics and Cultures* (with Karen Risager) and *Intercultural Experience and Education* (edited with G. Alred and M. Fleming), and he is the editor of the *Routledge Encyclopedia of Language Teaching and Learning*. He is a Programme Adviser to the Council of Europe Language Policy Division, and is currently interested in language education policy and the politics of language teaching.

Anwei Feng teaches and supervises Education Doctorate and PhD students in the School of Education at the University of Durham. His research interests include intercultural studies in education, bilingualism, international business communication and TESOL. He has published a number of journal articles and co-written or co-edited two books in these areas. Currently, he is leading a research project on synergetic culture focusing on experiences of students from Confucian heritage cultures studying in the UK and is editing a Special Issue on Chinese bilingualism for the *International Journal of Bilingual Education and Bilingualism*.

Mike Fleming spent 14 years teaching in schools before joining the School of Education in Durham in 1988. He spent five years as director of the initial teaching training secondary course and a further five years as

Director of Initial Teacher Training before assuming his present responsibility as Director of Research. His publications include three books on the teaching of drama and two books on the teaching of English. He has also edited books on interculturalism. His teaching is now largely focused on MA courses (Arts in Education) and doctorate supervision. His research interests are in the area of the teaching of English and drama, aesthetics and arts education, and intercultural education.

María del Carmen Méndez García is a lecturer at the Department of Filologia Inglesa, Universidad de Jaen. She was awarded a predoctoral I + D scholarship by the Spanish Ministry of Education (1997–2000) and has undertaken research in the cultural component in EFL material and intercultural competence and intercultural communication. She is the author of the book *Los Aspectos Socioculturales en los Libros de Inglés de Bachillerato* and co-author of the book *Foreign Language Teachers and Intercultural Competence* (Multilingual Matters). Individually or as a co-author, she has also published articles in, among others, *Intercultural Education*, *Journal of Multilingual and Multicultural Development*, *Language and Education* and *Language and Intercultural Communication*. She is currently participating in two international projects: 'International Competence for Professional Mobility', Leonardo da Vinci Programmes; and 'Intercultural Competence for Professional Mobility ECML', European Centre for Modern Languages, Council of Europe.

Gerhard Himmelmann just retired from his chair as Professor of Political Science and Citizenship Education ('political education') at the Technical University of Braunschweig, Germany. His special interest is to transform 'political' education in Germany into a broader sense of democratic citizenship education, which includes more modern, practical, and experience-based teaching and learning democracy in schools. He is speaker of the section Political Education in the German Society of Political Science and board member of the new association German Society of Democracy Pedagogy. His research interests focus on modern challenges of individualisation in contrast to globalisation and the demands of social cohesion, democratic cooperation, and mental consciousness for democracy in schools. His theoretical references go back to the inspiring works of John Dewey on Democracy and Education.

Manuela Guilherme is a senior researcher at the Center for Social Studies, University of Coimbra, Portugal. She received a PhD in Education from the University of Durham, Great Britain. Previously, she taught both at university and secondary-school levels and is an experienced teacher educator. She is the author of *Critical Citizens for an Intercultural World: Foreign Language Education as Cultural Politics* (Multilingual Matters, 2000) and coeditor of *Critical Pedagogy: Political Approaches to Language and Intercultural Communication* (Multilingual Matters, 2002). She is currently coordinating and participating in two European projects in the field of intercultural education, namely: (a) ICOPROMO: Intercultural Competence for Professional Mobility (Programme Leonardo da Vinci and the European Centre of Modern Languages, Council of Europe); and (b) INTERACT: Intercultural Active Citizenship Education (VI European Framework, Priority 7, and Fundação Calouste Gulbenkian). She is a member of the Editorial Board of the journal *Language and Intercultural Communication*.

Wing On Lee is at present a professor at the Faculty of Education and Social Work and Director of International Development at the College of Humanities of Social Sciences, University of Sydney. He is also Honorary Professor of the Hong Kong Institute of Education. He has been involved in research, teaching and teacher training in the areas of civic and moral education for over 10 years. In Hong Kong, he started the M.Ed. in Values Education programme at the University of Hong Kong in 1994. He participated in drafting the 1996 Guidelines on Civic Education in School and the 1998 Civic Education Syllabus, and was twice appointed to the Committee on Promotion of Civic Education in Hong Kong by the Hong Kong Government. He has published extensively in the areas of civic and moral education, including *Citizenship in Asia and the Pacific*.

Stewart Martin's background is in secondary education, where he worked for over 30 years, and in educational consultancy in the UK and Canada. He has also served as a company director in the private sector. He moved into university research and teaching in 1999 and is currently Director of the EdD at Durham University School of Education, an international doctoral programme taught in the UK and overseas. His research interests are in the role of organisational leadership in bringing about educational change, the educational use of computer technology, computers and traditional approaches to learning, and the relationship between cognitive/learning styles and technology.

Lynne Parmenter is a professor at Waseda University, Tokyo, Japan. She has lived and taught in Japan for the past 13 years, at junior high school and university levels. Her research focuses on the relationships between education, citizenship and identities, particularly in intercultural and global spheres.

José Manuel Pureza is a Professor of International Relations at the University of Coimbra. He teaches international law, human rights and global governance. He is also a researcher at the Centre for Social Studies, where he coordinates the Peace Studies Group. His fields of research include cultural peace and the challenge of multiculturalism to human rights. He is author of *Para uma cultura da paz* [Towards a Culture of Peace] (Coimbra, 2001) and *O património comum da humanidade. Rumo a um Direito Internacional da solidariedade?* [The Common Heritage of Humankind: Towards an International Law of Solidarity?] (Oporto, 1998).

Phyllis Ryan is a professor in the Department of Applied Linguistics of the Center for Foreign Language Study at the Universidad Nacional Autónoma de Mexico in Mexico City, Mexico. She has taught courses in intercultural communication, sociolinguistics, the politics of language and qualitative research methodology in the Master's degree in applied linguistics at this university while also directing doctoral students in the areas of intercultural communication and the maintenance and displacement of indigenous languages in Mexico. Her interests involve research with the Mexican participants in the Programa para la Mobilidad en la Educacion Superior en America del Norte (PROMESAN), a tri-country grant offering students the opportunity to participate in academic exchanges with universities in Canada, Mexico and the USA.

Maria Walat studied English at the Adam Mickiewicz University, Poznań, Poland and taught it for a number of years before becoming a teacher of British and American studies at the Teacher Training College of Foreign Languages. She then took a PhD in Applied Linguistics and is an adjunct at the English Philology Department, Kazimierz Wielki University, Bydgoszcz, where apart from cultural studies, she also teaches in the masters' degree programme. Her research interests include intercultural education, material development for British studies and implementing of the notion of otherness and elements of Critical Theory in the teaching of foreign language culture.

Leung Sai Wing completed his PhD in sociology, specialising in political sociology, at the Australian National University. His current research is on social indicators, sociology of food, and identity in Hong Kong. He has been teaching in the Department of Applied Social Sciences of The Hong Kong Polytechnic University. Teaching areas include methods of research and Hong Kong society. His major publications include *The Making of an Alienated Generation: The Political Socialization of Secondary School Students in Transitional Hong Kong* (Ashgate, 1997), 'Social

Construction of Hong Kong Identity: A Partial Account' in *Indicators of Social Development: Hong Kong 1997* (Hong Kong Institute of Asia-Pacific Studies) and 'Tea Café and Hong Kong People's Identity' in *Hong Kong Cultural Studies* (Hong Kong University Press, 2006).

Introduction

Being Intercultural

The main focus of this book is to apply theory and concepts of interculturality/of being intercultural to citizenship education. Interculturality is a concept that is receiving increasing attention as societies become ever more multicultural in composition. Geographical mobility is frequent and a cause of concern for some people, as they see apparently homogeneous societies changing fundamentally in less than a lifetime. What appeared to be mono-ethnic, -cultural and -lingual societies are now complex multi-ethnic, -cultural and -lingual polities, which in turn become hosts to 'new arrivals', the strangers who 'come today and stay tomorrow', as Simmel put it a century ago. A response is expected by all concerned – hosts and guests and their political representatives – not least from education systems, which, as ever, are expected to be readily managed and changed to meet new challenges and provide solutions. Thus labels such as a 'multicultural education', 'pluralist education' or 'intercultural education' refer to a range of responses.

Our understanding of interculturality, of being intercultural, has developed mainly from traditions of foreign language education but has been enriched from other disciplines including counselling psychology, the pedagogy of drama and literature, and ethnography. We have pursued this process of enrichment in an earlier collection of papers (Alred *et al.*, 2003), where we emphasised that being intercultural involves:

- questioning the conventions and values we have unquestioningly acquired as if they were natural;
- experiencing the Otherness of Others of different social groups, moving from one of the many in-groups to which we belong to one of the many out-groups that contrast with them;
- reflecting on the relationships among groups and the experience of those relationships;
- analysing our intercultural experience and acting upon the analysis.

In applying our theory of interculturality to citizenship education we shall see a stronger focus on realising the consequences of being

1

intercultural through action, as education for citizenship involves encouraging learners to become active citizens prepared to engage with the different communities to which they belong.

Because citizenship education is usually related to and even synonymous with education into a national identity, and allegiance to a nation-state, it is also important to state clearly from the beginning what relationship we see between education for interculturality and education for citizenship in a nation-state. What we are advocating is a particular way of being, of having a national identity – of having for example an intercultural French, or Chinese, or Norwegian identity. We are not suggesting that people should acquire further identities, additional to or replacing national identity, in the form of 'global' or 'cosmopolitan' citizenship. If we were, we would have to explain the relationship between the two social identities involved and the two groups – the national group and the group of 'all human beings' – from which national and global identity and citizenship derive.

On the other hand the concept of being, for example, an intercultural Chinese is not simple. For the experience of being intercultural is challenging and not always comfortable, in any social identity – e.g. as an intercultural able-bodied person vis à vis a disabled, or a Northerner vis à vis a Southerner, or a West Coaster vis à vis an East Coaster. In any of these identities, being intercultural involves questioning the taken-for-granted conventions within which one lives, seeking to empathise with the experience of others, reflecting on the impact of this upon oneself and one's own identities, allegiances to and experiences of one's various groups. This can be an unsettling experience. It involves a disappointment of the narcissistic assumption of the superiority of 'us' over 'them'. It challenges us to be willing to become involved with Otherness, to take up others' perspectives by reconstructing their perspectives for ourselves, and understanding them from within. Being an intercultural Chinese, then, is challenging and may be perceived as a threat to simply being Chinese, even though we want to argue that it will provide a deeper and enriched understanding of one's national identity, not undermine it. For it does not imply abandoning our own perspectives but rather becoming more conscious of them.

Education for Intercultural Citizenship

As we argue that intercultural citizenship is not an alternative to national or other kinds of citizenship (for example European citizenship), the potential impact of our position on education for citizenship needs

to be examined, and we have chosen to do this from a comparative perspective, which is in itself a characteristic of being intercultural. We have asked our fellow authors to compare citizenship education in two or more countries, or to present a case study, in the light of a set of criteria that operationalise our understanding of being intercultural. Readers can then compare for themselves.

We need to look at citizenship education as it exists in different countries because an intercultural perspective raises questions about educational practices that take too much for granted. It questions what is often unquestioned, for instance the assumption that confidence and self-esteem for the individual are always and inevitably positive. It does so by juxtaposing these notions with humility and conformity. By juxtaposition with East Asian democracies, it questions too the facile claim that Western democracy is the culmination of progress, which has been and continues to be disseminated to the rest of the world.

An intercultural perspective on citizenship education also identifies ethical issues more clearly. There are questions for the teacher about the moral stance and judgements the individual learner makes about others and although such questions are already met by teachers of citizenship education, they are related to 'our' communities, to the in-groups whence we take our identities. An intercultural perspective requires reflection on comparative morality. Teachers also have to ask themselves whether they should encourage action, and whether they should participate in action inside and/or outside the classroom. A focus on education for intercultural citizenship places this in the broader context of political action in, for and with the communities of which learners are members. An intercultural perspective thus implies that moral debate and political action should take place in all cross-community groupings – groups of able-bodied and disabled, groups of males and females, for example, which are intercultural groups but not visibly so. An international cross-community project however is visibly intercultural and makes participants aware, by comparison, of the intercultural nature of male/female and other groups. The literature in social psychology suggests this will lead to the creation of new identities and adherences, reducing the prejudice that otherwise exists between groups.

These are the challenges and suggestions for the classroom that are raised in this book by comparative study, but they are also questions that need to be addressed in curriculum design and syllabuses, as will be evident from our case studies.

The Structure and Argument of this Book

We realise that many readers will read some chapters and not others, searching, for example, for information on a particular country. The book is however more than a collection of chapters, and even the reader who selects only some chapters ought be aware of the function of each within the whole.

Put briefly, the purpose of the book is to develop from a theory of interculturality a concept of 'intercultural citizenship', and to investigate if and how education systems in several countries are moving towards a citizenship education that will include the development of intercultural citizenship in young people.

We do not see this as the exclusive purpose of education for citizenship – in whatever form it takes: permeation or specific subject – as will be evident from our discussion above, but we believe that it must be a crucial dimension of education for citizenship in all education systems, and it is for this reason that we have included case studies from East Asia, from Europe and from North and Central America.

The book has three parts. The first deals with questions of identity and its complexity and the difficulties this poses for education for (national) citizenship. The second deals with the specificity of concepts of citizenship education and the difficulties of translating both literally and metaphorically from one context and language to another. The third puts forward a definition of intercultural citizenship that is sensitive to complexities of identity, of concepts and of translation, and analyses the degree to which intercultural citizenship is present or emergent in contemporary education systems.

In Part 1, the first chapter, by Ryan, demonstrates the complexity of identities and challenges any simple concept of national identity. Ryan does this by close analysis of ethnographic data from interviews with several 'Mexicans', and shows that this simple designation of Mexican is inadequate in representing the experiences and processes of identification her interviewees have undergone.

In the second chapter, Leung and Lee write about Hong Kong and the significance of language as a marker of identity. They demonstrate how a language can become a locus of resistance to the imposition of a political identity, whether it is a colonial identity embodied in English or a 'neocolonial' imposition of a Chinese identity with a new language, Putonghua, from mainland China. In doing so, they contrast Hong Kong and Singapore. In both locations there has been a search for a lingua franca that will draw people together within the geopolitical space in question. In the first case English has been rejected, though its usefulness in a globalised economy is acknowledged, whereas in the second case English has been embraced as one of the tools for creating the unity of identity in a country of mixed ethnicities.

In the third chapter, Martin and Feng focus on Singapore in more detail and argue that this is a case where a sense of identification can be deliberately and forcefully created. They show how English has been part of this process, as a symbol of a shared identity, reinforced by its instrumental value in a global marketplace. They also show how the spectre of external threat has been used to strengthen identification with Singapore, and how the education system has been and is at the heart of this process.

The chapters in Part 1 thus remind us that national identity and citizenship are two very complex terms, that education for citizenship has to be understood in its historical context and that language is a powerful indicator of citizenship and/or identity that can be manipulated by political authorities but also resisted by populations.

In Part 2, the question of language is addressed from a different perspective. The two chapters in this part demonstrate the difficulty but also the necessity of an understanding of the terminology of citizenship education. Himmelmann analyses models and concepts of citizenship and education for democracy in Western Europe and the USA. There are underlying similarities in the models of objectives proposed in Britain, the USA and Germany but there are also significant differences. Here again, it is only a historical analysis that can provide understanding and overcome the difficulties of translation. Himmelmann remarks from the beginning how he is aware of these issues because he is writing in English whereas he normally writes in German. His chapter is thus, *inter alia*, a display of the characteristics of the intercultural person able to mediate meanings from different languages.

Feng is in a similar but not identical position as a native speaker of Chinese who usually writes in English. His chapter pursues the theme of elucidating terminology, this time in Chinese, without which an understanding of education and citizenship in China is not possible. He also argues that existing approaches are being challenged by a new perspective on China and by new rationales for citizenship education. The most recent of these, based on a concept of interculturality, is scarcely evident in practice in the education system but present in the academic discourse which is seeking to instigate change.

The purpose of Part 3 is to define and illustrate the concept of intercultural citizenship, while acknowledging the difficulties of identities, of concepts and language and the importance of a historical awareness of the development of education systems presented in Parts 1 and 2. In doing so, we do not propose that young people should acquire a new identity, as we said above. We are proposing a way of dealing with intercultural experience within citizenship education, adding a new dimension to whatever kind of citizenship education already exists.

The first two chapters introduce the concept. Byram and Fleming write from starting points in different areas of the curriculum, Modern Languages and English respectively, but both discuss the central issue of citizenship education: values and morality. Byram places this in the context of determining objectives and Fleming demonstrates the relationship with aesthetic and moral education.

A statement of 'axioms and characteristics' of education for intercultural citizenship, which evolved from a symposium at the University of Durham in 2004, can be found in the Appendix. They act both as definition for planning of education for intercultural citizenship in whatever form deemed desirable, and as criteria for evaluating the degree of intercultural citizenship education already present in existing education systems.

The following chapters then analyse particular education systems on the basis of these criteria/axioms:

- Parmenter writes on Japan and, following the criteria closely, comes to the conclusion that Japan still falls short of the criteria with its strong emphasis on national identity in citizenship and with little indication of any elements of education for intercultural citizenship.
- Walat focuses on the importance of an understanding of a society under change – the end of a centralised authoritarian system; she too follows the criteria and demonstrates how a close analysis of curricula – combining qualitative and quantitative approaches – can be used to analyse an education system, in this case Poland; her conclusion is that there are few indicators of the characteristics and axioms currently present and therefore she ends with suggestions as to how the situation might be changed.
- Méndez García presents citizenship education in Spain where the complexity of autonomous regions – an outcome of the end of another authoritarian regime, under Franco – within a national framework is analysed and the conclusion is that there is more education *about* citizenship than the development of active citizens in an intercultural spirit, and she too suggests a way forward.

- Guilherme *et al.* present a third country in transition as a consequence of revolution – the Carnation revolution of Portugal – and a society experiencing major change from emigration to immigration; these authors show the importance of the interaction with the past in understanding how Portugal has, at least in its policies, pursued an education which has strong elements of interculturality at its heart even if practice does not always follow policy.

Four of our cases in Part 3, and Hong Kong and Singapore in Part 1, are studies of societies in transition, and in fact emerging from some kind of subjugation, to a colonial power or a dictator or a dictatorial regime. Some of them have developed education for citizenship that reflects the emancipation or at least has the potential to do so and to promote a national citizenship of free, participating and active citizens. They are all moving towards the intercultural rationality that promotes intercultural citizenship, although to different degrees. The Singapore study shows how it is possible to accompany emancipation from colonialism with a new centralised and technical education for citizenship that does not allow freedom but creates and enforces a strong sense of national identity and fear of Otherness. Although it is not in the same situation as the others – unless one argues that it is now beginning to emerge from dominance by the USA, a colonial power in all but name – in Japan, there is nonetheless a similar emphasis on national identity, although with different origins.

We note these characteristics as tendencies and nothing more. What this book shows above all else is the danger of generalisations about education for citizenship, not least because of the problem of concepts and translations. It also suggests that any attempt to promote a new 'global' identity and a concept of global or cosmopolitan citizenship will be interpreted very differently in different circumstances. It is for this reason that we have emphasised three elements of education for intercultural citizenship: experience, reflection and action on the basis of experience, and attention to values. The latter is crucial. We have argued that a relativist perspective on values is not tenable but we recognise, not least from the diversity of our cases, that a simple universalism is not attainable either.

One way towards resolving the impasse between relativism and absolutism in matters of value is through the process of democratic debate and negotiation, which is usually considered the province of politics rather than morality. As chapters by Feng, Fleming and Himmelmann show, although the development of moral values is often thought to be important for citizenship education, this is often conceived only in terms of the inculcation of *particular* values and is often contrasted with other aspects of citizenship development such as 'political literacy'. Developing political literacy involves acquiring knowledge such as how systems of government work and skills such as the ability to argue, defend a point of view and negotiate towards consensus. In contrast, the development of values is often seen in individual rather than communal terms and as the acquisition of values that are fixed and universal. However ideas of 'absolute' and 'relative' values are not helpful here; moral values evolve within communities and need to be resolved and negotiated in dialogue. It is in this sense that the development of moral values and the political process are not as far apart as sometimes assumed. An intercultural approach does not mean abandoning value positions but it means recognising the importance of understanding and negotiation. It also involves developing insight into how legal and political processes both nationally and internationally are significant for individuals within a society; this in turn has important implications for education.

Part 1
Identity and Citizenship

Chapter 1
Interculturality, Identity and Citizenship Education in Mexico

PHYLLIS RYAN

Introduction

The purpose of this chapter is to raise some questions about the relationships between identity, interculturality and citizenship education. The focus will be on Mexico, a unique country with abundant cultural diversity, a developing country with a 1000-mile-long border with its economically powerful northern neighbour, the USA; Mexico is a country with complex multilingualism and rich potential for the development of interculturality from the learning of foreign languages. At the same time, the complex identities present in Mexico are a test case of how citizenship education needs to take identity issues into consideration. In many countries, citizenship programmes, like the rest of the curriculum, are based on the assumptions of a homogeneous nation-state, a myth that is convenient but false in most countries, not least in Mexico. By considering the Mexican case we shall raise questions that all education for citizenship has to address, and lay the ground for the development of intercultural citizenship presented in other parts of this book.

In contrast with the efforts of some education systems in Europe to work with intercultural communicative competence, intercultural education and intercultural citizenship in foreign language education, Mexico is only just initiating efforts to structure an intercultural education that will meet its needs. At first glance it might be said that intercultural education is in its infancy in Mexico. At the level of formal definition, this might be true, but within the linguistic/cultural composition of society sporadic attempts have been made to address this problem, starting from efforts of the classroom teacher in a struggle toward interculturality of untutored indigenous inhabitants in *provincia* forced on them by circumstances. The latter, it should be mentioned, is almost unknown in contemporary Europe. It can be argued that features of interculturality have been part of the Mexican multilingual/multicultural scene for centuries, but the educational scene today is in the process of establishing positions and policies. Muñoz Cruz (2001) describes the four types of programmes of the Secretaría de Educación Publica de México aimed at indigenous people, of which intercultural education is the most recent. Bilingual education (*educación bilingüe*) in the 1930s pursued a policy of integration of indigenous groups into the mainstream *mestizo* society. This paradigm was replaced by *educación bilingue bicultural* based on diversity as a resource. The third orientation is *educación intercultural bilingue*, which includes indigenous education and multicultural education. The paradigm sees diversity as a right, and this discussion will consider diverse identities and how they aid in understanding the issues intercultural education addresses.

Intercultural Identity: Sibilina

What are the features of intercultural education in the social context of Mexico, where foreign language learning, especially university education, contributes greatly to Mexico's entry into the international arena of globalisation? Extremes play a role in national identity and larger group identity in Mexico. Extremes of wealth and poverty are seen in urban and rural population centres throughout the Republic. Geographical location also plays a large role in understanding how inhabitants are socialised into membership in cultural groups. For instance, a person from a *pueblito* (small town) or a large urban centre such as Mexico City, Guadalajara or Monterrey projects different images or identities. For instance, a *chilango* (Mexico City resident) visiting a *pueblo* is automatically characterised as a *chilango* of the Federal District at the sight of his car and licence plates. At the same time the *pueblito* resident, when talking about someone from the next *pueblo*, can be heard saying: 'He isn't a Mexican, he wasn't born here!'

The images people project are also ones that Mexicans have of themselves and are ones that are strongly held. Consider Sibilina, a Zapotec woman whose dual identity as a Mexican and as a Zapotec illustrates the issues in practice. Sibilina lives in Mexico City and works at both the National Autonomous University of Mexico (in the Departmento de Bienes Artísticos y Culturales de Patrimonio Universitario [Department of Artistic and Cultural Artefacts of University Heritage]) and at a government research centre, the Centro de Investigación y Estudios Superiores in Antropología Social (CIESAS) [Centre for Research and Studies in Anthropology]. She received a degree in

Oriental Studies from the University of Arizona where her sister and brother-in-law, an anthropologist, live.

I first met Sibilina on the steps of the Sala Netzahuacoyoatl auditorium, a central spot in the cultural centre of the National Autonomous University where we work. We sat on the stone steps to talk about how she perceives interculturality and how she describes her cultural identity. She immediately talked about her youth growing up in a small village, San Francisco del Norte, in the high mountains of Oaxaca and her life up to her present life in Mexico City. She strongly identifies herself as a Zapotec woman and also with her Zapotec language. She longs to return to her village to live. The interview focused on the question of interculturality and how her life is related to her perceptions of it.

Her father and his experience working in the USA strongly influenced his life and the lives of the members of her family. She recalled how her father left when she was very young to work in Omaha, Nebraska:

> I think that a lot had to do with the fact that my father – I don't remember if it was the exact year I was born or a year later – What happened was that my father went to the United States and unfortunately he got sick there. He was in a hospital in Omaha, Nebraska. It was not a happy experience, but in any case this experience of contact with another culture, with other people, widened his vision of the world very much. And when he came back, at that time many children were dying of epidemics that were devastating the children. My father was not ready to have us die and said to my mother, 'Would you like to see them, even if it is only from time to time, or would you rather take flowers to their graves?' And my mother had to say 'No. It would be better for us to leave [the village].' At that time my mother was totally against us going to Oaxaca. She would cry for days and days. She said her favourite phrase of that time to my father. 'Tomorrow you won't have anyone who will give you a glass of water, and when you're old, there won't be anyone to give you a glass of water.' Then, my father said to her, 'Well, when that day comes you will have to give it to me.'

Sibilina said that his vision of the world and of his own life changed through his contact with the USA. She explained how the decision to leave the country and work affected her. Her father's dream was to have his children study and return to the pueblo, but he knew that this was impossible. She said that once her mother scolded them, saying that she wanted them to marry and live there, to which her father responded

'Dejales, dejales, yo prefiero verlas felices aunque sea lejos.' [Leave them alone, leave them alone, I want them to be happy, even if they are far away.] If he hadn't intervened, she thought, she would have married, stayed in the village and had many children.

She explained more about her Zapotec identity and how living with her three children in Mexico City has not changed her desire to return to her *tierra* ('homeland'), but had enriched her life. Sibilina said that she hopes that God will return her to the *sierra* ('mountains') because that is where her roots are.

> If someone asks me where I am from, someone from outside the country, or even from here ... there are people who automatically, if you say you are Zapotec, say 'Ah, from Oaxaca.' I answer, the State of Oaxaca, yes, I am from Oaxaca. Usually I do not say that I am Oaxacan, usually I say I am Zapotec from the northern *sierra* of Oaxaca. Almost always I refer myself to my community, to the sierra, not to the city of Oaxaca. Because in the city of Oaxaca I in fact, have relatives, but my home, my identity is in the *sierra*. Of course, if I am in the US and someone asks me where I am from, I do say that I am Mexican, from Mexico, but a Zapotec from the northern sierra of Oaxaca.

She illustrates the micro nature of the cultural setting in Mexico. Her desire to be open to other cultural settings and her awareness of her own values, beliefs and behaviour are evident. Her adaptability and respect for other culture(s) are visible in talking with her. She reiterates that 'Mi cultura adoro, lo valoro, porque es lo mio. No voy a cerrarme a otros culturas. No, No!' [My culture I adore, I value it because it is mine. I am not closed to other cultures, No, No!]. At the same time she is in contact with other cultures:

> It is the contact with other cultures that has brought us to what I am. There are even things that appear strange and exotic to me in the behaviour of people in my village. I recognise that there is no single way of seeing things, or perceiving things. There are so many languages and cultures. You have to see it, value it and respect it. At the same time you are expanding your vision of the world.

She adds that she believes that in some way a national culture should value and respect indigenous languages in Mexico. She herself felt she made a great error in not speaking Zapotec more with her children as they were growing up. Her daughters reproach her for not teaching them to speak Zapotec well. Her youngest daughter, Natalia, has acquired the best facility with the language and has strong ties to the *sierra*, as Sibilina does. Tone and intonation, she points out, are extremely important to the language and slight changes can cause much laughter. Natalia, her youngest, makes many funny mistakes as she speaks Zapotec in their home: 'Gracias, ya comí a mi abuelita ya mi abuelito. Le da mucha risa de mi papa.' [Thanks, but I already ate my grandmother and grandfather. It makes my father laugh.] Her children's accent is obvious to native speakers.

Sibilina ended the discussion about her family and their lives by identifying what is most important about being intercultural. She said, 'Intercultural . . . a person who is not prejudiced who can communicate with other people without being prejudiced, with people of different cultures who have different ways of thinking and doing things.'

The direct contact her father had living and working abroad she believed created a *cadena* ('chain') that each member of her family added to over the years. It has spread to her daughter now. Sibilina laughed, 'Una de mis hijas, la chiquita, dice, no hablas de la muerta, pero yo cuando me voy, voy a ir a la sierra también. Así como existe este víncula.' [One of my daughters, the youngest, says not to speak of death, but she says when I leave, I am going to the sierra also. This is how the connection exists.]

Mexican Identity, Its History and Citizenship: Francisco

To explore further the strength of identity in how Mexicans perceive of themselves and others, I turn to the perspectives of two other multicultural researchers who carry out research on indigenous languages. Francisco Brambila is a Mexican applied linguist studying Náhuatl (Aztec) dialects throughout the Republic. His direct contact with cultures outside of Mexico has been through studies in France and Canada. Harold Ormsby is also an applied linguist. He, however, was born in the USA, and lived in the north of Mexico during his childhood before spending his early adult life in California. For the past 30 years he has worked with indigenous groups throughout Mexico.

Francisco's reflections about his identity are summarised in a statement he made that is similar to Sibilina's: 'Outside of Mexico one says, "I am Mexican." Inside the country one says "I am Oaxacan" [from the state of Oaxaca] and in Oaxaca one says, "I am Zapotec".' For Francisco, the significance of his example of the Zapotec lies in Mexico's social structure and in its historical context as states were formed. A nation-state was only formed in the 19th century and people began to identify themselves with the state, an identity still strongly felt today. For Francisco identity depends on the circumstances of 'belonging' to one's social context. He used as an example a rural area in the State of Mexico where he lives:

> What happens is that it depends on the circumstances in which one speaks of 'belonging'. I live in the State of Mexico [a state bordering Mexico City] in a rural area where the political authorities of the township (there is no law, only tradition) are perceived of as necessarily being from the principal town of the township. So, saying that this person is not from here takes on a functional meaning, making him eligible or ineligible in the context of local elections. In other towns the fact that a person speaks the language of the community gives him certain rights. For example, the right to a traditional post and such a traditional post has practical benefits. The *mayordomos*[1] have the right to use a particular water-well. The usage of this water leads to economic benefits, no? In some cases it is important, in others no – for example, someone who wants to start a business in a town. In many places it is not necessary to know exactly whether he comes from the town or not. That sense of belonging depends heavily on the place and regional context. Near large cities it is very difficult to keep this type of identity. The further one is from large urban centres the more value this type of identity has.

Francisco finds a dichotomy created between being Mexican and being indigenous:

> Mexican identity is very complex. There are studies of it from different parts of the world with different focuses. It is not an identity that integrates historical, cultural, linguistic and religious aspects in one whole. Because in historical terms one aspect of Mexican identity is that it is not an identity as a member of an ethnic group. Being Mexican and being indigenous is not the same. This causes conflict.

In colonial times there were two sets of laws: one set for indigenous people and one set for white people, he explains. A labour of the 19th century was the forging of the *mestizo* ('mixed race') identity, which went along with a great increase in the number of *mestizos*. The historical figures of that century, once independence from Spain was achieved, discussed the inequality of the law and searched for a way in which a race, a culture and everything new could emerge in this new country of Mexico. Fernando points out that:

In legal everyday terms, a new tendency emerged. You can see in the census the demographic proportions of Mexicans of Spanish origin, *mestizos*, and Mexicans of indigenous origin. Throughout the 19th century this ethnic composition was modified. By the end of the 19th century the changes in the proportion of the population that was *mestizo* is impressive. It had become a massive majority. The indigenous population declined and the racially European population also. *Mestizaje* ('racial mixture') increased and was reflected in customs and culture. In the 20th century one sees a revival of indigenous aspects. For example, all Mexican mural painters recognise their pre-Hispanic past, but in a new sense. They did not simply try to revive the pre-Hispanic past, for they said, 'Let us revive elements of our pre-historic culture'.

Today indigenous elements are emerging with the impact of the Zapatistas and their 1994 movement. Attitudes are beginning to change and small minorities are no longer seen as inferior groups, but are recovering their identity. Francisco includes urban society as well:

> The Zapatista army emerged in the jungles of Chiapas, but it has a very strong influence in urban areas, even internationally. It has an influence that often is not seen in the jungle. Demonstrations by university students in the cities supporting Zapatistas are much larger than in the jungle itself. A demonstration by 2000 persons is a strong statement.

Identity and Intercultural Education: Harold

Identities as an indigenous person and as a Mexican are evolving, but local settings with their ethnic mixes still remain strong. Harold, when I asked him about his own identity, said that he was a member of a minority group in Mexico. As a member of a minority group in Mexico he points out he does not remember a day when he was monolingual. In fact, he doesn't understand not being bilingual. 'I don't say that I am born intercultural; that is a different thing. I have one culture. That's me. It's like an ideo-culture.' He finds that part of the process of being aware of one's minority status in the face of a majority society is being aware that one is multicultural:

> There is a process of our awareness of our minority status in the face of the majority society. Now, when you have education among minority members, their teachers are born multicultural even though

some were monolingual as children. Often children know that the language that they don't understand well is Spanish. In Michoacan they can distinguish between Spanish and English, the other language they come into contact with, although they have no proficiency in either one. I have had four- and five-year-olds ask me through a parent if the language I am speaking is Spanish or English. In that sense, they are born multicultural, even though in a testing sense they are monolingual. In addition, in Michoacan, with the Purépecha groups, there are bunches of them that have three languages from being very small, because relatives who come to visit them from the States have Purépecha and English.

Harold continued to explain the idea of bilingual education in Mexico, saying that it is based on a false assumption; namely, that a person is monocultural and becomes bilingual. He points out that, 'It isn't the way it works for millions of people in the world.' Moreover, he calls for intercultural/bilingual education in Mexico to encourage awareness of one's cultural mix at any age of development:

A primary goal of interculturality is to try to help them [students] be aware of the different cultures they have, however many they happen to have. I would think the first thing anyway is to be aware of your own cultural mix. Who am I? And what does my ideo-culture consist of? What are my cultural ingredients? And this is not what intercultural-bilingual education in Mexico is doing.

I think in schooling, child and adult processes are probably different. An idea might be to draw a line. To say that the cultural awareness process and cultural development process changes palpably when people cease to be child learners of language and become adult learners of language. Now, I know that is a fuzzy line, but we know that there is a line there. No one denies that there is a line. They argue about what it is about. The point here is, wherever that line happens to be, it is very individual. An individual starts to cross that line to become a cultural adult; they are becoming a linguistic adult and their learning processes change also. So when we are dealing with young kids who are still in that language acquisition time, it may well be difficult to get them to become fully aware of their cultural ingredients, just as it is difficult to get them to become aware of linguistic components.

He finds that people who are well integrated into the majority culture are better attended to by the educational system: 'The educational system is more comfortable with them. And the educational system is not comfortable with or for linguistic minorities. I think that is an absolutely fair statement, and also true in most countries of the world.' Establishing this position, he points to how indigenous teachers perceive of authorities:

> I have had Indian teachers tell me. 'Look, if we really like it they won't let us do it. So we have to do it under the water [secretly].' I have talked with teachers about publishing their proposals and they say, 'No, because if we let them know what we are really doing, they will try to stop us.' Well, they are probably right. I have been told not to say what I have seen in schools because they don't want the 'system' to feel that they have the right to stop them. I have seen that when the inspectors show up, the school changes. Sure. A *mestizo* comes in and, boom, the school changes. We all know that the minorities all over the world have their way of keeping . . . of protecting themselves from the power of the majority.

In addition to seeing Indian culture as monocultural, he states that authorities also view *mestizo* culture as the national culture (*la cultura nacional*). 'The goal of the authorities is to simplify things. The reality is not that the Indians have Indian culture and no other and that the national culture is a monolith – one monolith versus another monolith.' When asked about intercultural education, Harold maintained that interculturality is already taught with some indigenous groups: 'I think that there are Indian cultures that teach their people to be intercultural, if you like. The signs of this are very subtle, but as one interacts over time with different groups, one begins to see patterns.'

Identities as a Challenge for Citizenship Education

One's identity is formed through the process of socialisation and continues to develop depending on one's experiences in many social settings. The ideas and perceptions of the three people we have seen in this brief discussion have touched on elements that are part of the multicultural/lingual setting in Mexico and some of the identities found in this setting.

Sibilina is intense when she talks about feelings for her *tierra* that will remain strong all her life. She is aware of her family and how each member adds to the intercultural *cadena* they are creating. Aware of her identity as a Zapotec, she can also identity with larger group membership in social contexts in Mexico and outside the country. She can move

within groups and still be a Zapotec. Interculturality to her means not
having prejudices.

Francisco deals with citizenship in a more impersonal manner, relating
it strongly to identity. Identity for a Mexican is seen in relation to the
state and the history that created the state. The identity he chooses to
discuss is the regional context of the State of Mexico with the influence
of pre-historic culture and minority and majority cultural identity.

For Harold, knowledge of his cultural mix is his identity. As a
researcher who has travelled extensively throughout the Yucatan and
worked with teachers of indigenous groups in many parts of Mexico,
he feels knowledge of one's cultural mix is important for indigenous
groups. He raises strong questions about how bilingual education is
serving these groups. The reality is that the system serves the needs of
the majority *mestizo* population with little sensitivity for indigenous
bilingual education. Part of this reality he suggests is that some of the
indigenous groups teach their people to be intercultural.

When talking about indigenous groups and the tolerance they show
toward cultural groups they are in contact with, Francisco and Harold
immediately mention defence mechanisms of group members to ensure
group perpetuation and compactness. For Francisco these mechanisms
rigidly maintain a protective shell maintaining the group's existence. He
finds it difficult to apply one of the goals of interculturality, that of
stepping outside of one's culture and being able to view it and other
cultures critically, to members of indigenous Náhuatl groups with which
he is familiar. Harold, on the other hand, notes a range of awareness
shown by indigenous groups toward members of other groups, an
awareness ranging from multilingualism to multiculturalism. He, in fact,
attacks labels of monocultural being given to these groups: 'Although the
Indians may be seen as monocultural, the truth of the generalisation is to
be found in the shades of grey in between.'

Mexican identity is a complex identity that has its roots in a social/
historical context where the mixture of Spanish and indigenous cultures
has created what might be called a multifaceted identity. There is both a
natural and intellectualised mixing of these two cultures. Belongingness
is also deeply involved in perceptions of Mexican identity and there is a
tendency for a person to be strongly tied to certain regions or areas of the
republic and at times to exclude those who are not from the same area. In
fact, there are examples of Mexicans not recognising others as Mexicans
when they are from outside of a geographic area. The *pueblito* ('small
village') serves the function of creating a feeling of belongingness that
stabilises personal and national identity while also being a political

structure for its inhabitants. Fernando gave the example of the Mexican who said 'I am Mexican', 'I am Oaxacan' or 'I am Zapotec', depending on whom this Mexican is speaking with and where he is at the time. This example hints at the three such concentric circles that represent their identity in some way. Of course, such circles exist in any country and one can find narrowing circles of belongingness, but in Mexico it is especially strong. Even so, we might conclude that a conscious effort at various levels is being made to increase the range of belongingness for all citizens by groups within the society.

The process of becoming intercultural creates a heightened sense of self constantly being challenged through contact with different cultures. Adler (1975) takes the multicultural person beyond sensitivity to other cultures and cultural knowledge into an evolving psychocultural pattern of identity that differs radically from the relatively stable forms of self process found in more local cultural identity patterns. Learning about oneself involves the change from a monocultural to an intercultural frame of reference, which he points out transcends the boundaries of ego, culture and thinking. Paradoxically, the more one is capable of experiencing new and different dimensions of human diversity, the more one learns about oneself. As a result the core of cultural identity is an image of self and culture intertwined in the individual's total conception of reality. The intercultural person is neither completely part of nor completely apart from their culture, but lives on the boundary or edge of their thinking or culture. This person has a style of self-consciousness that is capable of negotiating ever new formations of reality while being capable of negotiating the conflicts and tensions inherent in cross-cultural contacts. This person undergoes personal transitions that are always in a state of flux with continual dissolution and reformation of identity and growth. It is the adaptive nature that distinguishes them from other human beings.

If we now consider this account of identities in the context of education for citizenship, we find difficulties. Citizenship is often related to belonging to a community or being a member of a group or groups of people who recognise that they have something in common. The notion of the nation-state as an 'imagined community' (Anderson, 1991) perpetuates this and the assumption that there is one community to which all belong.

Yet the people discussed here illustrate how false and illogical it would be to have education for citizenship in Mexico based on that assumption. They all have different degrees and kinds of intercultural experience and identity; and in their multiplicity and complexity are representative of Mexicans in general. What is needed in Mexico is an education for citizenship that takes account of all this; but as we said initially, the Mexican situation is not unique in its complexity even if every situation and country is unique in its particularity. All of these people have intercultural experience, see themselves as intercultural people. People like them need a citizenship education that recognises their interculturality and builds upon it, rather than ignoring it.

Note

1. 'Community leaders': a *mayordomo* is a leader that the village selects for a year to lead festivals for the community. Although there is a relationship with the Catholic Church, he is a leader selected by the members of the local community.

Chapter 2

National Identity at a Crossroads: The Struggle between Culture, Language and Politics in Hong Kong

SAI WING LEUNG and W.O. LEE

National Identity at a Crossroads

The issue of national identity was almost nonexistent throughout the period of Hong Kong's colonial history. According to Lee and Constas' (1996: 37–41) study of civic education in Hong Kong (as a part of the IEA Civic Education Study 1995–2001), they found that national identity was almost unmentioned in textbooks of civics-related subjects such as Economic and Public Affairs and Social Studies. For instance, a Form 1 EPA textbook says:

> Our identity is who we are and what we are, for example: I am John Chan; I am a Form One student; I am a Hong Kong citizen. This is our identity.

Another textbook writes:

> The meaning and importance of identity: it is important that you are able to prove who you are, or identify yourself. In Hong Kong, people do this by showing their identity cards. For example, if you go to a bank, apply for a job or a library card, you are required to show your identity card.

As is evident from these expressions in the textbooks, the concept of identity is basically one confined to citizen registration rather than national identity. Interestingly, when Hong Kong's identity is discussed, the textbooks even refer to Hong Kong's international identity (by using such descriptions as 'a cosmopolitan city', 'a world city' and 'an international trading and financial centre') rather than national identity.

Moreover, people in Hong Kong tend to distinguish between their national *identity* and *national* identity, with the former referring to the national passports they wish to hold, and the latter referring to the psychological national affiliations. In their interview with students, Lee and Constas (1996) found that 45.8% of the students preferred to hold British passports, 12.5% other overseas passports, 29% Chinese passports, 8% Special Administrative Region passports and 4% with no preference, although in general they identified themselves as Chinese or Hongkongers.

The identity question becomes more complicated if people are asked to choose their identity between Chinese, Hongkongers or their combinations, such as Chinese Hongkongers or Hong Kong Chinese. In the same study by Lee and Constas, an interviewee said:

> I would identify myself as a Chinese but not a foreigner. However, I increasingly feel that I am a Hongkonger. On some occasions, like the Olympic Games and the World Cup, I would identify myself as a Chinese, but when the China team is competing with the Hong Kong team, I would side with Hong Kong. [...] In Hong Kong, the choice between the two is becoming more difficult. (Lee & Constas, 1996: 327)

This kind of ambivalence has prevailed in Hong Kong for a long time, even after Hong Kong's handover to China. Lee (2003) has tried to track studies that captured national identity changes in Hong Kong by summarising survey findings on the various types of identity since the handover, as shown in Table 2.1.

Table 2.1 comprises findings from 13 different studies between 1997 and 2002. As the sample size, target respondents and the type of questionnaire varied, the figures were basically incomparable with one another. However, it still generates some information about how people in Hong Kong perceived themselves in terms of national identity. In general, if the questionnaires did not force the respondents to choose between Hongkonger and Chinese, they had a tendency to choose both identities. If they were forced to choose either Hongkonger or Chinese, the proportions fluctuated and no identifiable trend was found. This shows how national identity has continued to be an issue, or a struggle, among Hong Kong people. The more uncertain Hong Kong people's national identity, the more governmental effort is expended to provide and strengthen national identity education.

According to the latest study on national identity in 2004, conducted by the governmental Committee on the Promotion of Civic Education (CPCE, 2005: 27–28), the picture of national identity in Hong Kong

Table 2.1 National identity of people in Hong Kong

Year/ month	Hongkonger (%)	Chinese (%)	Hongkonger > Chinese (%)	Chinese > Hongkonger (%)
1997/8	60	38	–	–
1998/1	50	50	–	–
1998/10	–	–	57	29
1998/11	33.9	39.9	15.8	10.4
1999/6	62	34	–	–
2000/5	–	–	40	49
2000/5	–	–	52.9	37.7
2000/6	82.8	83.3	–	–
2001/9	–	–	54	38
2001/10	60	19	–	–
2002/8	25	21	–	–
2002/9	50	40	–	–
2002/9	51	48	–	–

Source: Lee (2003: 122)

remains unclear. The survey report identified that the respondents could be grouped into two clusters, with the younger (below 40), more locally born and more highly educated (university or above) respondents merged into Cluster 1 and those of the others into Cluster 2. Overall, the survey found that a majority of the respondents (74%) 'saw themselves as Chinese', but just more than half of them (53%) 'saw themselves as a Chinese citizen', and just less than half of them (49%) 'respect political and legal systems in China' (p. 27). The difference between the two clusters is more revealing. In Cluster 1, only 21% of the respondents 'feel being a Chinese', 12% 'feel being a Chinese citizen' and 17% 'respect political and legal systems in China'.

It is quite obvious that Hong Kong people's national identity continues to fluctuate, especially among the young, despite the efforts made by the government to strengthen national identity, showing that people tend to define identities for themselves rather than have them identified by the government.

(Inter)cultural Imperatives and National Identity

The continued ambivalence in national identity among Hong Kong people has attracted quite a number of studies and conjecture on the reasons behind this phenomenon as well as the implications for future policy making. Not surprisingly, most of the discussions are focused on political explanations, attributing the causes of identity problems to political changes, and largely to the former colonial rule. However, as the rest of this chapter will show, attributing identity problems to political reasons can be a rather trivial and lopsided perspective. Leung (2003) has conducted a survey on patriotic orientations among Hong Kong people, and he found multiple dimensions of nationalist orientations. Namely, he found among his respondents anticolonial nationalism, civic nationalism, totalitarian nationalism, cosmopolitan nationalism and cultural nationalism. Leung's major finding is that cultural patriotism is one that most Hong Kong people feel comfortable with, as far as developing a linkage in terms of identity to the motherland, and thus Leung's study has hinted for the need to employ a cultural perspective in understanding national identity, even when national identity is inseparable from politics.

The need for a cultural perspective is also expressed directly or indirectly in the literature on citizenship education. According to Kymlicka and Norman (2000), as many societies have become increasingly diversified, the issue of the rights and status of different subgroups, dividing along gender, ethnic, linguistic and religious lines, needs to be addressed. In their study of multidimensional citizenship, Kubow *et al.* (1998: 116) highlight eight citizen competencies that they think policy makers should give urgent consideration and attention to during the next 25 years:

- the ability to look at and approach problems as a member of a global society;
- the ability to understand, accept, appreciate and tolerate cultural differences;
- the willingness to resolve conflict in a nonviolent manner;
- the ability to be sensitive towards and to defend human rights (e.g. rights of women, ethnic minorities, etc.);
- the willingness and ability to participate in politics at local, national and international levels.

They have obviously pointed to the need for developing the kind of citizenship competence that can accommodate cultural differences, rights for the ethnic minorities and articulate local, national and international concerns.

When a cultural perspective is employed, it soon opens up the need to address cultural differences, and the corollary of addressing cultural differences is the need to develop an intercultural perspective on national identity and citizenship. As Kymlicka and Norman (2000: 41) put it, '(c)ritics of minority rights can no longer claim that minority rights inherently conflict with citizenship ideals; defenders of minority rights can no longer claim that concerns about civility and civic identity are simply illegitimate attempts to silence or dismiss troublesome minorities.' The need for developing pluricultural awareness and intercultural competence are stipulated in the *Guide for the Development of Language Education Policies in Europe*, as follows:

> Developing pluricultural awareness also has a linguistic dimension, both cognitive and affective; it therefore has the function of managing the cultural misunderstandings which may result from lack of linguistic understanding, lack of knowledge or difficulties accepting other ways of behaviour or doing things due to ethnocentric assessments. The purpose of pluricultural education is to create a degree of adaptation to other cultures so as to establish with members of those communities forms of communication as free of prejudice and stereotypes as possible ... The purpose of creating intercultural competence is to manage relations between oneself and others. This competence ... can be broken down into elements such as:
>
> - knowledge, in the sense of knowledge of other societies
> - the ability to learn, understood as the ability to develop knowledge about a society on the basis of what is known and to inform oneself by searching for and processing new data; in other words, the capacity to identify the relevant information and sources of information
> - the ability to interpret and assess, understood as the capacity to give meaning to cultural objects of whatever kind on the basis of a framework of reference (historical, sociological, anthropological, etc.) and values (such as those on which human rights are based, etc.) ...
> - attitude and personality factors underlying the ability to suspend one's judgment and neutralise one's representations about others, and detach oneself from one's culture (by explaining what is implicit or questioning consensus views) so as to perceive it from a (fictive) external point of view comparable to the way those foreign to the community view it. (Beacco & Byram, 2003: 68)

Guilherme (2002) explores the development of critical cultural awareness with educators engaged in the process of teaching foreign language education. By critical cultural awareness, she refers to 'a reflective, exploratory, dialogical and active stance towards cultural knowledge and life that allows for dissonance, contradiction, and conflict as well as for consensus, concurrence, and transformation' (p. 219). She sums up her work by referring to the issue of language and culture in education:

> In sum, Human Rights Education and Education for Democratic Citizenship, all three components – Cultural Studies, Intercultural Communication and Critical Pedagogy – and more particularly the conceptualisation and adaptation of the 'operations' identified above comprehend both a theoretical and a practical dimension that makes for an understanding of a critical approach to foreign language/ culture education and respective teacher education as praxis which involve the search for (inter)cultural knowledge via committed and insightful experience, investigation, reflection and dialogue. (Guilherme, 2002: 225–226)

Alred *et al.* (2003) make a distinction between 'intercultural experience' and 'being intercultural'. The former refers to the experience of Otherness in a range of ways that will help to create a potential for questioning the taken-for-granted assumptions in one's own self and environment. The latter, however, goes beyond experience. It refers to the capacity to reflect on the relationships among groups and the experience of those relationships. It is not only the experience of Otherness, but also the ability to analyse the experience and act upon the insights into the self and others that the analysis brings. Bredella (2003: 237–238) offers a succinct elaboration on what it means to be intercultural:

- Being intercultural means to reconstruct the others' frame of reference and see things through their eyes in order to overcome our ethnocentric tendency to impose our categories and values on their behaviour.
- Being intercultural means to enhance our self-awareness as cultural beings.
- Being intercultural means to be able to accept the others' beliefs and values, even if we cannot approve of them. Therefore tolerance plays an important role in the intercultural experience.
- Being intercultural is based on a concept of culture which does not determine the individuals' behaviour but enables them to mediate between contradictory values and to pursue their interests.

- Being intercultural comprises both involvement and the reflection on this involvement. Hence the classroom is not only a kind of substitute for direct intercultural contact but a necessary place where students can reflect on their intercultural experiences since such reflections are often impossible in direct contact.
- Being intercultural means to be aware of disquieting tension in the intercultural experience. On the one hand, we must recognize the other culture in its difference. [...] we cannot rest content in relativism but must mediate between different frames of reference in order to create a better one.

On the basis of the above discussion, we would argue that political explanations *per se* are insufficient in understanding the complexities of the issue of national identity in Hong Kong. To arrive at a better understanding of the issue, it is necessary to explicate the issue from the cultural and/or intercultural perspective. Further, cultural identity is inseparable from language, as culture groups are very often language groups. That is to say, a cultural perspective requires an intercultural perspective, which further implies the need to adopt a language perspective in understanding the cultural (or intercultural) identities.

Language and Identity: A Two-way Interaction

Research on language and identity has been growing in momentum, as reflected in the number of doctoral dissertations as well as special issues in journals (Norton, 2000: 5–6). As argued by Le Page and Tabouret-Keller (1985: 248), 'National, ethnic, racial, cultural, religious, age, sex, social class, caste, educational, economic, geographical, occupational and other groupings are all liable to have linguistic connotations. The degree of co-occurrence of boundaries will vary from one society to another; the perception of the degree of co-occurrence will vary from one individual to another.' In a special issue of *TESOL Quarterly* on language and identity, Norton (1997: 419) summarises the common viewpoints shared by the five contributors as follows:

- the notion of identity is complex, contradictory and multifaceted;
- identity is seen as dynamic across time and place;
- identity constructs and is constructed by language;
- the construction of identity must be understood with respect to larger social processes, marked by coercive or collaborative relations of power.

All these viewpoints are illuminating, but what is most relevant to our study is the idea that identity constructs and is constructed by language. How is identity constructed by language? Different scholars put forth different arguments for this relationship. For Bourdieu (1977: 651), language is a kind of cultural capital:

> Discourse is a symbolic asset which can receive different values depending on the market on which it is offered. Linguistic competence (like any other cultural competence) functions as linguistic capital in relationship with a certain market. This is demonstrated by generalised linguistic devaluations, which may occur suddenly (as a result of political revolution) or gradually (as a result of a slow transformation of material and symbolic power relations, e.g., the steady devaluation of French on the world market, relative to English). Those who seek to defend a threatened capital, be it Latin or any other component of traditional humanistic culture, are forced to conduct a total struggle (like religious traditionalists, in another field), because they cannot save the competence without saving the market, i.e., all the social conditions of the production and reproduction of producers and consumers.

To broaden the scope of Bourdieu's theory, Ben-Rafael (1994) argues that in modern societies where diverse codes coexist, the greater the profit the knowledge of a language can provide, the more likely the privileged groups will view this knowledge as a desirable object. Thus, 'status of linguistic resources should correlate with the status of the carriers of these resources' (p. 42). When English proficiency, or even English in Received Pronunciation, is required for entering government and business, this language can create a sense of identity among those who can master this language. Milroy and Milroy (1985: 55–59) argue that only when people opt for status rather than solidarity will they choose the standardised or high-prestige form of the language. In their research in inner-city Belfast, it was quite rare for a person in those working class groups to prefer status to solidarity. In other words, the cultural capital of a language constructs identity, as well as social network. Edwards (1995: 126) further points out that 'to the extent to which language remains as a valued symbolic feature of group life, it may yet contribute to the maintenance of boundaries [of identity].'

How does identity construct language? From the linguistic point of view, the practice that many non-native speakers of English blend the vocabulary, syntax and intonation of their languages into English will pose a threat to the future of English. From the identity point of view, however, mixing codes in using English is a good example of how identity constructs language. As McConnell (2000: 145) argues,

> Many Asians insist that English belongs to all its speakers. They reject the idea that the standard varieties such as British, American, Canadian, or Australian are the only correct models. In their opinion, English must reflect the reality of their world. In this way, English fits into the pattern of multilingual societies like Singapore or the Philippines. These New Englishes are helping Asians to forget the unpleasant associations of English as the language of colonial oppression and cultural imperialism.

Whereas McConnell speaks for Asians, Lanehart (1996: 329) speaks for African Americans:

> What I am saying is that language use is a choice, and the choice for African Americans has been very limited historically because we have been told that our experiences do not matter, or that they are not relevant, because they are different and therefore inferior. We are again and again told that we have to assimilate; we have to accommodate another's socio-cultural and historical context because ours is not acceptable. This is not acceptable.

Both McConnell and Lanehart pinpoint a coercive relation of power that is at work during the construction of identity. To assert their identity, they insist on their way of speaking English, and they do not care whether they are speaking English in Received Pronunciation.

The language situation in Hong Kong is very complicated in that probably everyone has to face the following language choices or dilemmas from childhood to adulthood: English (a legacy of the UK and an international language in the era of globalisation), colloquial Cantonese (spoken by a great majority of the local population), mixed code (mixing English and Cantonese, popular among bilinguals, middle class, youth), standard and formal spoken Cantonese, dialects (for example, Hakka, Chiu Chau, Fukien, Shanghainese and so forth), formal spoken Putonghua, written Chinese in traditional characters, written Chinese in simplified characters and a distinctive written Cantonese. In real life, the language choice is mainly between speaking English, Cantonese or Putonghua, and between writing English or standard Chinese. What we aim at answering in the present chapter are: (1) How does the uniqueness of Hong Kong identity manifest itself in linguistic terms (a question asked by Joseph, 1997: 71)? (2) What is the implication of Hong Kong people's linguistic identity for national identity in Hong Kong?

Language and Identity in Hong Kong: The Case of English

By the treaty of Nanking, Hong Kong became a British colony in 1842. As a colony, English in Hong Kong was beyond a shadow of doubt the most important linguistic cultural capital. As observed by Cansdale (1969: 347), 'probably the most immediate and important effect of the British administration is that the key to the best jobs and the most influential positions is a command of fluent English.' Lin (1996) provides a more detailed portrait of how English could act as 'a language of power and the language of educational and socioeconomic advancement'. First, there had been an English-medium higher-education policy in Hong Kong for many years. Second, there was the British-based accreditation system of professional qualifications (for example, accountancy, medicine, engineering and so on). Third, there had been the policies upholding English as the official, legal and government language. Fourth, there had been the imposition of an English-language requirement on individuals aspiring to join the civil service. All these focused on the instrumentality of the English language in the colony. In reaction to that, there were many remarks from the governors, university heads and English department senior academics reminding people not to forget the cultural implications of the English language.

Our brief historical account starts with the establishment of the University of Hong Kong in 1912. The university was proposed to be set up by Governor Frederick Lugard with an aim to increase British influence in higher education in China and to train up graduates to serve the administrative and business interest in the colony. In expressing his view on adopting English as a medium of instruction in the university, Lugard's speech touched upon the issue of intercultural understanding: 'On the contrary, we desire to promote a closer understanding of the two races, and this can best be done by the acquisition of the English language. We believe that language is the best medium for imparting Western knowledge, and that by acquiring a fluency in it students will best fit themselves for success in after life whether they adopt a profession or become officials in the service of their country at the Capitals or abroad' (cited in Poon, 2003: 40). This view was echoed by Vice-Chancellor Sir William Brunyate of the University of Hong Kong in the early 1920s: 'If we are to take advantage of our exceptional position I think we are bound to make a most serious attempt to do something towards finding a way to mutual understanding between the two civilisations, and that, I think, will mainly be done in the arts subjects' (cited in Poon, 2003: 102). As a matter of fact, under the leadership of R.K.M. Simpson, Head of English Department between 1920 and 1951, English in the university was treated as a gateway to Western civilisation and culture of general knowledge. Many years later, Roy Harris, Chair of English Language of the Department, presented an inaugural lecture entitled 'The Worst English in the World?' at the University in 1989. He once again referred to the cultural implications of the language:

> (T)here was something much more important, and something which only a university could seriously attempt to provide than vocational English, or business English, or technical English ... To furnish a student's mind with English at this level requires serious engagement with some of the outstanding works and some of the finest minds that the long tradition of English writing affords ... The English to which university students need access is the history-rich language which articulated the tropes, the metaphors, the arguments, the concepts which shaped the minds of some of the world's best poets, scientists and philosophers. That is the English worth having: not as a nostalgic memorial of the past but the mental equipment of the present. (cited in Poon, 2003: 117)

Quite coincidentally, in 1987 the vice-chancellor of the university, Wang Gungwu (1987: 9) expressed a similar view in his speech 'Language Policy and Planning in Bilingual Hong Kong':

> Because of the ever-expanding domains of knowledge, as an international language English provides the greatest aid to the acquisition of the most updated and most advanced knowledge. However, we need to pay more heed to how students absorb English culture, and thought and communicative behaviour related to English.

With respect to English learning in secondary school, according to the syllabuses of English Language of the Hong Kong School Certificate Examination from 1952 to 1965 (Hong Kong English School Certificate Syndicate, 1952–1965), students had to prepare to sit for a section called 'General English' (changed to 'General Reading' in 1958).[1] Set books containing selected works from prose, poetry and later drama were assigned for one of the three subsections. The syllabus changed in 1966 and from then onwards it seems that only students taking English Literature could have the joy of reading literature in English. The number of students taking English Literature, however, remains very low in comparison with those taking English Language, mainly because not many secondary schools offer this subject. Recent figures from 1996 to 2004 show that whereas the number of students sitting for English Language of the Hong Kong School Certificate Examination rose from 109,389 to 129,103, the number for Literature in English rose from 730 to 849 (Hong Kong Examination and Assessment Authority, 2004: 98–99).

The repeated reminders not to ignore the cultural dimension of the English language reflect the degree that English is seen as an instrumental language by Hong Kong, rather than being seen as an integral part of the language and culture in the territory. This is even reflected in the development of teaching approaches. From the 1970s onwards, English language teaching in Hong Kong has been undergoing transformation from the oral-structural approach (emphasising structural knowledge and accuracy in speech before writing) to the communicative language teaching approach (emphasising accurate and fluent language use in both speech and writing) and now to the task-oriented approach (emphasising fluency, accuracy, appropriate and creative language use) (Chow & Mok-Cheung, 2004).

The interesting question however is not so much whether the development of English language teaching has been shaped by Hong Kong people's instrumental view of this language. Rather, it is more interesting to ask, why didn't Hong Kong people's full appreciation of English as an important linguistic capital lead to a language shift in Hong Kong? Why, with a clearer emphasis on language use in English language teaching, has the standard of English still been criticised for several decades as declining? Görlach (2002: 109–110) offers a very apposite observation:

> Although the British presence in the former Crown Colony lasted for more than 170 years, the functions of English were, societally, that of a second language, and although knowledge of the world language was of eminent importance in a community that so much depended on trade and technology, English in a way never took root. Typical functions of an ESL, such as its spread outside trade, administration, law, and higher education, appear to be largely lacking, and there is only limited use in creative writing and no distinctive spoken variety with an independent local norm. This surprising fact – in which Hong Kong contrasts strikingly with Singapore – obviously has to do with the virtually monolingual speech community of Hong Kong:

not only are 98% of the population Chinese, but most of these also speak one variety of Chinese, namely, Cantonese.

Görlach's observation about the language composition is an important one, and his comparison of Hong Kong with Singapore to highlight this perspective is particularly helpful for understanding why English is being treated differently between the two cosmopolitan cities. Echoing Görlach's view, Lam (1994: 190–193) offers further deliberation on the issues:

> Unlike the Singaporean Chinese population, which is made up of some seven or eight dialect groups, there is only one dialect group in Hong Kong – Cantonese; except for a negligible minority of speakers from other provinces in China, who will also be able to speak Cantonese, all Chinese use Cantonese exclusively in everyday discourse, with some words of English intermingled. There is, therefore, neither necessity nor home support for learning English ... It is not that Singaporeans want to integrate themselves with the native English-speaking communities but that they need English to integrate themselves as one community.

According to Joseph (2004: 160), the declining standard of English in Hong Kong and the emergence of Hong Kong English are two sides of the same coin. The problem is '(t)he idea of such a language is not one which Hong Kong people take seriously – not yet, anyway.' Why have Hong Kong people not taken Hong Kong English seriously? We would venture to say simply that English is merely an instrument in Hong Kong, not a language forging Hong Kong identity. As a result, speaking or writing English in the Hong Kong way will be criticised as bad English, and no one will defend themselves as speaking 'Hong Kong English'. It is exactly because of the lack of 'necessity nor home support for learning English (in Hong Kong)' and because English is not the linguistic identity of the majority of Hong Kong people, that Hong Kong students' motivation to learn English is hardly strong (Tsang, 2000).

The fact that English fails to take cultural root in Hong Kong is very telling in terms of national identity in the territory. As much as there is a problem of national identity in terms of being a Chinese, Hong Kong Chinese or Chinese Hongkonger after 1997, there is a problem of identity with British rule. The fact of colonial rule and consequential significance of English as the dominant official language, as the dominant language in the University of Hong Kong and as the dominant language in the Certificate of Education examinations could explain that the English language is important only in achieving political and economic ends, but these political and economic ends have not been able to counterbalance the power and influence of the dominantly monolingual language of the territory, Cantonese. Cantonese, as the *de facto* daily lingua franca in the territory, has created a significant identity adherence among Hong Kong people that is far stronger than has been generally realised. This adherence has created a strong cultural identity among Hong Kong people that will further impact upon the preference in national identity.

Language and Identity in Hong Kong: The Case of Cantonese

Bauer (1984: 309) predicted that after the unification of Hong Kong with China, the 'importance of Putonghua can be expected to soar in the years to come and eventually eclipse Cantonese, which will be reduced to the regional dialect status it now has in the PRC'. His prediction has not come true. Cantonese continues to keep its role as a dominant language in Hong Kong eight years after 1997 and shows no sign of decline. As shown by census statistics: in 1991, 88.7% used Cantonese as the usual language; in 1996 it was 88.7%; in 2001 it was 89.2% (Census and Statistics Department, Hong Kong, 2002: 46). A daily life observation can tell how dominant Cantonese is in Hong Kong. In 1997, the Hong Kong Bible Society published a Cantonese version of the bible, entitled *New Cantonese Bible*.[2] To take this dominant status of Cantonese before and after 1997 for granted will miss the historical context for the understanding of national identity in Hong Kong, not only during the past 150 years of British colonial rule, but also in the years after Hong Kong's handover to China. As a colonial power, the British attitude towards indigenous dialects was quite different from that of the French: 'The English language was highly privileged, to be sure, but other roads to salvation were also available: you could remain Muslim, Hindu, Malay, or Chinese and use your native language and not necessarily feel pressured to be somehow British if you wanted to prosper in the colonial possessions themselves' (Wardhaugh, 1987: 8). When Hong Kong became a British Crown Colony, people spoke different indigenous dialects, including Hakka, Tanka and Po-an Cantonese. When more and more people from the Pearl River Delta region began to gravitate towards Hong Kong, the standard Cantonese based on the norm of Canton became the language of culture for the Chinese in this area. In post-war years, the census data show that about a quarter of the population did not speak Cantonese at home. The figure dropped to 15% by the mid-1960s and further dropped to a very small percentage a decade later (T'sou, 1985: 15–16). Many people have expected the rising importance of Putgonhua after 1997. However, there was no 'Speak Mandarin' campaign initiated by the Hong Kong SAR Government or the Central Government of the PRC, nor was Putonghua regarded as the mother tongue in the 1998 language policy that strongly enforced mother-tongue medium of instruction in the majority of schools in Hong Kong.

In other words, the thriving development of Cantonese in Hong Kong has been almost a natural social process without much interference from the colonial or the PRC administration over the last 150 years. Indeed, not only has there been no sign of decline of Cantonese in Hong Kong whether under British or Chinese rule during the last one and a half centuries, but Hong Kong people have even vitalised the dialect and elevated its language status beyond an ordinary dialect, in terms of the functionality of the language and its popularity in usage. In terms of its functionality, linguists have observed that Cantonese has become a 'high' language, high in the sense of becoming a more formal language beyond its colloquial functions. Luke (2003) points out that Cantonese today can be classified into High Cantonese, which is used by better educated people and on formal occasions, such as ceremonies, public announce-ments, news broadcasts, formal speeches, lectures and as a medium of instruction in schools, and Low Cantonese, which is basically a colloquial language used on more informal occasions, especially at home, for friendship and in the neighbourhood. Being an instruction medium not only in school but also in university, Cantonese has evolved into a language sophisticated enough to become an academic language, much more than most other dialects can achieve. Its formality has become enhanced, when colloquial expressions have been adopted in the written form in Hong Kong newspapers. While Hong Kong people in general do not realise the amount of Cantonese expressions in local newspapers, many Putonghua speaking non-Hongkong Chinese complain that they do not understand the Hong Kong papers. Hong Kong people have quietly, though also naturally, mixed the local expressions into the standard Putonghua-based written language, and created the Hong Kong-style written language.

By converting Cantonese into High Cantonese, the language strength-ens the cultural identity among Hong Kong people, and thus the national identity, but simultaneously the increased popularity of the language has further strengthened Hong Kong identity. To be more exact, it was the rise of Cantonese popular culture from the 1970s onwards that succeeded in cultivating a sense of Hong Kong identity among Hong Kong Chinese

(Chu, 2003; Leung, 1999; Ma, 1999). Although the great majority of the Chinese population in Hong Kong were using Cantonese as their usual language at that time, only with the rise of Cantonese popular music, Cantonese TV programmes and Cantonese movies in the 1970s could Hong Kong people have something in common to share together and to take pride in. Choi (1990: 106) summarises succinctly the significance of this rise of popular culture on identity formation in Hong Kong:

> The late seventies saw the emergence of an indigenous culture in the form of mass entertainment, including TV production, popular songs and films. These are highly significant because, not only is their audience drawn from across the social spectrum, but that they reflect life-patterns and values that are peculiar to the Hong Kong community itself.

Written Cantonese began to get its wide currency with the rise of local popular culture. With the rise of TV, and thus a tremendous expansion of the entertainment business, the 1970s witnessed a significant rise of popular songs either as theme music for soap operas or as a key component of entertainment programmes. Further, not only did written Cantonese appear often in popular song lyrics, Cantonese increasingly entered into other parts of the cultural life of Hong Kong, such as comic books, advertisement captions, popular newspapers and other forms of folk literature, and all these enhanced the opportunity for Cantonese to be expressed more. Snow (2004: 172–173) concludes his study of written Cantonese by enumerating the following significant development: more and more written Cantonese is adhering to spoken Cantonese norms than to standard Chinese vocabulary; written Cantonese seems to lead to a growing Cantonese literacy among the public. Over the years the appearance of written Cantonese has had a slow but consistent increase in the genres and subject matters of texts; written Cantonese has transformed into a written language used in texts for middle class and particularly for young people. Snow goes on to argue that this rise of written Cantonese is an indicator of Hong Kong people's acts of identity (p. 189). We would rather argue that if Cantonese popular culture demonstrates how language constructs identity, written Cantonese is perhaps a case demonstrating how identity constructs language in Hong Kong. Whereas in the past commentators criticised Hong Kong as a 'cultural desert', Hong Kong people are now proud of the genres of popular culture that the city has exported to other countries. Of course, what we portray here is at best an outline of a complicated process. In real life, the complication can be found in a renowned columnist of

Hong Kong Economic Journal, a representative Chinese newspaper specialising in finance news, who has been writing his column in Cantonese for the past 30 years. He explains that due to his poor training in standard Chinese and poor standard of English, he felt more comfortable writing in Cantonese than in standard Chinese. This style of writing is, however, very attractive to younger businessmen, of whom a great majority also feel inadequate in standard Chinese. He was encouraged to keep this style of writing by his press (Wu, 2003: 36–50); such an endorsement of his style of writing has far-reaching implications and the local identity has become strengthened at the same time.

Another important indicator of how identity constructs language is the ubiquitous use of Cantonese–English codemixing in informal conversation in Hong Kong (Tse, 1992). According to Pennington (1998a: 12), codemixing in Hong Kong has been undergoing a shift from translation of meaning (the expression of equivalent messages in the two languages), through alternation of meaning (the expression of nonequivalent messages in the two languages), to the extension of meaning (the expression of new messages by the combined use of the two languages). From the linguistic point of view, Cantonese–English codemixing cannot be claimed to be a third language structurally. However, from a sociolinguistic point of view, it does serve specific communicative functions and may thus be considered a third language code (Chan, 2003: 211).

Li (2002: 87–95) proposes four specific motivations for codemixing in the Hong Kong Chinese press, namely, euphemism, specificity, bilingual punning and principle of economy. But for a number of scholars, Cantonese–English codemixing has something to do with local culture and identity. In Gibbons' (1987) study, three complementary approaches yielded similar corroborative findings that Cantonese was perceived as a marker of group and ethnic solidarity. In Lai's (2001) survey of 134 senior secondary students, 56% of those of middle-class background liked to use mixed code mostly and 43.8% of them thought that mixed code best represented Hong Kong. Pennington (1998b: 18) regards it as 'an innovative amalgam of the linguistic resources available to Hong Kong speakers'. He thinks it represents 'a creative and inherently flexible resource – and certainly not only an equivalent to English or Cantonese. Rather it is a new variety to match the emerging new generation, their middle class culture, and their pull towards modernisation of their language.' (Pennington, 1994: 102). In Tsang and Wong's (2004) analysis of codemixing in a renowned comedian's stand-up comedy, they think codemixing helps to project a dual identity, which reflects and constitutes the shared complex and ambivalent 'Hong Kong identity'. Moody (1997: 217) echoes this view by pinpointing that codemixing in Hong Kong serves to 'reinforce Chinese ethnicity while providing direct contrast to the national identity of the PRC, which would be symbolised by its national language, Putonghua'.

What codemixing indicates is a very complicated relationship between identity and language in Hong Kong. Some scholars argue that codemixing serves as an outlet when there is a strong sanction against the use of English for intraethnic communication (Gibbons, 1987; Li, 2002). As a matter of fact, Cantonese is so dominant a language in Hong Kong that it is regarded as inappropriate for Hong Kong Chinese to communicate in English. The Cantonese ethnocentricity of Hong Kong, along with the political and demographic changes as aforementioned, has resulted in schools that are strongly monolingual and monocultural. In Johnson's (2003) review of studies on codemixing in the classroom, he concludes that there has been an increasing approval of mixed code use in the classroom, and the younger the speaker, the more frequent the use and approval ratings. The situation is similar in Hong Kong universities. Li (1996: 25) recalls his experience at the City University of Hong Kong, when some English major students wondered why they should continue to talk in English during the break. Jackson's (2002) ethnographic study of 25 full-time English majors reports the following:

- students believe that they can maintain the 'richness' and uniqueness of their culture by using Cantonese;
- they think codemixing is natural; they feel particularly at ease with using Cantonese;
- and they assigned a limited and a clearly defined role for English in their lives.

In the colonial period, Hong Kong people recognised English well as a cultural capital, so they wanted to acquire English as an asset for success. Exposure to English culture was seldom their concern. Nowadays, because of the linguistic identity with Cantonese and the cultural identity with local culture, English learning has even more emphasis on its vocational function, or as an examination subject. Roy Harris' aspiration for 'the history-rich language which articulated the tropes, the metaphors, the arguments, the concepts which shaped the minds of some of the world's best poets, scientists and philosophers' is seldom heard in the new millennium Hong Kong. Students' responses in Jackson's (2002) study give us the following scenario. With respect to talking to each other in English, students make a clear boundary between Cantonese and English, as shown in the following interview (p. 47):

> For Hongkongers, the mother tongue is Cantonese and they are supposed to use this language for communication too. This concept can explain why there are many Chinese students who are English majors primarily use Cantonese, not English, when communicating with each other . . . Since my classmates and I are native-Cantonese speakers, and, more important, we share the same cultural background, we feel comfortable when using it . . . The most direct way of communicating is using the same communication medium. It must be Cantonese, our mother tongue, and it forms strong resistance to English.

Cantonese is so predominant and powerful in the society that it also results in the reluctance or even opposition to adopting Putonghua as a teaching medium in schools. In Yau's (1992) study, in answering the question, 'Would it be reasonable to designate Putonghua as Hong Kong's "legal vernacular" after 1997?', 66% of secondary form four students, 49% of polytechnic students and university undergraduates replied 'no', though only one third of the school principals held this view. On the contrary, over half of the respondents (and over 70% of the secondary students) affirmed the significance of keeping Cantonese as the 'legal spoken language' in post-1997 Hong Kong as a crucial factor in maintaining the status quo of the Hong Kong social system.

Would the predominance of Cantonese in society make Hong Kong monocultural? At a first glance, it is unlikely to be the case, being an international city and given the well developed information infrastructure of the city. However, Margaret Ng, a renowned Legislative Council member and a barrister, thinks otherwise:

> A few years ago, the streets of Central teemed with people of every race and colour. Now, the crowd is almost uniformly Chinese and local. Bilingualism used to be the rule in street signs and public notices, now they often are in Chinese only. Although the media has always consisted of more Chinese than English, now a non-Chinese speaker might stay unaware of even major news . . . In the Legislative Council, English speeches are given little coverage. Subtly but certainly, non-Chinese-speaking people find the Chinese speakers around them less prepared to make allowance for their disability. Their areas of activity and awareness have diminished. Barristers who have no Chinese more frequently find themselves out of work.

Patriotism and nationalism are the prerequisite for political advancement. Only Chinese food is politically correct for official functions.
The best people swear by Chinese medicine. The only jarring note
is that most senior civil servants (all of whom are Chinese) send
their children to Britain and the US to be educated. (cited in Bolton,
2002: 13)

Ng's observation does not seem to be purely a personal feeling.
Although media consumption does not prove that Hong Kong has been
growing towards a monolingual society, the importance of the English
media in the city does show a declining trend. According to the *Hong
Kong Annual Reports* from 1997 to 2003, the number of Chinese-language
dailies decreased from 38 in 1997 to 28 in 2003 and the number of
English-language dailies decreased from 12 in 1997 to 11 in 2003. In terms
of circulation, English-language newspapers pale in comparison to the
Chinese-language press. According to AC Nielsen's Media Index, the
most representative English-language daily, the *South China Morning
Post*, ranked only eighth place, with 5% of the total daily circulation
figures, and another major English-language daily, *Hong Kong Standard*,
ranked thirteenth place, with only 1.8% of the total daily circulation
figures.

The declining importance of the English language in the media is also
manifested in television. There are two commercial television stations,
each broadcasting one channel in Cantonese and one in English. The top
10 programmes of the TVB Cantonese channel command at least 75% of
the audience share. Although the two English channels are not rated, a
1998 survey shows that these two channels could only have 5.2% of the
audience share. To balance the impact of popular television programmes,
Radio Television Hong Kong has launched the election of 'Good Quality
Television Programmes'. According to *Media Digest*, from 1993 to 2003,
English-language programmes seldom entered the list of the top 20, with
the exception of English-learning programmes like 'Learning English
in One Minute' in 1993 (ranked 7th) and 1995 (ranked 12th), 'Tour in
English' in 1999 (ranked 20th), and 'Funny English' in 2000 (ranked 10th)
and 2001 (ranked 18th).

On the basis of the information from various studies and various
sources, we seem to have a solid ground to conclude that whereas
Singapore is a bilingual society in which there is a language shift from
ethnic dialects to English, in Hong Kong the importance of English has
been overshadowed by Cantonese in almost all aspects of people's daily
life. But to what extent does this predominance of Cantonese signify an

ethnolinguistic identity? To compare Hong Kong with Quebec of Canada may give us some ideas. First, it took Quebec a lot of effort to sustain its being the only French-speaking state in Canada. In Hong Kong, Article 9 of the Basic Law (the mini-constitution of the Hong Kong SAR) grants official status to both the Chinese language and the English language. Secondly, French is a majority language in Quebec but a minority language in Canada. This is exactly the situation of Cantonese in Hong Kong and in China. However, French and English are two different languages and have two different cultural traditions; Cantonese is only one of the Chinese language varieties that share the cultural root of China. Consequently, whereas French in Quebec 'had clearly replaced the Catholic religion as the primary symbol of Quebec society' (Thomson, 1995: 75), and the independence of Quebec from Canada is still a lingering issue in Canadian politics, in Hong Kong there is neither the need to fight for the official language status of Cantonese nor any outcry for the independence of Hong Kong. In other words, the predominance of Cantonese in Hong Kong is not a consequence of external threat to indigenous language, but a cultural choice of its inhabitants. Politically, Hong Kong people might have had an identity crisis 'between maintenance of a unique, superordinate Hong Kong identity and a shift to primary allegiance to China as a superordinate group identity' (Brewer, 1999: 194). In terms of language, however, there does not seem to be a society-wide linguistic identity crisis caused by the overshadowing of English or Putonghua by Cantonese.

Conclusion

Civic education in Hong Kong has always been subject to criticism. The *Guidelines on Civic Education in Schools* in 1985 was criticised by Leung (1995) as being depoliticised and trivialised from policy making to implementation. The *Guidelines on Civic Education in Schools* in 1996 was criticised by Tsang (1998) as inculcating a subject political culture, conservative in political reform and irresponsible in its implementation. In comparing citizenship education between Hong Kong and Taiwan, Law (2004) points out that English is still not strong enough in either area to become part of their citizens' global identity. More relevant to our line of analysis is his following observation:

> Similar to the case of Japan, in both of the Chinese societies discussed in this article English is promoted as an instrument for global competition rather than global identity. English instruction is more concerned with how to use the language properly than with

understanding the cultures from which it developed. In contrast, the promotion of local dialects or the national language is associated with fostering local or national identity and preserving culture.

On the basis the above analysis, we further argue that there seems to be a parallel development of the predominance of Cantonese and the declining importance of English to an extent that there are indicators showing the development of Hong Kong after 1997 towards a less plurilingual and pluricultural society. This is clearly an obstacle for the development of intercultural citizenship education in Hong Kong. Being intercultural, as we have outlined previously, requires a person to be open to, reflective on, critical towards, curious about and tolerant of other cultures. Taking curiosity as an example, we do have the notorious record of Hong Kong students, from primary to university, lacking enthusiasm to read books outside the curriculum: in one survey, 50.8% of 1999 primary students spent less than half an hour a week doing noncurriculum reading; another 7% did not read any books outside of required school reading (*South China Morning Post*, 23 April 2004). In another survey, 76% of 4882 interviewed parents said that their children spent less than one hour daily on noncurriculum reading, but spent three hours or more on watching television and playing computer games (*Tai Kung Pao*, 26 April 2004). Moreover, in a survey of 332 university undergraduates, about 20% did not have any noncurriculum reading, and 50% of those claimed they had spent only an hour a week on reading (*Hong Kong Economic Times*, 19 January 2005). Also, Hong Kong people are not enthusiastic to keep themselves informed of what is going on in China. The social indicators survey of 795 respondents in 2004 had the following findings: 90.9% of the respondents did not or seldom read magazines published in mainland China; 87.9% did not or seldom read new books published in China; 68.9% did not or seldom listened to or watched Chinese current affairs programmes; 90.3% did not or seldom surfed forums on mainland Internet. We cannot assert that this lack of curiosity towards the outside world is caused solely by the predominance of Cantonese. But the anti-intellectual tendency in Cantonese media does arouse concern (Yiu, 2002). The impact of these Cantonese media on students' language code and their attitude towards culture may be greater than we have expected. Consequently, although students in Hong Kong nowadays seem to have benefited from a very well developed information network, other than their possession of much piecemeal information on the West (especially that about consumption), their cultural literacy is weaker than the older generation.

The struggle of language in Hong Kong as reviewed in this chapter offers a significant perspective to understand the struggle of identity in Hong Kong. While the changing political situation in Hong Kong might be a cause of struggle in national identity, the explanatory power of politics obviously becomes less significant once the cultural explanation comes into place. If politics is the key reason for putting Hong Kong people's national identity at a crossroads, we do not understand why the struggle is not between a British identity and a Chinese identity, but between Chinese and Hongkongers and/or between Hong Kong Chinese and Chinese Hongkongers, given Hong Kong's political context as a colony, which was decolonised after 1997. Our review shows that culture offers a more convincing explanation for the identity dilemmas of Hong Kong people. It is the struggle to maintain their choice of lingua franca that has made both English and Putonghua fail to take root in Hong Kong. What is more, our review shows that throughout Hong Kong's history, Cantonese has grown into a stronger language in the territory, being transformed into High Cantonese, and becoming a stronger literary language. From a political point of view, it is difficult to understand why Putonghua fails to become the 'mother tongue' when the government enforced mother tongue to be the dominant medium of instruction in school in 1998. However, from a cultural point of view, it shows the power of the dominant language of the territory, which has overshadowed the coloniser's language in the colonial period and the motherland's language afterwards. This is a cultural choice, and the force of cultural choice has overshadowed the political force. It is the struggle of maintaining this cultural choice in the territory that puts Hong Kong people's national identity at a crossroads, vis-à-vis the political power above it.

Notes

1. In Hong Kong, passing five subjects of the Hong Kong School Certificate Examination, of which English is a compulsory one, is a necessary condition for all secondary students, having finished five years of study, to secure a place in their two-year post-secondary education. There is a proposed change to the present structure from 5 years secondary and 2 years post-secondary to 3 years junior secondary and 3 years senior secondary. The earliest past syllabuses of the Hong Kong School Certificate Examination in the Hong Kong Collection of the University of Hong Kong's library we can find is from 1952. There is an interesting finding that in early years, foreign languages such as French, Portuguese, Hindi and Urdu were included in the Hong Kong School Certificate Examination.

2.   In China, or in Chinese communities all over the world, the dialects may be
     totally different, but the written form of Chinese is universally based on
     Mandarin, the so-called standard Chinese. The publication of the bible in
     Chinese is normal. A Cantonese bible, however, may indicate the church's
     motivation to promote the bible to Cantonese-speaking Chinese as well as
     Cantonese emerging as a written vernacular. Bruche-Schulz (1997) offers
     a brief account of the linguistic difference between Putonghua (on which
     modern standard Chinese is based) and Cantonese.

Chapter 3

The Construction of Citizenship and Nation Building: The Singapore Case

STEWART MARTIN and ANWEI FENG

Introduction

People in many parts of the world perceive Singapore and its people very differently (Kwok, 2001; G.B. Lee, 2001). To those with little geographical knowledge, Singapore may be imagined as a small part of China. To many, the country is simply a tiny dot at the tip of the Asian mainland, a nation struggling for its very survival. Those who have seen or studied the country tend to describe it as a small city-state with no natural resources but one which enjoys a strategic position, a superb infrastructure, a strong economy and a powerful government. The three major ethnic groups, Chinese, Malay and Indian, are thought to communicate well and to live harmoniously on the small island. The country is often characterised as an ideal multicultural home for all Singaporeans – even as a small utopia. Some critics, however, draw an analogy between Singapore and an orderly corporation under the efficient and skin-tight control of an authoritarian management structure.

It appears that some of these perceptions find expression as part of the Singaporean identity and are influential in conceptualising Singaporean citizenship and formulating national educational policy. It is these perceptions, in part, that are believed by many to have inspired its leaders to turn the island-city-state into a strong state (Gopinathan, 1997).

Citizenship Education and Building of a Strong Nation-State

Singapore's ethnic composition has had a significant effect on the direction and process of nation building and consequently upon its formal educational structures. Emergent nations usually seek to build a state-centred identity. Singapore has transformed from a small colonial island into a new sovereign nation and in doing so has sought to integrate its three major racial groups – the Chinese, the Malays and the Indians – into a coherent expression of citizenship. Whilst the size of these three groups as a proportion of Singapore's citizenry is not equal (Figure 3.1), it has remained very stable over time, with the last decade being typical of those since decolonisation (Singstat, 2000).

After WWII and the Japanese surrender in 1945, Singapore returned to its previous colonial status under British rule. The period after this was marked by the rise of anti-British feeling and in 1955 the rise of new political parties and some partial self-government eventually led, in 1959, to Singapore having its own prime minister and cabinet, although Singapore was still under British control.

In the process of forming the new nation-state of Singapore after the end of the colonial period and WWII, the ruling elites in Singapore found themselves under considerable pressure both from within their population and especially from some of their surrounding political neighbours to ensure that the new state did not fall under the influence of the Malayan Communist party, which wanted to dislodge both the prior colonial authorities and the regimes that followed them. Singapore began decolonising and the regime was under considerable pressure to create

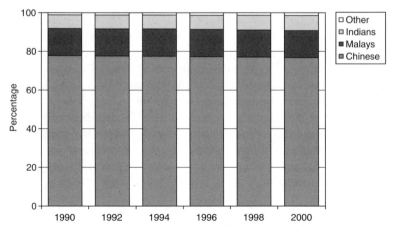

Figure 3.1 Population composition of Singapore over time, by ethnicity

a Singapore-centred identity and to blend its three major racial groups together. Chinese schools, meanwhile, actively developed Chinese patriotism and a world view very different from English, Malay and Tamil schools. The British considered such schools to be undermining Singaporean state formation.

From the early 20th century the Chinese government had used school education to promote patriotism in its own territory and this was reflected in the character of existing Chinese schools in Singapore. Chinese Singaporean students therefore often had a hostile view of colonial states. This was made all the more acute by the fact that Chinese students in Singapore (and in nearby Hong Kong) were effectively barred from higher education. As late as 1946 Singapore did not recognise qualifications awarded by Chinese schools for higher education or government employment (Wong, 2002). The British authorities in Hong Kong did not have in place any school-leaving qualifications for Chinese schools before 1952. Chinese students there-fore had no cultural capital that they could convert to political or economic advantage and Chinese schools continued to be seen as alien institutions within Singapore. China, in contrast, offered these schools financial support and actively recruited their students for higher education in China.

In the early 1950s, Chinese residents comprised 75% of the population in Singapore. The state sought to change Chinese schools to serve the interests of the ruling group. This process became more intense after the general elections of the mid-1950s, as the state depended increasingly on support from the masses for its legitimacy but, given its agenda, it had little capacity to compromise with the Chinese on educational policy and needed to blunt their cultural distinctiveness.

When the British colonised Malaya in the late 19th and early 20th centuries, they established a special arrangement under which they guaranteed that the sultan would be ruler of the territory and that the Malay people would be the only legitimate inhabitants. After WWII the Malays were therefore understandably anxious that 'Chinese aliens' would threaten this status quo in Singapore after the British left, especially as the Chinese outperformed the Malays economically and educationally. Britain was as a result compelled to adopt anti-Chinese policies in language, education and citizenship.

Even though Britain had never included the Singaporean Malays in these special arrangements (only about 10% of the population was considered to be Malayan), Singapore found itself under great pressure on this matter from Malaya, especially as at that time Britain planned to decolonise Singapore and amalgamate it and Malaya into one unit. Few thought that Singapore could become an independent country, so Singapore was strongly encouraged by Malaya not to become pro-Chinese, but was also under pressure to accommodate the Chinese within its school policy. Schools are able to shape these kinds of agendas profoundly for state formation. In Singapore the Chinese schools promoted alternate identities, bred social confrontation and blocked state formation. State builders seem to have felt compelled to subdue or reform them.

A comparison with the situation in Hong Kong is illuminating. During its colonial days, Hong Kong was used by the British as a bridge between China and the West. It was a largely monoethnic Chinese community and, perhaps because of this, the officials in Hong Kong were strongly inclined to learn Chinese and the regime was quite willing to incorporate Chinese-speaking elites into the government. But Singapore was still perceived by many to be part of the larger Malaya and the colonial regime took the Malays as its chief ruling partner and tended to see the Chinese as alien. State officialdom therefore felt more inclined to acquire the language and culture of Malaya than of China. The state in Singapore was also less willing to encourage the involvement of Chinese-speaking elites. The two countries therefore were different with regard to their relationship with the Chinese community and the policies of their Chinese schools. After 1945, therefore, the two states took very different directions in their political development – one went through decolonisation and the other remained a dependent territory until recently. In 1965 Singapore withdrew from the Federation of Malaya and entered a new phase of state formation.

In Singapore civil society has to this day remained fragmented by several ethnic communities – the state's relationships with any one of these is hamstrung by those it has with the others, especially the Malays. In particular, the Chinese and the Malays form two rival ethnic groups, whose antagonism has its roots in the brutalisation of the Chinese by the Japanese conquerors of Singapore in 1942. During this period the Japanese supported the Malays but also used their police force to brutalise the Chinese. After the Japanese were defeated, the Chinese, who until the fall of Singapore had always been anti-Japanese, exacted bloody revenge on the Malays. British and subsequent governments have therefore inherited a legacy of ill feeling between these two groups.

Singapore provides us with an example of how, when the school curriculum is used for explicitly hegemonic purposes, the curriculum becomes a defensive tool that tends not to effectively prepare people for self-government. In contrast, adopting a 'world history' approach often decentres the host culture, especially if this approach places the host culture within the context of Western history.

Both Singapore and Hong Kong had very difficult 'circles to square' in seeking to meet the needs of two different groups: in Singapore it was ethnic/racial (Chinese and Malays) and in Hong Kong it was political (Beijing and Taipei). The two states had different agendas and capacities to build their ruling power by co-opting their Chinese residents and adopted different approaches in seeking to exert their influence over Chinese schools. State building in these two contexts attempted to integrate peoples from diverse cultures and within this process education played and continues to play a key role.

Educational systems have a profound effect upon the pace and progress of state formation because they influence the formation and development of identity, social consciousness and social cohesion. The colonial legacy in Hong Kong and Singapore meant that many historical ingrained features of their respective educational systems made state formation more problematic. Singapore's attempt to unify its educational system and curriculum was compromised by differing rules for evaluation, the existing links with colonial educational systems and a parochial intellectual outlook. In Hong Kong problems centred on the strong links with Chinese schools, resources and pedagogy and were due to both the Chinese regime's support for overseas Chinese schools and the colonial regime's indifference to them.

State formation is a complex process and interventions made by the state to resolve particular difficulties may easily result in the making or unmaking of existing social identities and thereby change the direction and nature of state formation. In multiracial settings, especially when states are striving to develop an internally common conception of citizenship, it is important to discriminate between the two processes of incorporating and remaking the cultures of subordinated groups. Failure to address this problem can result in incorporated, or what Wong (2002) has called 'unmade', citizenship identities. Such unsuccessfully reformed populations may damage state or regime power and it can be argued that Singapore has experienced and continues to experience such problems in trying to remake its curriculum Singapore-centred.

The Concept of Singapore Citizenship

Singaporean ideas of citizenship since decolonisation have been constructed within the context of a permanent state of anxiety about the survival of the state (Lai, 1995). The political leadership has continually stressed the need for citizens to be dependent upon one another, on the grounds that their nation is surrounded by agencies whose values and activities, whether intentionally hostile or not, would bring about their destruction unless they were resisted at every turn:

> And one of the things we can do to get a little further down the road a little faster is to raise the spectre of total disaster as the alternative. . . . Within this context, sooner or later they (the citizens) will change. (Hill & Lian, 1995: 34)

The continuing success of Singapore as a nation-state is clearly and repeatedly identified by its political leadership in speeches, policy documents and political publicity as being due wholly to the good outcomes of its policies and activities. Admirable political leadership within this context is therefore implicitly defined as being any course of past action that has resulted in acceptable outcomes. Thus there is no explicit requirement that the process of making national political policy be an expression of, or be informed by, a previously articulated set of moral, social, religious or humanitarian values. Political credibility and worthiness can therefore be constructed in terms of retrospectively defined 'success' and all actions that have led to this are therefore automatically validated as acceptable and good, as is evident from an official website:

> **Test for results, not political correctness**
>
> Singapore's policies are guided by pragmatism, not dogmas. We sometimes buck the trend by implementing policies which we feel will bring results, even if the move is not deemed politically correct at that time.
>
> http://www.moe.gov.sg/ne/aboutne/govprin.htm

Because moral or political judgements within such a context are able to be made only about past events, the Singaporean political environment is not one within which meaningful, defensible judgements can be developed with regard to the desirability of any proposed future activity. The value of activity can be judged only post hoc. Indeed, political activity only acquires the capacity to accept judgement after it has run its course.

The meaning of citizenship within such an arena does not therefore embrace Westernised notions of active democratic participation, least of all dissent, and in many ways renders such activity unhelpful, irrational and even meaningless. It is wholly consistent with the political rationale in Singapore that its programme of National Education emphasises the need for young people to develop a convergent way of thinking about what it means to be a citizen and to be trained to accept instrumental conceptions of their role as a citizen. As an agent of the state, the educational system in Singapore is seen as having a clear and vital role to play in the social construction of a citizen:

> No child should leave school after 9 years without carrying the 'software' of his culture programmed into his consciousness. (Ong *et al.*, 1979)

Individual service and loyalty to the nation has been promoted in Singapore as being of paramount importance, as has the need for each citizen to continually display such loyalty in both public and practical ways. Individual citizenship is characterised and portrayed as something that must be continually revalidated in civil society.

In most Western democracies traditional models of citizenship can be encapsulated by the terminology of liberal individualism that prioritises the civic, political and social rights of the autonomous individual and is thus expansionary and emancipatory (Marshall, 1977; 1981). Some commentators argue that citizenship thus perceived may pose problems both nationally and internationally as citizens may tend to claim their rights and then retreat into their own privacy ignoring the community, the national and international public spaces (Ichilov, 1998). Some note that since the 1970s many democracies have in fact experienced crisis in maintaining the status of citizenship thus defined because of the erosion of conventional welfare provisions (Hill & Lian, 1995). This is not the case in Singapore, where democratic citizenship is construed primarily as a vehicle for serving the interests of the community and the state:

> the litmus of a good education is whether it nurtures citizens who can live, work, contend and co-operate in a civilised way. Is he loyal and patriotic? Is he, when the need arises, a good soldier ready to defend his country? ... Is he filial, respectful to elders, law-abiding

and responsible?[. . .] Is he tolerant of Singaporeans of different races and religion?

(Yip *et al*., 1997: 16)

As a natural consequence of the discussions and criticism of these ideas in recent times, many alternatives have been suggested and developed in the sociological literature in particular, to address the changing context of citizenship in terms of national interests and issues on globalisation. One of the notable discussions in the literature is the civic republican conception of citizenship suggested by Oldfield (1990), which firmly rejects 'welfarism' and in which the goals of collectivist activity take precedence over those that prioritise the needs and desires of the individual. In Singapore the notion of democracy is attached to a nonliberal socialist ideology in which the needs of the individual are sublimated to those of the state: 'Singapore believes that welfarism is not viable as it breeds dependency on the government' (http://www.moe. gov.sg/ne/aboutne/govprin.htm).

In the civic republican conception, citizenship is essentially seen as conferring duties and it becomes meaningful when those duties are practised by a responsible and participating individual supported by other similar individuals in a community. Citizenship for the individual is about supporting and engaging in practice. This concept of citizenship, according to Hill and Lian (1995), and Oldfield (1990), addresses the Singapore context appropriately.

We turn now to an examination of some of the relevant primary sources within which these competing perspectives on the nature and role of citizenship are examined and resolved in contemporary Singapore. We will also consider the nature of education for being intercultural in a society like Singapore, where democracy is explicitly aspired to but is not always characterised in ways familiar to those from other democratic nations, where apparently similar concepts and terminology are differently interpreted.

Singapore 21 and National Education

'Active citizenship' is the basis for Singaporean democracy and in 1997 the then prime minister, Goh Chok Tong, launched the 'Singapore 21' committee, whose brief was to articulate a vision of this for Singapore in the 21st century. The report of this committee (*Singapore 21*, 2003) identified five key challenges that it argued formed a vision for the future. These challenges embrace many of the paradoxes facing societies that wish to promote individual freedoms whilst developing an identifi-able, strong and politically coherent nation-state:

A less stressful life	versus	Retaining the drive
The needs of senior citizens	versus	The aspirations of the young
Attracting talent	versus	Looking after Singaporeans
Internationalisation/ regionalisation	versus	Singapore as home
Consultation and consensus	versus	Decisiveness and quick action

The report notes that many male Singaporeans defend the country through National Service whilst other citizens volunteer time and resources to community associations and welfare organisations. But it expresses concern that many individuals 'remain content' to let the government, or others, be the ones taking the active role in community and civic affairs. The report argues that for the good of all greater social cohesion is needed, as is more political stability and a greater public expression of collective will, values and attitudes. Active citizens are therefore defined as those who 'have a passion for and commitment to building a better Singapore' (*Singapore 21*, 2003: 14) and whose actions are 'enlightened by commitment to the values and principles that underpin Singapore society'. This active, individual, public and ongoing demonstration of nationalism is seen as enhancing 'ownership, passion and commitment' (p. 55).

The report stresses the need for each individual to demonstrate active citizenship, particularly in light of its own findings that in the previous year a survey the committee had commissioned found that only 15% of Singaporeans were willing to contribute to their community because they felt they lacked ownership over the issues and challenges facing their country, the lack of respect accorded to their views, and because of a lack of trust in the government. Behind this rationale for active citizenship lay an acceptance of political reality and, implicitly, of contemporary political unrest (especially amongst the young):

> As Singaporeans become better educated, they will want more autonomy and discretion. They want a greater say in national affairs, in the steering of the ship and in setting its direction.
>
> Younger Singaporeans complain that they are not consulted enough before, during or after policy-making. Even when their views are given, they lament the 'black hole' of obscurity and non-action into which their ideas may fade, or the 'black book' of notoriety into which their names may be recorded. (*Singapore 21*, 2003: Chapter 6)

Many other nations have grappled with the appropriate nature of education for being intercultural in a maturing society. The report of the *Singapore 21* Committee called for a restructuring of the education system and in particular for support for National Education, which had been launched in the same year in 1997.

National Education was conceived in order to revise the school curriculum to emphasise nation-building. Attention was focussed on introducing or revising Social Studies and Civics and Moral Education (primary school), Social Studies (secondary) and Civics (junior colleges). Other subjects' syllabuses such as literature and languages would be adapted accordingly. Schools would also be required to celebrate significant national events and organise regular visits to national institutions and economic facilities. The intention throughout was to stress 'how Singapore has overcome our constraints through sheer will and ingenuity' (Singapore Government Press Release, 1997).

> Many Singaporeans, especially pupils and younger Singaporeans knew little of our recent history. They did not know how we became an independent nation, how we triumphed against long odds, or how today's peaceful and prosperous Singapore came about. (Lee, 1997)

The wider purposes of this were set out in the previous year, when the spectre of external threats to the identity and existence of Singapore was again summoned:

> It is critical that we succeed in National Education. Then when our pupils hear or read about the warring in Bosnia, about the conflict in Sri Lanka, about the problems in Northern Ireland, about the many disputes and fights all over the world on account of race, religion or language, they will appreciate that these events in places far away are not irrelevant to Singapore. Rather, they are lessons for Singapore, for Singapore itself can easily slip into such a state. (Goh, 1996)

These concerns were developed in the *Desired Outcomes of Education*, where attention was turned towards the nature of Singaporean citizenship and individualism, seen as two quite separate identities that might often be in conflict with each other if the implicit tensions remained unresolved by appropriate educational preparation. Education was seen to do two things: develop the individual and educate the citizen. Both were seen in terms of responsibilities rather than rights:

> An educated person is one responsible to himself, his family, and his friends. [. . .] An educated person is also someone who is responsible to his community and country. (*Desired Outcomes of Education*, Ministry of Education, 2000a)

Education is characterised as being about nurturing the whole child, as in the traditional Asian understanding of the term, where education means developing the child morally, intellectually, physically, socially and aesthetically. What is different to similar conceptions and terminology elsewhere is the manner in which citizenship is interpreted and expressed through policy and action in Singapore. The Singaporean concept of democracy has been best characterised as a state in which 'anything not expressly permitted is forbidden' (Lee, 1999).

Civics and Moral Education

From 2000 onwards, citizenship education in Singapore has been steered by the Civics and Moral Education policy documents published by the Curriculum Planning and Development Division of the Singapore Ministry of Education. In these two documents, the government set out the 'desired outcomes' for young people in primary and secondary education. In primary schools children would be required to:

- Be able to distinguish right from wrong
- Have learnt to share and put others first
- Be able to build friendships with others
- Have a lively curiosity about things
- Be able to think for and express themselves
- Take pride in their work
- Have cultivated healthy habits
- Love Singapore

Five themes underpinned these outcomes, each of which was intended to reinforce identification with the social and political identity of Singapore: character building; bonding with family; sense of belonging to school; being part of society; national pride and loyalty. Assessment of this curriculum area was left largely in the hands of teachers themselves, although fixed amounts of curriculum time were prescribed (two periods per week, rising to three).

The emphasis throughout is placed firmly on developing loyalty and commitment to the nation as a citizen, on developing an emotional bond to Singapore, on promoting positive attitudes towards responsibility and teamwork and on absorbing and valuing Singaporean cultural tradition. The ultimate test of the programme's success is defined as being whether pupils demonstrate 'integrity of behaviour; respect and personal responsibility; graciousness and team spirit; civic consciousness; and patriotism' (Ministry of Education, 2000b: 8).

In secondary education two periods per week were devoted to the programme; assessment was again left to the discretion of teachers and the syllabus content was again grouped under five themes:

- Character building
- Family relationships
- Community spirit
- Our nation, our heritage
- Challenges ahead

Within these themes, acquiring certain attitudes and conduct was afforded equal importance to acquiring knowledge and skills. In the theme of 'character building', the key learning outcomes are developing integrity and being a good friend; in 'family relationships' contribution, responsibility and family unity are stressed; 'community spirit' encourages the demonstration of a sense of belonging (to the school and the national community); 'our nation, our heritage' aims to inculcate an appreciation of the achievements of the nation's forefathers (emphasising their pioneering spirit and their contribution to improving the well-being of others); and 'challenges ahead' focuses on Singapore's national icons (the national flag, anthem and pledge), the importance of 'demonstrating the ideals of Singapore' and the need for pupils to 'identify their duties and responsibilities as citizens of Singapore' (Ministry of Education, 2000c: 10). The goal of this programme is explicitly deterministic: 'the mission of our education service [. . .] is to mould the people who will determine the future of the nation' (p. 2).

The emphasis in both educational sectors is on contribution, responsibility and collectivism rather than on rights, freedom and individualism. This emphasis continues through the syllabus for Civics for Junior

Colleges and Centralised Institutes, where the objectives are set out as being to enable students to:

- Have conviction and commitment to lead and serve the nation
- Contribute to social cohesion
- Be committed to the efforts of the nation to defend itself
- Have confidence in the country's future

The main theme of this 30-h module is 'The Challenge of Leadership'. The key word of the purpose is again 'to mould' – 'to mould the future of the nation, by moulding the people who will determine the future of Singapore' (Ministry of Education, 2000d: 2).

Four components of 'The Challenge of Leadership' are identified: leadership, historical perspective, current situation and future scenarios. The learning outcomes required from these components include:

- propose and justify the qualities, knowledge and skills that the future leaders of Singapore must have to ensure her continued survival, stability and growth in a fast changing world;
- identify the challenge of leadership in Singapore and propose what can be done to address this challenge ('The leadership challenge in Singapore', Ministry of Education, 2000d: 6.)
- Analyse the policies that Singapore implemented to address the problems she faced as an emergent nation. ('Critical milestones in our nation's history', Ministry of Education, 2000d: 8.)
- Predict factors that can destabilise our harmonious multi-racial society. ('Lessons from the past', Ministry of Education, 2000d: 9.)
- Examine the significance and influence of national ideology in the development of nations.
- Anticipate the impact of some policies on the cohesiveness of our society and identify what might be done to address them.
- Examine how racial and religious fault lines can be exploited in different countries. ('Social cohesiveness', Ministry of Education, 2000d: 11.)
- Examine the implications of increasing global competitiveness on Singapore. ('Singapore's place in the current world situation', Ministry of Education, 2000d: 13.)
- Analyse how different countries handle the issue of national security.
- Propose what Singapore can do to sustain her economic success and survival in a fast-changing world.

- Identify the key values, attitudes and skills Singaporeans need to have to ensure the success and survival of the nation. ('Ensuring Singapore's continued success', Ministry of Education, 2000d: 16.)

The syllabus repeatedly draws attention to the continual presence of external and internal threats to the stability, continued existence and well-being of Singapore and emphasises that the appropriate response to this should be seen in terms of supporting existing political policies and social institutions and developing an explicitly collective and conformist behaviour towards the past, present and future. In this it extends and develops the approach to the training (or moulding) of citizens (Chew, 1998) found in the curriculum documents for Civics and Moral Education at primary and secondary level and in the civics syllabus for Junior Colleges.

The examples of National Education in civics and moral education programmes given in Chew (1998: 510–513) include:

- Module on *Becoming a Better Citizen* for Year 9 (15-year-olds)
- 1/3 of 60 h allocated for:
  - The concept of citizenship
  - Responsibilities of citizens
  - Responsibilities of citizens towards laws
  - Responsibilities of living in a democracy

The same themes are revisited at Year 10 under slightly different unit headings.

- Module on *Unity in Diversity* for Year 9 (15-year-olds)
- Objective: To foster cultural and religious appreciation
- The concept of celebration
- Festivals
- Major systems of beliefs in Singapore
- Expressions of beliefs in our daily lives (Unit 1 in *Becoming a Better Citizen* for Year 10 (16-year-olds).)

Included under 'Issues of national concern' are:

- An article entitled 'Looking Back ...', which summarises 'threats' to the nation.
- Transparencies: showing the achievements of Singapore
- A video entitled: The good life – Is it forever?
- A Teacher's Guide, which includes facts, cue questions and a detailed listing of teaching steps.

Chew (1998) concludes that the aim throughout such units is citizenship training that can be seen as a concerted effort to induce pupils into a convergent thinking mode underpinned by a dominant economical rationality and pragmatism.

Remaking Singapore

Given the political rhetoric of past decades and its continual emphasis on the success story that is Singapore, it would seem reasonable to suppose that a great deal has been achieved that is worth sustaining. It is curious, therefore, that politics in Singapore has recently become dominated by a strong and urgent expression of the need to remake Singapore in quite fundamental ways. Some might find it difficult to understand why this course of action should have come to be desired so suddenly, but within it can be found a clear legacy from past practice in the leadership and development of this nation-state. Within it can also be found a suggestion that at least some of the outcomes of Singapore's efforts to construct its own unique vision of citizenship have been found to have serious shortcomings.

In February 2002, the Singaporean government set up a 'Remaking Singapore Committee'. In its report, this committee argued for the need to remake Singapore and set out the evidence under four main headings for why this now was seen to be important. First, the committee argued that the Singaporean economy had now reached a turning point as a result of the forces of globalisation, the development of technology and the emergence of new economic competitors. Change was therefore imperative in the face of such external threats. Whilst this can be seen as a pragmatic and sensible perspective that has also been adopted by many other nation-states, it can also be seen as an approach that is in harmony with previous approaches to Singaporean nation-building in that it seeks to legitimate any consequent governmental action by raising the spectre of external threats to survival.

Secondly, the committee argued that due to the success of past economic policies within Singapore, greater disparities of individual income had emerged and unemployment had risen. These unwelcome developments were characterised as an inevitable fallout from the process of economic restructuring and not as things that could have been foreseen or mitigated. Thirdly, the committee noted that Singapore was witnessing a rise in religious and ideological extremism that was accentuating 'tribal' fault-lines within society, although there was no speculation as to why this might be so. Lastly, it was argued that previous developments within the economy, education and of the national infrastructure had been so successful that Singapore now boasted a more educated, sophisticated and mobile population. This citizenry had become one in which were found more complex loyalties and identities than had been the case previously and it increasingly now expressed rising demands for a more participative democracy (*Singapore 21*, 2003).

In the light of Singapore's previous anxiety to develop in its citizens a conformist unique Singaporean identity, this last argument is perhaps the most revealing. The committee's conclusion could equally well be interpreted as an acceptance that improved education and social mobility carry implicit threats to the success of an approach to the social construction of citizenship by means of 'programming', training, moulding or indoctrination.

Having outlined its rationale for the need to remake Singapore, the committee's thinking turned towards the required outcomes of such a process. Desirable objectives were classified into categories depending upon whether they would find expression at the social or at the individual level. The subtext for remaking Singapore is, however, entirely economic. The Singaporean government's Economic Review Committee argued that, at the level of the wider society and social policy, in order to ensure its continued economic prosperity Singapore must become: 'a leading global city, a hub of talent, enterprise and innovation' (http://www.channelnewsasia.com/remaking_sg/directions.htm), thus maintaining the economic argument underpinning the nature of citizenship. Singapore must also, it maintained, become the most open and cosmopolitan city in Asia; a creative and innovative culture that respects achievement in the sciences and the arts (ibid.). The drives to develop Singapore into a knowledge economy and to become the regional provider for workers in such economies are linked. Between them they may ensure that Singapore is more secure because its unthreatened existence then becomes important for the economic success of its more powerful political neighbours.

The Chinese typically value education and scholars above all and value merchants least, even after manual workers and farmers. This implicitly antientrepreneurial ethos is seen as being Singapore's most significant obstacle to economic progress. Singapore was, as we have seen, built on discipline and conformity. It is a country in which the government owns six of the ten largest companies on the Singapore Stock Exchange and exercises considerable control over the everyday lives of its citizens. The recognition by Singapore's political elite that greater individual freedoms have now become essential to the nation-state's survival is, we would argue, also a tacit recognition that entrepreneurialism and control are often mutually incompatible.

The remaking of Singapore has been made necessary by a combination of the globalisation of capital, the rise of new technology and, most of all, the rise of new economic competitors, especially China. Singapore has seen a worsening of its relative economic position since 1991 (Lam, 2000). Added to these factors have been those of a widening disparity of income amongst citizens and rising unemployment. The political leadership also worries about the emergence of religious and ideological extremism and the more complex political landscape of a nation-state in which some of the more educated, sophisticated and mobile citizens are demanding more of a say in the running of their country.

When setting out the goals that must be achieved at the level of the individual citizen, the Remaking Singapore Committee emphasised that they should seek to pursue their individual dreams through individual efforts. The ways in which Singapore could be remade into the necessary form were set out within four themes: a home for all Singaporeans; a home owned; a home for all seasons; and a home to cherish.

A home owned

The strategic thrusts within this section of the report focus upon:

- Enlarging space for expression and experimentation, refinement of censorship (less prescriptive and more facilitatory role for government), encouraging participation (accommodate a more diverse range of views) in national political processes and community life.

A home for all Singaporeans

Strategic thrusts:

- Enhancing identification with the ideals of the nation.
- Strengthening cohesion among people of different races, languages and religions.
- Enhancing our ability to integrate new Singaporeans, developing global networks of Singaporeans and strengthening their participation in national life.
- Harnessing diversity in talent, encouraging the entrepreneurial spirit and expanding opportunities for all Singaporeans.

A home for all seasons

Strategic thrusts:

- Promoting a gracious and compassionate society, encouraging community assistance and fine-tuning state safety nets for relevance to the emerging economy (a lesser role for government).
- Enabling full participation (more done by social and civic organisations) of all segments of our society.

A home to cherish

Strategic thrusts:

- Promoting equal opportunities (the patriarchal family must change).
- Strengthening families as a first line of support (as relief for 'the stresses of urban life').
- Preserving and building shared memories (heritage icons).
- Improving the environment for participation and fun.

Throughout these thrusts the explicit emphasis is upon handing more power and responsibility over to the citizen whilst maintaining loyalty to the state. Implicitly, there is an acknowledgement that current Singaporean society is showing the strains of economic and racial inequality and of civil unrest with the present restrictive regime.

Whilst welcoming the report of the Remaking Singapore Committee in 2003, the Prime Minister likened the relationship between the citizen and the state to that between a child and its parents. In Goh Chok Tong's vision of the citizen: 'There comes a point where you must take a risk and let go, in order for your child to grow and learn' (Goh, 2003). He was careful, however, to qualify his support for what he described as a 'participatory democracy' in 'a more participatory society' by explaining that where the government 'has to lead, or act without the benefit of consulting, it must explain its position'. There is no suggestion that such a paternalistic government is at any time accountable to the citizenry for any such decisions, merely that it should keep them informed of what it has done.

> Singapore is now facing one of the most critical periods in our history. Our economic relevance is being tested. The terrorist threat has put pressure on our social cohesion. And Singaporeans are wondering what part they have in the future of this country. The challenges are many, and complex. (Goh, 2003)

The spectre of external threats appears once more. The importance of education in developing concepts of citizenship has been well understood by the political leaders of Singapore. Like all political education, citizenship should lead to activity, to change in behaviour. This is a strong theme in the documentation we have examined. But citizenship should also lead to analysis and reflection. Whilst the Singaporean concept of citizenship has always emphasised individual activity, particularly that of the public demonstration of loyalty, support for and contribution to the society, it has not often encouraged wider analytical and reflective thinking in citizens. It has instead urged compliance, introspection, defensiveness and fear. The political leadership of Singapore has, over the years, demonstrated an implicit understanding of an important principle of state governance in this regard:

> Therefore a wise prince ought to adopt such a course that his citizens will always in every sort and kind of circumstance have need of the state and of him, and then he will always find them faithful. (Machiavelli, 1513: Chapter 9)

Singapore as a home is a powerful and recurrent metaphor in the political rhetoric in Singapore. The context for this is rooted in the island's recent history and in a political vision that emphasises 'belonging' over libertarianism. Allegiance to Singapore as a state, rather than as a collection of somewhat disparate tribes, is the ultimate political goal of its leadership and even Singaporeans overseas must therefore be encouraged to think of themselves always as Singaporeans first and foremost (Goh, 1999).

The context for the development of citizenship in any state is a combination of factors amongst the most influential of which are geographical location, the nature of one's neighbours, physical size, the supply of natural resources and historical legacy. None of these presuppose that any one particular expression of citizenship is more likely to emerge or will be more successful than any other in securing national survival or success.

The economic dimension is frequently to the fore in contemporary debate about citizenship in Singapore but in reality the desire of the political leadership for allegiance and conformity is at its heart. It is primarily a debate about citizenship in the service of, and as a means to achieve, a national identity. It is argued that nation-building requires the forging of a common basis of trust and identity among the populace – a single tribe whose members will put their allegiance to their homeland (and by implication to each other) above all else (Goh, 1999). The development of the Singaporean 'heartbeat' or 'heartware' (Singapore *21*, 2003) is therefore seen as the necessary precondition for continued national survival and economic success.

The notion of citizenship in Singapore at its heart serves the perceived need by the political leadership for a highly defined national identity that is essentially introspective, compliant and defensive. This nonliberal, democratic socialist model of citizenship is but one of many that could have emerged or been chosen and is in particular contrast to more multidimensional models, such as that of 'globalised citizenship' (Kubow *et al.*, 2000), which seek to endow the individual with significant political power and autonomy. It is the lack of this latter factor in particular that may make Singapore's search for greater participation in a globalised arena more difficult to achieve.

Part 2
Concepts of Citizenship Education

Chapter 4

Concepts and Issues in Citizenship Education. A Comparative Study of Germany, Britain and the USA

GERHARD HIMMELMANN

Writing in English as a researcher who is German and usually writes in German immediately raises a problem of expressing German terminology in English or of explaining what new problems and debates have arisen in Germany about my own newly launched approach to *Demokratie-Lernen* ('democracy-learning') as a contribution to the subject *Politische Bildung* ('political education'). By its very nature, this debate includes the question: what is the 'identity' or the 'leading idea' of 'political education' or of 'democracy learning'? Should the basic identity tend to more 'political learning' or concentrate on more 'civic', 'civil' or 'democracy-learning'? How can it be expressed and explained for international and intercultural understanding? Could international studies in this field of education help to answer these questions?

One of the first points to make in a study of intercultural education is that words and terms have a certain meaning and sense in every language. Terms are embedded in a certain culture. They emerge from that culture. They are modes of communication and ways of thinking in that culture. They symbolise certain contents and provoke certain connotations for those who are used to the words and terms in question. They are expressions of a certain culture, its mentalities and traditions, its collective self-understanding and sense of life (Kockel & Craith, 2004). So we have to involve ourselves in intercultural dialogue to find out what is meant by those words and of what we speak.

In this chapter, I shall address these issues as I compare three countries with different histories of education for citizenship/civics/political education, or whatever generic phrase we decide to use. There will also be some reference to the related programme of the Council of Europe (CE).

The Case of Britain: 'Citizenship Education', 'Citizen-literacy'

In Great Britain (more precisely in England and Wales, but I shall use the term Britain for convenience), one term seems to be widely accepted. It is 'citizenship education', as the National Curriculum defined it in 1999 (DfES, 1999). The previous Crick Report of 1998 also used the term 'teaching democracy' (QCA, 1998). Both terms characterise fairly well what is meant.

The British parliament passed a new Education Act in 1996, and as a consequence of that legislation, government introduced citizenship education in 1999 nationwide through a National Curriculum (NC). Related lessons should cover two hours a week or 5% of total curriculum time, and the new curriculum started to be implemented in September 2002. It begins with cross-curricular, nonstatutory guidelines (that is, as a recommendation but not a legal obligation from the central authorities) at Key Stages 1 and 2, that is, primary school, with pupils aged 5–11 years. It is taught in lessons of 'Personal, Social and Health Education (PSHE)' and is continued with statutory responsibilities (that is, legal obligation) and guidelines at Key Stages 3 and 4, which is Secondary School, with pupils aged 11–16 years (DfES, 2000a). The central aims, competencies and outcomes of this newly introduced 'citizenship education' were defined in the consultative report published in advance of the legislation as fostering the development of social and moral responsibility, community involvement and political literacy (QCA, 1998: 8). However, as the chair of the consultative committee, Bernard Crick, pointed out later, the term 'political literacy' was not beyond criticism, because this term proved to be 'too narrow' to cover the wide scope of what is meant by the terms 'civil', 'democratic' or 'citizenship education' (Crick, 2000b: 79). On the other hand, there seems to be a substantial body of opinion in Britain, that 'political' literacy or 'political' education are regarded with the suspicion that they are partisan, should not enter school and will therefore not be accepted (Frazer, 2000). As a consequence, in the National Curriculum competencies, abilities or 'outcomes' are defined in the triplet: knowledge, skills and understanding (NC). In other scripts we find the triplets of: knowledge, skills and values (Qualifications and Curriculum Authority – QCA) or knowledge, skills and attitudes (Department for Education and Skills – DfES).

The three above-mentioned terms seem now to be predominant as dimensions of teaching and learning in citizenship education. They have, in some way, the status of levels of competencies to be reached by pupils.

Their meaning is widely explained by pragmatic interpretation and listed in various booklets. The triplets differ only on the third dimension: 'understanding', 'values' and 'attitudes'. It seems that this third dimension of learning is intended to focus on the promotion of democratic attitudes, values, commitments, understanding, beliefs, feelings, habits, responsibilities and virtues. In other words, citizen education – besides 'knowledge' and 'practical skills' – is to provide opportunities to promote the spiritual, moral, social and cultural development of pupils. This seems to be a core intention, the underlying idea of citizenship education in the UK.

The development of practical 'skills' on the other hand includes skills of communication on a wide variety of social, political and community issues, the application of numbers and statistics in a social and political context, skills in using ICT, skills of working with others in responsible action in communities, skills of improvement of learning and performance, and skills of problem solving. The training of thinking skills, financial capabilities, economic abilities, work-related skills and education for sustainable development are other related aspects of the curriculum. Apparently, British citizenship education embraces not only ethical, moral or 'political' issues but also relevant social, economic and financial aspects of life.

The triplet of knowledge, skills and understanding (values/attitudes) is headed by high and ambitious targets and cultural aspirations. To quote the Crick Report (1998: 7): 'We aim at no less than a change in the political culture of this country both nationally and locally'. This claim shows that education for citizenship is not only an education policy but also a cultural matter. In this respect we may find direct links to language and cultural education and it should be an intercultural matter too (see also Alred *et al.*, 2003; Blunkett, 2001; Kerr, 1999a; McDonough & Feinberg, 2003; Osler, 2003; Osler & Vincent, 2002).

To implement citizenship education in Britain, strong emphasis is laid on a broad and clear cluster of 'attainment targets' that again explain the outcomes or competences, 'what pupils should be taught about', down to the last detail. All this is accomplished by teachers' handbooks, teachers' guides and a great number of clearly defined 'Schemes of Work' with proposed units for teachers to work with in lessons at school (DfES, 2000b). These schemes again clearly describe: the concrete objectives of each single unit, the concrete proposed activities and concrete planned outcomes of every unit-lesson, not to forget the 'Points to Note', which draw teachers' attention to combinations and links with other units or fields of learning. These schemes and units with contents and attainment targets of citizenship education in Britain are planned and worked out with great attention to detail and the teachers' needs, but in an empirical, pragmatic and interdisciplinary way. We find rather little theoretical framework such as a reference to a specific sector of science (philosophy, sociology, economy, political science or political theory). By this pragmatic and concrete approach teachers should know what to do. Learners should be capable of acquiring civic knowledge, skills and attitudes step by step from the first up to the fourth grade and further, if all this is really put into practice (further discussions in Arthur & Wright, 2003; Arthur *et al*., 2000; Crick, 2000b; Lawton *et al*. 2000; Lockyer *et al*., 2004; Pearce & Hallgarten, 2000; Potter, 2002).

Behind this new and courageous effort to introduce citizenship education in Britain we find a national 'Department for Education and Skills (DfES)' (that is, the Ministry of Education), a national 'Qualifications and Curriculum Authority (QCA)' and last but not least the 'Office for Standards in Education (OFSTED)' as a national inspection of schools and assessment agency. These institutions are joined by other specific government bodies like the 'Learning and Skills Development Agency (LSDA)'. This centralism, being a relatively new phenomenon in England since the 1980s, has now become an accepted fact, but in Germany and in the USA, not being used to deal with this kind of organisational centralisation, the idea is much more difficult to accept and understand.

Britain first started with citizenship education in 1990 by cross-curricular and nonstatutory efforts only. Britain now takes advantage of the following facts.

- that citizenship education in Britain – in comparison with Germany and the USA – came late (1999/2002) but it came effectively with clearly defined statutory responsibilities for schools and solid teachers' handbooks and schemes of work;
- that it is strongly backed by (New-Labour) Government;
- that it meets the mental, political and social crises of the so-called 'Second Modernisation';
- that it is sustained by the actual 'communitarian spirit' of the times; and
- that Britain, in England and Wales, has highly centralised educational institutions and organisations (Quesel, 2003).

On this basis, innovations such as 'citizenship education' can be implemented in a rather consistent and strict way, in a 'top-down model' of policy. Federalist states with more local or regional institutions and decentralised systems-organisations in the member states, look somewhat poor or at least more unorganised in framing what is meant by citizenship education, in contrast to Britain. What Britain, in comparison to Germany, however, may be lacking is a university-located and science-based study of citizenship education. By now there are various courses in initial teacher training for citizenship education in Britain. But this is only the beginning of a professional initial teacher-training *in* and *for* that subject. In future more connection and relationship with political and social science, based on modern theories of society and democracy, of civil rights and obligations and of civil affairs and public problems etc. are needed.

The Case of the USA: 'Social Studies'/'Civic Education'/ 'Civic Literacy'

The USA is, in contrast to the UK, organised in federal states, with autonomy in cultural affairs such as education. The 50 member states of the USA have their own educational systems and their own curricula, which differ, not unexpectedly, on a wide scale. There is, in consequence, no official national curriculum. Even the terms that are used to give this field of education an adequate name are various. Educationists speak of: social studies, citizen education, civic education, civics, civic learning, education for citizenship, education for democratic citizenship, education for democracy, community education, political education or (simply) government (Fields & Feinberg, 2001; Heater, 2004a; Parker, 2003; Sehr, 1997; Sliwka, 2001; Soder *et al.*, 2001).

In my further discussion I shall use the term 'civic education' to characterise the approach in the USA in general. However, it is important to note that all these terms mentioned are not really interchangeable. They may differ from district to district and are often linked up with different 'approaches'. Koopmann distinguishes the following dominant approaches: issue-centred learning (conflict pedagogy), problem-solving, experimental learning and service learning (Koopmann, 2001). Not mentioned in this list is the traditional approach of 'history learning' with the traditional patriotic appeal, involving memorising traditional texts such as the Mayflower Compact (1620), the Bill of Rights (1776), the Declaration of Independence (1776), Federalist Papers and the studying of the Constitution, American history and governmental institutions.

Civic education in the USA goes back to the foundation of the USA and has as ancestors Thomas Jefferson, James Madison and John Adams, who at an early stage defined the 'civic mission of public schools' (Gilreath, 1999). They expressed the notion that 'popular government' could not be stable, alive and significant without an enlightened and responsible citizenry. They argued that even well designed institutions are not sufficient to sustain democracy enduringly. Today it is concluded that 'A free and democratic society must rely on knowledge, skills and virtues of its citizens' (CCE, 2003b: 1). The first academic effort to establish civic education in the USA was made by Francis Lieber at the end of the Civil War, in the period after 1865, to overcome the social disruptions of the war (see Heater, 2004). However, civic education began to grow only at the end of the 19th century, and especially with an emphasis on 'education for democracy' as a consequence of the writings of John Dewey, particularly in his *Education and Democracy* in 1916 and the rise of the 'progressive-education' movement in the USA (Evans, 2004). After WWII the Deweyan inspiration declined and the behaviourist school of American social science became predominant. At that time, the term 'social studies' began to dominate the field, but in the 1970s social studies went through a period of idealistic, ideological and partisan politicisation. A conservative backlash followed. From the neoliberal, neoconservative and religious-fundamentalist point of view there was an attempt 'to lay social studies in its grave' (Evans, 1997: 197). As Amy Gutmann reports (1999), these neoconservative and religious-fundamentalists attacked civic education in school as being suspected of political indoctrination. Following a doctrine of privatisation, they tried to exclude all aspects of ethical, moral and civic education from public school, arguing that these should be a private, parental, family or church affair. Even today, Ronald W. Evans (2004) speaks about 'the social studies war'.

Since the middle of the 1980s and strongly in the 1990s, efforts to re-envisage, reinvent, reaffirm or revitalise and recivilise 'social studies' developed and gained a counterdominant position. This movement, trying to give an answer to the mental crises in the USA, was headed by leading communitarians and various private foundations (for example, Barber, 1998; Barber & Battistoni, 1999). Evaluation reports on previous 'social studies' had noticed the neglected status of civic education in society and at schools and identified 'conceptual fuzziness' in social studies/civic education at schools in the 1980s. Diffuse intentions, goals, syllabuses and methodological approaches were noted even though some version of patriotism-based education was always a part of school life in the USA. In 1987 the Center for Civic Education in Calabasas (CCE), Calabasas/California, was founded. It is a nonprofit, nonpartisan education corporation, which is voluntarily dedicated to fostering the development of informed, responsible participation in civic life by citizens committed to values and principles of American constitutional democracy and has gained a leading position by proposing a framework for civic education with the volume entitled *CIVITAS: A Framework for Civic Education* (CCE, 1991) and by establishing *National Standards for Civics and Government* (CCE, 1994/2003). The former publication, published as Bulletin No. 86 of the National Council for the Social Studies in 1991, emerged from a joint project of the Center for Civic Education and the Council for Advancement of Citizenship, which itself is an umbrella organisation of 90 national and regional organisations dedicated to voluntarily fostering civic participation and citizenship education. *CIVITAS* was developed and formulated by an impressive number of contributors and stresses the following goals:

- Civic virtue: goal to foster among citizens civic dispositions and commitments to fundamental values and principles required for competent and responsible citizenship;
- Civic participation: goal to develop among citizens participatory skills required to monitor and influence the formulation, amendment and implementation of public policy, as well as to participate in voluntary efforts to solve neighbourhood and community problems;
- Civic knowledge and intellectual skills: goal to provide citizens with the knowledge and intellectual skills required to monitor and influence ... public policy ... (CCE, 1991: XXVII).

In his personal preface to *CIVITAS*, R. Freeman Butts addresses teachers, officials and curriculum developers in the USA. He points out that *CIVITAS* 'cannot go into detail about the usefulness of *CIVITAS* in the continuing wars over the best approach to civic education. But I would like to wager that *CIVITAS* will not only be useful but essential to be reckoned with by all major disputants and ideologies' (CCE, 1991: XXI). It should be noted that *CIVITAS* stresses three major contents:

- institutional design and history of democracy, public policy and law, and constitutional government;
- the broader society: problems, issues and conflicts in community and neighbourhood;
- the personal aspect: civic attitudes, dispositions and commitments.

In 1994, the Center for Civic Education published the *National Standards for Civics and Government* (CCE, 2003b). More than 600 contributors worked on this project; official representatives of departments of education in the federal states or of private foundations and

academics and teachers, aided by international reviewers. In addition to
'civic education', the terms 'civics' and 'government' are also mentioned
in this book; the leading terms still differ. The *National Standards* starts
with the 'civic mission of schools' citing famous phrases from Thomas
Jefferson, Martin Luther King, John F. Kennedy and other famous
Americans. Secondly, it explains the 'need for increased attention to
civic education' today. Thirdly, it names the institutions and groups of
persons to whom the standards are addressed and of use: standards for
students, standards for teachers, standards for schools and standards
for state and local education agencies. Fourthly, it offers a definition of
skills to be attained. They are twofold:

- intellectual skills (identify, describe, explain, evaluate a position,
  take a position and defend a position);
- participatory skills (capacity to influence policies and decisions by
  working with others, clearly articulating interests, building coali-
  tions, negotiating, compromising and seeking consensus, managing
  conflicts).

What is missing here is the dimension of values, attitudes or social and
moral abilities, more prominent in the British documents. Participatory
skills should be developed by providing students with opportunities to
practise these skills. These opportunities include:

- monitoring politics and government by tracking an issue in the
  media, researching in libraries, gathering information, interviewing
  people, observing meetings and so on;
- influencing politics and government by working in groups; taking
  part in classroom governance; simulation: town meetings, hearings,
  judicial trials, lobbying, campaigning and voting; observing governmental agencies; presenting positions in debates and to student
  councils; writing letters to newspapers; performing services in
  school and in communities directly related to civic life.

The fifth focus is on the 'content-standards', which are outlined in
terms of five main questions: What is government and what should it do?
What are the basic values and principles of American democracy? How
does government established by the constitution embody the purpose,
values and principles of American democracy? What is the relationship
of the USA to other nations and world affairs? What are the roles of the
citizen in American democracy? These five questions are the leading
content-focus, and are repeated at every grade.

The systematic nature of the *National Standards* combines the content-standards with outcome-standards for grade K4, for grades K5–8 and for grades K9–12. In this manner, the book defines what contents should be known and what learning outcomes are expected at the end of grade 4, through grades 5–8 and through grades 9–12. The higher the grade, the more complex the contents and outcomes, and there is a defined system of contents with outcomes at each stage and finally three levels of performance (basic, proficient and advanced).

The volume follows its own logic, rationale and systematic structure. It is solid, impressive and logically convincing: but rather complex, often rather cognitive and not uncomplicated. Thus, many questions arise. How can all this be put into practice? Isn't it just a theoretical exercise or publicity event? How is it transferred into the state curricula and to schools? How can it be taught to teacher students or to teachers in in-service courses? Doesn't it contain an overload of contents and attainment targets? Isn't it often rather idealistic and in many ways too US-patriotic? Can students in school really influence the formulation, implementation, amendment and enforcement of public policy? Perhaps the main objective of the CCE is to present a comprehensive account of what can be meant by 'civic literacy', 'civics' or 'government'; the umbrella is widely stretched. In comparison with UK schemes, the approach of CCE may not be as attractive and 'handy' to meet teachers' direct needs. However, these two publications give an impression of what a majority of authors understand 'civic literacy' to be, whilst leaving the door open for various approaches and methods in civic education in the USA.

The Case of Germany: 'Political Education', 'Political Literacy'

The case of Germany seems to be more complicated than the British, American or European cases. Germany is a federalist union (Bund, FRG) with 16 member states (Bundesländer) that have autonomy in cultural affairs such as education. These 16 member states each have their own educational curricula. There is no official national curriculum, and there are no schemes of work as in Britain or even a voluntary recommended curriculum or system of goals and contents like *CIVITAS* in the USA. There are some 160 different school books in use, accompanied by various commercial collections of schemes of work and supplementary units. Twenty-three different terms cover how the subject is named and what is proposed in school curricula. Even in the single member-states the terms vary according to the type of school and the grade of class, just like in the USA. In the different curricula there are different combinations of politics, history and geography, of politics and law, of society and economy or politics and environmental studies. In some cases the subject is named *Politik* ('politics'), in others *Gesellschaft* ('society') or even *Wirtschaft/Politik* ('economics/politics'). Beyond school, in public, in politics and in adult education the term *Politische Bildung* (political education) is dominant. *Politische Bildung* is used in the field of teacher education and even teacher associations use that term in their titles. A very influential institution of the federal government, beyond the cultural autonomy of the member-states, is the so-called *Bundeszentrale für Politische Bildung* (Federal Centre for Political Education, newly translated as 'Federal Agency for Civic Education, Germany'), which produces various books on the subject, organises events and funds conferences. Academic experts in the didactics of *Politische Bildung* in universities often use the term *Politikdidaktik* (politic-didactics) or 'didactics of political education' (Roberts, 2002). To sum up the 'fuzziness' of the terms, what elsewhere is called 'citizenship education' or 'civic education', *Politische Bildung* is best translated as 'political education' (as a mode of instruction) or 'political literacy' (as an outcome).

The subject *Politik* is not taught in primary schools (*Grundschule*) explicitly and has an uncertain existence in Grades 5– 10 in the tripartite secondary school system, where it is mostly taught in combination with history and geography. Later, in Grades 11– 13, the subject acquires more attention and is usually taught for one or two lessons per week, often in combination with law or economics. In the syllabus, many contents, goals and standards seem in practice to be rather similar and in a broad sense interchangeable, but in many cases they are not at all. Furthermore, there is a great difference between theory (political didactics) and practice (in schools). Nevertheless, research on the curricula contents in the 16 states revealed four main fields of practical teaching:

(1) way of life and shaping social relations (family, school, communities, local government incl. media . . .);
(2) political-governmental-democratic system (with relevant sub-subjects incl. international affairs . . .);
(3) law and the judicial system (human rights, rule of law, state constitution, law in every-day-life, youth and law . . .);
(4) social market economy, labour market, vocational education . . .

In the theory of didactics (in Germany a highly rated academic discipline), the most general goal of this kind of education could be called 'political self-awareness' or 'self-realisation' (*politische Mündigkeit*) in the idealistic tradition of Kant. This includes: knowledge (*Wissen*), capacity for political judgement (*politische Urteilsfähigkeit*), issue-centred learning, problem-solving, conflict resolution and capacity for political action (*politische Handlungsfähigkeit*).

In the theory of political education (political didactics), little attention has been given to the dimension of affective, ethical and moral commitment, of habits and attitudes or of cultural, national and patriotic values. Patriotic values, especially, are under deep suspicion. This may be explained by the German experience that 'political' education in Germany since the 19th century has gone through several stages of highly patriotic, state-centred, idealistic and normative-ideological, even race-centred teaching. The English term 'citizen' always meant in German: 'state-citizen' (*Staatsbürger*) and has not the civil and civilian connotations that it has in Anglo-American language and cultures.

After WWII the American and British authorities tried to re-educate the German people 'fallen into disease' (1933–45) and introduce a pragmatic approach to democratic and social education for citizenship in Germany, in the tradition of John Dewey's philosophy of education. The terms used for this new subject for teaching of democratic culture in schools were *Gemeinschaftskunde* ('community studies') and *Sozialkunde* ('social studies'). Today these terms still have their roots in the pragmatic and civic attitudes of the American and British education policy in Germany in the late 1940s and early 1950s. However, this civic/civilian approach was not really accepted by German educationists, teachers and politicians. The subject continued to be called *Staatsbürgerkunde* or *staatsbürgerliche Erziehung* ('state-citizen-upbringing') over a long period of time. Later, in the 1960s and 1970s, the terms 'political didactics' and 'political education' acquired a leading position in academic circles (Gagel, 1994, 2000) whereas the terms *Gemeinschaftskunde* ('community education') and *Sozialkunde* ('social studies') were further in use to characterise the subject in schools. During the 1970s again a kind of ideological, political and partisan push shook the subject in Germany, as it did in the USA. In 1977 several political-didactics experts in teacher training at universities met in a little town near Stuttgart and established an accord on how to deal with the problem of politicisation (the Beutelsbacher Konsens). This accord stated that:

- it is not permitted to overwhelm pupils with the political or ideological opinions of the teacher;
- what is in dispute in science and politics should be dealt with controversially in school lessons;
- pupils should be encouraged to formulate their own interests in political questions and try to influence a political situation according to their own interests. (Schiele & Schneider, 1987)

Following this accord, German didactics experts have tended to deal with 'political' key questions in a rather 'neutral' way, leaving pupils to find their own answers and judgements in the field of political problems or questions. Various German didactics experts of today reduce political education to being 'rational', 'analytic' and nonpatriotic. Some warn against 'moralising' in education. Even teaching democracy is under suspicion of 'alarmism' and 'ideology' (Sander, 2001; 2003). As a consequence, many experts in political didactics concentrate on the 'analysis of *Politik*'.

As a consequence of this, another problem arose: there is and has been the question in German political science and political education of what the term 'the political' could really mean, what it is and how it could be identified. As there is in German only one term for the subject called *Politik*, leading authors discovered that in English there are three terms to characterise 'the political': the triplet of polity, policy and politics. This threefold meaning of: 'the political' was adopted by the didactics of political education and interpreted as: 'polity' – framework of the institutional system; 'policy' – fields of political contents (according to policy analysis); and 'politics' – strategies, tactics and processes of power, governance, interests and decision-making. Thus, leading theorists on 'political didactics' see the task to foster the three corresponding elements through political education: knowledge or awareness of polity, policy and politics (*Form, Inhalt und Prozess*) (Massing & Weißeno, 1995). On this interpretation of 'the political', the core term *Politik* deals with state polity, state policy and state politics, with 'high' problems and key questions of the times, and tries thereby to prepare pupils and students to become involved in the reality of '*Politik*'.

Furthermore, it is important to note that student-teachers study, at universities – besides pedagogy and psychology – mainly the subject of political science. Contemporary German political education, therefore, has political science as its main reference-discipline at university. The theory of didactics, like political science, is state-centred as well as issue-centred, often has a cognitive bias, and sets its sights mainly on the higher grades of education in Gymnasium (Grades 11–13). Some authors in political didactics, being in opposition to the mainstream, argue that centring all the efforts of 'political' education around the term *Politik* and fostering 'political' knowledge, 'political' judgement and 'political' capacities for 'political' action leaves little room for personal 'self-learning' or 'social learning' in the tradition of Dewey. The approach of 'social learning' is, in the mainstream, considered to be 'un-political learning', should be avoided and therefore not be the subject of 'political' education in schools. To meet democracy not only as a form of government but also as a 'way of life' or to give *Lebenshilfe* (personal help 'how to live' in this complex society) or to promote social experimentalism seems to be outside this mainstream theoretical approach. It seems that in this orientation German *Politische Bildung* has more to do with German political state-centred culture in comparison with English or American cultures with their stronger roots in civil society or in democratic traditions, commitments and morality. In Germany, political education is in no sense patriotic but there is a lack of terms similar to English terms such as 'civics' or 'civilian education' or 'citizenship education'.

In contrast to the approach of 'political education', as it is taught by 'political didactics' at universities in Germany, new German approaches in this field have devoted themselves to 'democracy-learning'. They try to embrace, and combine:

- the development of a 'democratic self' in behaviour, commitments, values and habits, from the beginning of Grade 4 up to the top Grades 12–13;
- the promotion of 'social awareness' by 'social learning' to foster nonviolent, cooperative, empathic and community orientated behaviour and skills; and
- the development of political awareness and of 'democratic-political' knowledge and learning in a broader sense, including the political system of democracy, national and international institutions and environmental issues.

This approach tries to put 'democracy' instead of 'Politik' more into the centre of civic education in Germany (Breit & Schiele, 2002). It finds its backing in a fourfold scientific approach to democracy-theory defined as: democracy as a form of living/way of life, democracy as a form of society, democracy as a form of governance and democracy as a global project (Himmelmann, 2004).

The teaching of 'democracy/learning' (and living) aims to encourage: self-learning and self-competence, social learning and social competence, and political learning, democratic awareness. The last outcome should be: democratic competence with defined degrees of focus at each stage (Infant/Junior School (1–4), Secondary School I (5–10) and Secondary School II (10–12)). In this respect, 'democracy learning' has strong ties to a Federal Government programme entitled 'Democratic Action'/ 'Democracy Learning and Living' (Beutel & Fauser, 2001). It is strongly attached to the programme of 'Education for Democratic Citizenship (EDC)' that has been launched by the Council of Europe (CE) in 1997 and worked out in many documents since the year 2000.

Council of Europe

The Council of Europe set up the project 'Education for Democratic Citizenship' in 1997. This is a project to promote democratic citizenship in the Western European countries as well as in the new democracies of Eastern European countries. Meanwhile a great number of 'work-programmes', 'documents', 'All-European-surveys' and 'conference- and activity-reports' have been published. Particularly important documents are those dealing with 'sites of citizenship', 'strategies for learning democratic citizenship', 'basic concepts and competencies for education for democratic citizenship' (all published in 2000, see, for example, Duerr, 2000) and 'school – a democratic learning community' (Duerr, 2004). These documents of the 'Council for Cultural Co-Operation (CDCC) of the Council of Europe' give an exciting outlook. Including the project of 'citizenship education' in the UK and the above-mentioned works of the Centre for Civic Education, they seem to be a 'treasure chest' for further evaluation, innovation and development of 'democratic citizenship education' in other countries.

Conclusion: Reflecting on the Terms and Concepts

To come to a conclusion, we can identify the main differences when comparing 'citizenship education' in Britain, 'civics' or 'civic education' in the USA, 'education for democratic citizenship' in the Council of Europe and 'political education' in Germany. The differences can be seen first in the leading terms that express the 'inner philosophy' of the related concept and subject, and second, in the trend to a more civic/civilian, or a more democratic-patriotic or a more political education. To acquire more knowledge about the subject it would be necessary to undertake more empirical research to know if these assumptions about concepts are in fact put into practice in schools. As public education tries to transfer the nation's culture, its tradition, ideas and beliefs to the next generation, the different kinds of civic/civilian, democratic-patriotic or political education reflect specific cultural aspects and aims of education in the country in question.

Our brief comparison of different systems and approaches to civic or citizenship-education shows differences and similarities. Even such comparison gives, without more solid empirical research, only a small insight into the broader problem of intercultural understanding, which is the focus of this volume. If we look behind the use of terms and try to reveal the real sense of different terminologies, in addition to empirical research we have to search for the underpinning meanings and connotations of the terms in each culture. In English, for example, we find connotations of 'citizenship' to 'city': orientated to town, to municipality and community, related to the Latin use of 'civis' and 'civitas'. It does not directly refer to state or politics. The term 'civic' in British custom has the collective memory of 'Roman citizenship' (*civilis*): to be of honour, be part of a city or municipality, having rights and liberties, having civil virtues like respect for others. The term 'civil' means: to be gregarious and fair, belonging to a shared community, obeying laws, being polite, not rude, being not criminal, not using force, not being ecclesiastical and living without official religious ceremony. The term 'citizen' itself is connected to: freeman, *Borgess*, civilian, member/inhabitant of a state (here the 'state' comes in) (Oxford Dictionary). German dictionaries transform 'civics' (in contrast to English) into *Staatsbürgerkunde* ('state-citizenship') (*Langenscheidts Wörterbuch*).

Recently the problem of use of language and translation was shown very clearly. The Council of Europe proposed in 2000 the concept of 'Education for Democratic Citizenship'. This term was translated in Germany into *Demokratie lernen* ('learning democracy') whereas in Austria it was translated into *demokratische (Staats-) Bürgerschaft* ('democratic (state-)citizenship'). The Federal Centre for Political Education (*Bundeszentrale für politische Bildung*) translates the term 'Education for Democratic Citizenship' (word for word) into *demokratische Bürgerschafts-bildung* ('democratic citizenship-education'). The *Bundeszentrale* has recently begun to use this in the translation of its own denomination, the term 'Federal Agency for Civic Education, Germany' and speaks of *Bürgerschaftsbildung* ('citizenship education') instead of *Politische Bildung* ('political education').

In my view it seems that the English term of 'citizenship education' tends in many ways to a more civil/civilian education than to political education or to patriotic education. The English approach to citizenship education tends more to foster civil, social and sociable commitments and behaviour than German political education. English authors, on the other hand, seem to dislike American 'civics' (estimated to be too low-based) as well as the 'patriotic' missionary sense in American schools (estimated to be too intrusive).

When David Kerr published his international comparison of the new development of citizenship education in Europe, which he identified as a 'civic megatrend' (Kennedy, 1997), he found the following influential factors for the different meanings of civics or citizenship education:

- the historical tradition of a country including its specific values, culture and tradition,
- the cultural-geographical-religions position,
- the sociopolitical structure,
- the related economic system,
- the organisation of and responsibilities for education,
- the culturally based educational values and aims, and
- the specific regulatory arrangements. (Kerr, 1999b)

If we not only look at Britain, USA, the Council of Europe and Germany, but include Portugal, Spain, South Africa, Japan or Hong Kong, the different cultural backgrounds can easily be revealed even more (Lee *et al.*, 2004; Print, 1997). The future task of intercultural understanding in this field should be to identify the meaning of the terms in different languages and cultures – even more if foreign authors use English terms – and to find some common definitions and concepts of civic education, citizenship education or democracy education that are compatible with different cultures and still express their universal and intercultural perspective (CCE, 2003a;b; 2004; Patrick, 2003). Cultures themselves are developing communicative systems expressed in language, meanings, traditions and beliefs. So we need more multilingual communication with one another and international communications about different cultures to find a common ground for citizenship education or teaching and learning democracy in the future. This process has just begun (Kockel & Craith, 2004).

The leading question in this process is: 'What are the ties that hold democracies together?' Could and should there still be nationalistic, patriotic, racial, ethnic or religious values in different cultures? Or shouldn't there rather be universal values, intercultural commitments, civic dispositions and democratic-citizenship attitudes. The question is the 'question of identity' of the future democratic societies, of the future democratic culture and of the future democratic self. It is the question of 'self-legitimisation' of democracy after the end of East–West confrontation. It is a moral, cultural and political question. This question is not limited to one country, nation or state. It leads to the question of how the educational system can help our young people to cope with all the open questions of our times peacefully, cooperatively and open-mindedly and, in this way, to keep the very idea of democracy alive, vivid, enduring and inventive. Our task is to find ways to foster democratic citizenship in an endangered and vulnerable culture of freedom, peace and justice and in a world of rapid change, a world of intercultural conflicts and global uncertainties. It is the question of forming intercultural identities at home and abroad (CIRCLE, 2003; Sünker *et al.*, 2003).

Chapter 5

Contested Notions of Citizenship and Citizenship Education: The Chinese Case

ANWEI FENG

Introduction

While the general aims of education are often under debate in many parts of the world, China has for nearly half a century had a clearly stated goal for general education, which was proclaimed in 1957 by Mao Zedong, the former paramount leader (Mao Zedong, 1977) and inherited with only minor modifications by his successors, Deng Xiaoping and Jiang Zeming. Mao stated that 'Our general policy in education is to enable the educated to become *workers* who have thoroughly developed *morally*, intellectually and physically and have gained *socialist conscious-ness and culture*' (Mao Zedong, 1977: 385, my translation and italics). This educational goal is incorporated into various official documents includ-ing China's Education Law[1] adopted in 1995. The definitive outcome of general education in the Maoist era was to mould characters of a 'socialist worker' in order to serve 'proletarian politics' and was slightly modified in the post-Maoist era 'to cultivate a socialist successor' to 'serve socialism and the people' (Shu & Tang, 2003). To achieve this general educational aim, schools and universities all over the country have long been running compulsory courses such as 'socialist morality', 'socialist ideology', 'political education' and 'Marxism, Leninism and Mao Zedong's thought' and organising a wide range of extracurricular activities to promote socialist ideologies, patriotism, collectivism and morality.

The concept of citizenship is by no means new in China in the literature of sociology, political education and other social sciences. The discussion of the concept has gained momentum in the post-Maoist decades both inside China and internationally. While some authors still devote their attention to historical perspectives of the concept (e.g. Fogel & Zarrow, 1997; Wong, 1999), many focus their work on the conceptual changes in postliberation China since 1949 (see Goldman & Perry, 2002, for a collection of essays). Many Chinese and international educators have also actively engaged in discussions on the aim and ideology of citizenship education, despite the aim statement as cited above and numerous policy documents and official publications elaborating the aim statement. The notions of citizenry and citizenship and the practice in education are earnestly debated and contested.

This chapter will first provide some linguistic evidence of this contestation by giving an account of the terminology relevant to the notion of citizenry. As in any other linguistic system, different terms in Chinese that appear to refer to the same concept can have immensely different implications for education as well as for the sociopolitical life of citizens. A review of the conception of citizenship and models adopted in citizenship education will draw upon evidence of contestation from official documents and academic publications. All these will lead to the final discussion where the significance of this contestation will be discussed from an intercultural perspective.

Chinese 'Equivalents' to Citizenry

Byram (in this volume) points out that linguistic complexities in communication should not be overlooked in discussions of complex concepts such as citizenship among people of different languages. This is also the case with Chinese as several terms can be taken as equivalents, including the seemingly precise counterpart but elusive *gongmin* ('the public people'), the relatively conventional *guomin* (literally, 'the people of the state'), the fairly political *shimin* ('the city people') and the powerful *renmin* ('the people'). They all seem to refer to membership of the nation-state, but each has its own intricate etymology and specific connotations in contemporary China. In discussions of Chinese citizenry, the terminology issue needs to be examined with reference to the political dynamics of the country.

Guomin was coined more than two millennia ago to refer to residents in rival warring states, thus, more to subjects under the jurisdiction of feudal states than to nationals in the modern sense. Ironically, the term lost its popularity and gradually disappeared after China became a unified empire ruled by Qin Shihuang, the first emperor of China. The term *chenmin* ('subjects') was predominantly used for many centuries. At the turn of the 20th century, *guomin* quickly gained its popularity again when late Qing dynasty reformer Liang Qichao reintroduced it by borrowing the Chinese characters back from Japan where the term had been adopted to capture ideas imported from the West (Shen & Chien, 1999). Liang defined the term, *guomin*, as state-conferred membership to encourage full participations in the modern nation-state. His main aim was to promote nationalist spirits so as to transform an imperial state into a modern nation-state, rejecting as impractical 'anarchist' human rights and universal ideals of international harmony. His interpretation had a great impact on Chinese society as a whole. The term soon entered state-sponsored textbooks and the concept of *guomin* was later adopted by the Chinese Nationalist Party and used in its name, *Guomin Dang*.

Another term that is all-embracing is *gongmin* ('the public people'), the origin of which can be traced back to the time of Confucius when the character *gong*, meaning 'public', was used, as opposed to *si*, which means 'individual'. The term was used on and off until the late Qing period when some Chinese intellectuals such as Kang Youwei (mis)took it as an Eastern progressive concept and (re)introduced it to China (Zarrow, 1997). *Gongmin* thus can be interpreted as a Chinese counterpart of the Habermasian 'public sphere', which refers to wide-ranging elite traditions of local activism (Rankin, 1993). Since the founding of the People's Republic of China in 1949, the term *gongmin* has gradually replaced *guomin* for the obvious reason that the latter is indicative of *Guomin Dang*, the Nationalist Party. Though *guomin* is not entirely forgotten,[2] *gongmin* is used more and more in legal and official documents as well as popular parlance to refer to people who are recognised constitutionally, not necessarily politically and legally (as we shall see below), as members of the state. It is much more commonly used to refer to general membership of the state in the last two decades or so and has become more of an equivalent term than any others to the English 'citizenry'.

The term *shimin* is used exclusively to refer to 'urban populace'. However, it is this term that most suggests a balance of citizen rights and obligations owing to the rise of new urban classes – industrial workers, professionals, businesspeople, students – who have played key roles in the history of 20th-century China. Goldman and Perry (2002) note that from the 1911 Revolution to the protests in 1989, manifestos demanding greater popular participation and human rights have been issued in the name of *shimin*. In the same way, governments have also used the term to call upon urban residents to maintain social stability and uphold civic virtues.

Though subtle, the distinctions between the three Chinese terms defined above are fairly evident to many people, academics, politicians or even ordinary people. The concept of citizenry has been made immensely complicated by *renmin* ('the people'), which was particularly widely used in official documents and ideological discussions during the Maoist era, and is still used today. The seemingly neutral but highly politicised term was used in political documents to refer to those that belong to the working class in cities, the poor peasant class in the country and other patriotic elements in the society who were reportedly trusted by the communist government. *Gongmin* differed from *renmin* in that the former did not only, theoretically, include the latter but also those 'reactionary' and 'counter-revolutionary' social classes such as bourgeoisie, landlords, rich peasants and rightists who were, in short, *renmin*'s enemies. All *gongmin* had to perform duties as citizens but those reactionary class *gongmin* were not entitled to legal and political rights allegedly enjoyed by *renmin* (Yu, 2002). In the post-Maoist era, as struggles between these social classes are seemingly less emphasised and the neo-bourgeois social classes, the newly formulated economic elites, are increasingly politically recognised, the distinction made between *renmin* and *gongmin* seems to be waning gradually. Nevertheless, the distinction is not forgotten. In the latest 1982 Constitution, still applicable today, the *renmin* and *gongmin* distinction still remains though the definition of the former is extended to include the 'majority' of Chinese (*The Constitution*, 1982). Article 34 deprives certain *gongmin*s of their rights of voting and being voted for, though these certain citizens are not explicitly defined.

As in official documents, academics and people in China in general are beginning to accept the term *gongmin* as an all-embracing formal term to refer to membership of the state. The politically prestigious term *renmin* has left its deep mark on all fronts including education. *Renmin* still remains a key word in titles of government organisations such as *Renmin Zhenfu* (People's Government), *Renmin Daibiao Dahui* (People's Congress), *Renmin Fayuan* (People's Courts), *Renmin Jundui* (People's Army), *Renmin Jincha* (People's Police) and so on. Most widely circulated official journals, newspapers, magazines, books and documents have *renmin* as the prefix. The Party's flagship newspaper is *Renmin Rebao* (People's Daily) and the monthly journal in education distributed nationwide is *Renmin Jiaoyu* (People's Education). This journal has been and will remain the official journal of the Ministry of Education to direct the country's education for years to come. Jiang Zeming (2002: 265), at a national congress of education held in 1999, stated that 'education must serve socialism and the people (*renmin*)'.

The contested notion of citizenry described above explains why some scholars such as Li and Zhong (2002) are cautious in academic discussions. They are aware that the terms are still value-laden and aim to clarify the terminology before discussion.

Citizenship Contested

The concept of citizenship in China can be traced back to the Confucian thought of *minben* (people as the basis). Serious discussions, however, did not start until the late 19th century when influential intellectuals like Liang Qichao and Kang Yuwei as mentioned above pondered the concepts of *guomin* and *gongmin* under foreign influences (Zarrow, 1997). In the 20th century, the Chinese view of citizenship has primarily been associated with notions such as duties and obligations, loyalty to the country, public moralities and civic virtues. Rights have generally been considered as given by the state, not as inherent natural rights (Nathan, 1985). This view was particularly salient in the Maoist era when all ordinary Chinese had to make every effort to show their loyalty and civic virtues in order to identify themselves with members of *renmin* (the people), because failing to do so would result in their being aligned with the enemies of the state. Citizens' rights as a whole were only symbolically written in the constitution.

In the last couple of decades, according to some observers, citizenship has evolved in subtle but significant ways in China. The changing attitude of the people, particularly intellectuals, towards political rights in citizenship is obvious enough from the democratic movements in the post-Maoist era. Sinologists and historians, such as Goldman (1994) and Black and Munro (1993), agree that from the democracy wall movement in the late 1970s to the 1989 *Tiananmen* event, the Chinese people demonstrated an increasingly strong will in asserting political, civil and social rights, as defined by Marshall (1950). From similar perspectives, many authors in Goldman and Perry (2002) examine the subtly changing perceptions of urban dwellers and villagers in contemporary China and portray a largely evolving situation in citizenship construction. In describing government positions, Yu (2002) notes that the provisions for citizens' rights in the 1982 Constitution are placed in a more prominent position than in its predecessors. He believes that this reflects a changing attitude of the government towards citizenship. Subsequent partial amendments to the 1982 constitution, Yu states, have further demonstrated the attitude shift. In a similar manner, Dowdle (2002) examines the structure and dynamics in the National People's Congress and concludes that new political norms including the concept of citizenship are inadvertently and gradually being formulated.

A recent policy document, however, seems to show that the change in official conception of citizenship is less evident than Yu and Dowdle indicate. *Gongmin Daode Jianshe Shishi Gangyao* (*Gangyao* hereafter) (the Implementation Guidelines to Construct Civic Virtues of Citizens) is a document issued in late 2001 by the highest government body, the Central Committee of the Chinese Communist Party, through the government flagship newspaper, *Renmin Ribao* (People's Daily), to all party units, organisations and the ordinary people throughout the country. *Gangyao* explicitly specifies what the Central Committee (the government) takes citizenship to mean. In its 40-paragraph guidelines grouped into eight parts, the document devotes most of them to citizens' obligations and 'moral standards', which are highlighted in 20 characters arranged in five paralleled, four-character phrases which can be literally translated into:

> in the whole society, the *basic moral standards* that should be vigorously promoted include: *patriotism and legal consciousness, civility and integrity, social harmony and friendliness, frugality and self-strengthening, and readiness to dedicate and contribute.* (*Gangyao*, 2001: 1, my translation and emphasis)

Citizenship in this context is clearly equated with socialist ideology and political morals. 'Socialist citizens', according to *Gangyao*, should possess these moral standards and perform duties for the country unconditionally and must be educated generation after generation.

Gangyao was promulgated less than two months after China was admitted into the World Trade Organisation. The social, economic and psychological impacts of becoming a WTO member state and of globalisation in general had been felt in many areas of the country. People from all walks of life seemed to expect reforms and changes to meet the challenges brought about by globalisation and internationalisation (Lardy, 2002). The promulgation of *Gangyao* at this point in time was apparently meant to send a message to the whole country that reforms and changes in the country's economy and other domains may be inevitable but socialist ideology in general and 'socialist citizenship' construction in particular will remain firm and unaffected.

In the 40-paragraph text, Paragraph 7 touches upon citizens' legal rights:

> *(A citizen's) personal legal rights must be aligned with his/her obligations and commitment to society.* On the one hand, we should ensure that a citizen has political, economic, cultural and social rights. We should

encourage people to gain material benefits through honest work and legal business. On the other hand, we must guide them to conscientiously fulfil their obligations specified in the constitution and other governances and actively perform their social duties. (A citizen) must know how to integrate rights with duties. He/She must *always put the national and people's interests first* while enjoying personal legal rights. In short, a citizen needs to build up his/her socialist rights-and-duties outlook. (*Gangyao*, 2001: 2, my translation and emphasis)

The government's position on citizens' rights is crystal clear. Personal rights or interests are conditional. Only when citizens fulfil their obligations and perform their social duties and only when there is no conflict between the nation's and the collective interests and their own can they start thinking about political, economic, cultural and social rights. A second point worth noting is the mentioning of 'material benefits' in this paragraph. The sentence with this phrase suggests the government's willingness to confer economic rights in an ethical way. On the other hand, the lack of elaboration on political, cultural and social rights makes economic rights, at least vaguely, less relevant.

Judging from the official position demonstrated in *Gangyao*, one can conclude that the official conception is a *collectivistic socialist citizenship* model in which citizenship could be viewed as membership in a socialist and collectivistic society and the moral standards and responsibilities, obligations and loyalty to the country that go with it. Social and political rights of citizens are permitted on condition that their commitments to the nation and the society are fulfilled and there exists no conflict between the national or collective interests and individual rights.

Yang (2001) claims that the promulgation of *Gangyao* is in effect meant to implement the government slogan of *Yide Zhiguo* (to govern the country with morals). Recent literature from educational research has recorded vigorous discussions on the correlation between citizenship and moral construction. Some scholars give their full backing to *Gangyao*, interpreting it in detail and listing implementation measures (X.F. Wang, 2002). Discussions on inculcating morals, patriotism and collectivism are often given with frequent references to Marxism, Leninism and Mao Zedong thoughts, and other current official views as backings of arguments (Zhan & Xu, 2002; Zhang, 2002). Many of these discussions argue for further research and systematisation of moral education for primary, secondary and tertiary levels and recommend ways to further permeate moral education across curricula.

There are no explicit critiques of the fundamentals of the official conception. However, some education scholars are beginning to bring up issues such as human rights and democracy that were hardly found in the literature of citizenship before. Li (2003) states that 'citizenship education' should include the study of topics such as human rights, democracy, freedom, legal and political systems. Li (2000) also argues for a move from 'country as the base' to 'human rights as fundamental' in conceptualising citizenship. As opposed to collectivism, He (2001) proposes placing at the centre awareness of individual rights and values in conceiving citizenship in China because collectivism as traditionally preached in education and consequently internalised by the masses reduces individual values and rights to almost nothing. The transition from collectivism to individual rights and values is thus the transition from the traditional totalitarian society ruled by morals and social elites to a postmodern society to be ruled by laws for which China is striving. From a historical perspective, Jin (2000) attributes the country's under-development to the failure to place individuals as the centre in the traditional social order but, unlike He, he argues for a pluralist perspective in citizenship education bringing to the fore both the individual values and rights and the well-being of society, which is multidimensional in terms of ethnicity, culture and social groups.

Recently, an increasing number of authors have added a world dimension to discussions on the meaning and teaching of citizenship and many of them adopt a comparative approach, introducing international conceptions and placing the Chinese debate in a wider context. In a fairly comprehensive review of parallel notions such as nationalism and democracy, liberalism and republicanism, globalisation and world citizenship, Zhao (2003) argues for directly addressing and adjusting tensions between nationalism and liberalism and emphasising individual awareness of rights and participation in citizenship education. She asserts that citizenship with a world dimension sets a new scene for citizenship education, negating to a certain degree an emphasis on nation-state and ethnocentrism.

Multiculturalism is a theme that appears in many discussions. Chen (2003) states that multiculturalism as a natural consequence of ever-increasing intercultural communication poses a clear challenge to traditional moral education in China. Policy makers, institutions and practitioners have no other options but to face the challenge by reforming the current practice. This view is presented in more detail by Wan and Wang (2003) on the basis of their review of major models of citizenship and literature on multiculturalism. They conclude that the concept of citizenship for the new era has to build upon greater tolerance of individual freedom of social identification and more acceptance and respect for diversity.

Challenged Models for Civic Moral Education

As citizenship is bound explicitly in policy documents with morality, social obligations and patriotic ideology, citizenship education has been traditionally conducted in the form of moral education, and political or ideological education. While these types of education have often been used interchangeably in documents and publications,[3] moral education has become more dominant in recent years because of the seemingly ever-honourable and all-encompassing nature of the notion of morality as the chief aim of general education. On the other hand, political/ ideological education has apparently lost its usual appeal in contemporary China for the obvious reason that it is often associated with indoctrination, which usually carries a negative connotation (Shan, 2003). Moral education as an all-encompassing term easily fits into and effectively accelerates the national campaign of *Yide Zhijiao* ('to run schools with moral education'), which corresponds with the government slogan *Yide Zhiguo* ('to govern the country with morals') as mentioned before. Yang (2001) asserts that moral education covers topics such as social morality, professional morality and family values and is thus the basis of citizenship education.

This is evident in *Gangyao* though the new term 'civic moral education' is adopted in an obvious attempt to integrate morality with the concept of socialist citizenship. Paragraph 20 in this document specifies how moral education for socialist citizenship should be conducted in schools:

> Schools are important avenues for systematic moral education. Educational institutions of all levels and of all types must follow the educational policies of the Party and promote quality education and combine knowledge teaching with good citizen education. They should also scientifically stratify contents for moral education according to age groups and learning stages and must standardise students' daily behaviour so as to create a good school spirit. Teachers should be role models for the students and try to permeate moral education to all school subjects and activities. Educational institutions should make students participate appropriately in manual labour and social activities and help them understand the

society and the country and realise their social obligations. (*Gangyao*, 2001: 3, my translation)

This paragraph touches upon many traditional notions that are often seen in discussions on approaches and contents for civic moral education. The first and the third sentences suggest systematic transmission of standard moral codes; the second and the second half of the fourth stress civic moral education across the curriculum; the first half of the fourth emphasises education by role models; and the last lists contents for education such as the value of manual labour, collectivism, loyalty and social obligations. Since *Gangyao*, these notions have been more discussed in the recent discourse on civic moral education, to which I now turn.

On the basis of data collected from a nation-wide project, Wan (2003) summarises three major weaknesses in moral education. In terms of methodology, the common approach of teaching morality and political education as knowledge leads to an overemphasis on superficial under-standing of moral codes at the expense of development of awareness and characters of good citizens. With respect to purposes, the aims set up for students of all levels are vague, abstract and idealised and thus detached from the real-world experience of the students. This detachment is unlikely to bring about internalisation of the civic morals taught and lead to moral transformation. As far as content is concerned, Wan points out that civic moral education should be a form of basic education with a focus on fundamentals of an ordinary human being. The current practice, on the other hand, stresses qualities of social elites. This is evident in the numerous role models included in textbooks as part of the content of civic moral education. Wan's findings do not seem to provide support for government visions of civic moral education in *Gangyao* as quoted above, but they do present a brief account of the major issues under debate in recent years.

As morality and political ideology are taken as hard knowledge that can be transmitted or spoon-fed, *Guanshu* ('indoctrination') is often adopted as an appropriate pedagogy for moral or ideological education. Indoctrination is usually used to refer to purposeful inculcation of a certain set of beliefs, values, attitudes and loyalty in pupils by a teacher or other knowledgeable figures or significant others. It is largely seen by Western philosophers of education as a negative and coercive process in which pupils are taught what to think rather than how to think (McLaren & Pruyn, 1996). This negative connotation is also evident in the Chinese literature (Xiao, 1999). Nevertheless, *Guanshu* is still passionately defended in recent discussions on moral education. The reason behind this is simple: *Guanshulun* ('the theory of indoctrination') is an important part of Marxism, Leninism and modern socialist citizenship education. C.M. Wang (2002) and Xiang (2003) cite Marx and Lenin as saying that indoctrination is necessary as concepts such as socialist democracy and consciousness cannot be acquired by the working (proletarian) class themselves. Lenin is further cited as asserting that without external indoctrination by intellectuals, unionism is perhaps the best the working class can achieve. In the same line of preaching, Mao Zedong also made similar remarks on the importance of indoctrinating political conscious-ness into soldiers and officers of the army. Because of this, the notion of indoctrination has been used explicitly in official documents including *Gangyao*, the 21st-century document on civic morals. In Paragraph 18 under a subheading of 'Greatly enhance civic moral education of citizens', *Gangyao* states:

> It is important to persistently carry on moral education among all citizens and to consistently indoctrinate socialist ideologies and moral codes into the members of the Party, the officials and the general masses. (*Gangyao*, 2001: 2, my translation)

Therefore, pro-indoctrination scholars such as Wang and Xiang maintain that the theory of indoctrination be adopted as a matter of principle, that is, to refute the theory is to refute guiding principles of Marxism. However, in most cases, these scholars are aware of the negative connotation of the term and thus make a distinction between dogmatist spoon-feeding and 'scientific indoctrination' often defined as an approach to combining knowledge transmission and active engage-ment of pupils in the political learning and morality developing process. C.M. Wang (2002) further remarks that indoctrination in this sense means that at the theoretical level of moral or ideological concepts, knowledge transmission must be unidirectional because socialist or communist theories such as Marxism and Leninism are categorical guiding princi-ples. Any attempt to promote pluralistic ideology must be prohibited. In terms of methodology, Wang continues, the unidirectional indoctrination should become two-way interactions, moving from coercive inculcation to nonforceful stimulation and character infiltration and from stressing the outcomes to an emphasis on the process. Evidence in official documents and academic discussions in the literature suggests clearly that the practice of *Guanshu* is determined by the Marxist ideology the country follows and the political/ideological educational culture the country develops. The tenet of indoctrination is not debatable in this education culture and the space for discussion is left only for methodol-

ogists who clearly have the ultimate aim to enhance the ideological and moral knowledge spoon-fed unidirectionally, and thus to further develop the theory of indoctrination.

Despite the firm ideological stance of the pro-indoctrination camp, an increasing number of scholars in the field of education argue explicitly against indoctrination. In Xiao's (1999) words, *Guanshu* takes morality as static and exclusive knowledge that can be compartmentalised for transmission or spoon-feeding from the teacher to pupils. He argues that *Guanshu* is itself not moral as it treads on an individual's rights, dignity, freedom and intellect. The consequences of indoctrination can be dire: creating enslaved citizens who are always obedient and regard doctrines as ultimate; producing hypocrites with double faces, feigned compliance and whose deeds mismatch words; and eventually developing nihilists. Wang (1998) sees indoctrination as the most chronic illness in moral education. In a similar tone, Li (2001) asserts that indoctrination is oppressive education that puts pupils in an entirely passive position and leads to hypocrisy. As an example, he notes that in examinations even the answer to the open examination question, 'How do you interpret the notion that the constitution is the guarantee of citizens' rights?', is rigidly standardised. Any personal interpretation different from the standardised answer would result in zero marks. In many such cases, pupils are rewarded as long as they can put in their essays those phrases and words in which they have been indoctrinated without demonstrating any real understanding or their own views. This, Li says is 'collective cheating'.

A second notion long used to characterise moral education in China is *Bangyang Jiaoyu* ('education by role models'), in which role models mainly consisting of national heroes and heroines and other outstanding individuals are used as the desired outcome of moral education and their behaviours, morals and beliefs the content for indoctrination. It is, in Wan's (2003) words, a form of elite education. Though under serious debate, *Bangyang Jiaoyu* is promoted vigorously in official documents such as *Gangyao*. The official faith is evident in many places, particularly in Paragraph 26 which stipulates that:

> We must mobilise the masses to *learn from our outstanding role models*. We must be good at discovering and making use of moral role models that look close, respectable, believable and learnable. (*Gangyao*, 2001: 3, my translation and emphasis)

The faith government leaders and educators in China have had in the effectiveness of this philosophy is reflected by the catchphrase, 'the power of role models is infinite', which is often used in both formal and informal domains. In Mao's era, the paramount leader personally set up numerous role models and launched many campaigns in the country to learn from them. Role models chosen and propagated ranged from ancient heroes in legendary stories, soldiers who died for the communist cause in wars, to ordinary people, dead or alive, of all walks of life. Through education, campaigns and mass media many names of these role models were made known in every household throughout the country. Morals and ideologies associated with the role models in Mao's era mainly consisted of patriotism, selflessness, loyalty and obedience to the Party, love of labour and readiness to dedicate and contribute. The approach adopted in schools to promote these morals and ideologies is often seen as dogmatic and authoritarian. After Mao's death, due to Deng's 'open-door' policy to the outside world and his economic reforms towards 'commodity socialism', people became increasingly suspicious and weary of political propaganda and began to openly question the role models promoted. Many regarded the values and beliefs of role models as incompatible with the times and the role models as political tools used by rulers to manipulate the people (Wang, 2003). The country seemed to move away from a 'virtuocratic' state towards a system that is ostensibly 'meritocratic' (Shirk, cited in Reed, 1996).

Apparently because of the 'faith crisis' (Reed, 1996) and student movements in the 1980s in China, the central government and education authorities returned in the 1990s to the usual themes by issuing directives and publishing handbooks for enhancing and reforming civic moral education (Lo & Man, 1996). These documents kept most of the traditional codes of civic morals but placed more emphasis on character building and less on love of labour and selflessness. In defending education by role models, some educators (Lin & Liu, 1998; Nai, 1995) associate this practice with child behaviouristic psychology represented by Bandura's (1963, 1977) social learning theory, despite a clear difference between the two. The latter deals clinically with the process of socialisation with an emphasis on children's imitation and identification of social behaviour of significant Others: peers, teachers and other adults around them, and under the influence of mass media. *Bangyang Jiaoyu*, on the other hand, primarily aims to inculcate moral and ideological codes in a pupil's mind through repeated teaching and propagating the moral deeds of past and present role models (mainly distant and seldom local). The role models may look remote but when their deeds are nationally propagated, and when those people replicating their deeds are rewarded and those doing otherwise condemned or punished, education by role models is found effective at all times, though the power of them may not be as infinite as before (Wang, 2003). In contemporary China, this practice will still play an effective role in modelling for and stimulating the educated so long as the educated can comprehend the behaviours of the models, discern the values and psychological orienta- tion behind the behaviours, identify with the values and behaviours, empathise with the role models and eventually bring identification and empathy to action (Dai, 2002).

One of the most representative and dominant role models created in the official culture of moral education is the name of Lei Feng who has been used since his death in 1962 as a model for civic moral education in the country (Reed, 1996). All the major civic morals, political values and beliefs the communist party wish to promote are reflected in the behaviour and spirit of this ordinary soldier who died at the age of 22 in an accident while at work. The most propagated character in Lei Feng is metaphorically called *Luosiding Jingsheng* ('the spirit of a little "screw"'), which basically refers to absolute allegiance and obedience to the Party and the country. This spirit was revealed in 'Lei Feng's Diary' published by the PLA propaganda department after his death in which he drew an analogy between his relationship (as an individual) to the Party to the function of a little screw in the running of a machine (the country). That 'I'll do whatever the Party tells me to do' is the trademark phrase of this spirit which was forcefully propagandised and upheld in Mao's era and is still promoted vigorously, with some modern touches, by mass media and education authorities. Besides a top-down political agenda for cultivating more 'Lei Feng-type' citizens, a firm reason behind the everlasting campaign to 'Learn from comrade Lei Feng' launched more than four decades ago by Mao Zedong, Reed (1996) argues, is that the Lei Feng spirit in fact overlaps with Con- fucianism in many virtues such as loyalty, filial piety, self-cultivation, benevolence, modesty and frugality. The overlapping clearly helps maintain the appeal of this role model as Confucianism is culturally rooted in China. This explains why ordinary Chinese today perceive Lei Feng as 'at least a good person', though many may not wish to follow his beliefs and way of life.

Academically, however, this spirit is seriously challenged. Jin (2000) remarks that the *Luosiding* notion is, on the surface, a concept for cultivating devoted citizens who fulfil their duties. At a deep level it reduces an individual to nothing but a component that can be cast in a standard mould and used or placed at will in any place in the nation- state machine. Such individuals are dependent on the state and the collective and have no freedom of even choosing their own jobs, no rights to create themselves opportunities and in short no individuality. He/she lives to demonstrate absolute allegiance and subjectivity to the collective but is deprived of individual value and basic rights. The notion of *Luosiding* is, in fact, extreme-leftist collectivism that puts the private life of an individual under strict collective monitoring and control and leads to slavish mentality. The education for this type of individual, called *Luosiding Jiaoyu*, is thus, in Jin's words, an extreme-leftist 'servility' type of education that forces the educated to identify their own interests with 'the common interests of the society' or 'collective interests' and to make a wholeheartedly selfless contribution to the society and, if necessary, to sacrifice their own interests and lives for the collective interests. Historically, Jin cites Lu as saying, there has never been a lack of political swindlers who make use of seemingly beautiful notions such as 'the interest of Chinese in the whole country' and 'the interests of the majority' to manoeuvre the masses in order to achieve their own selfish purposes. For the general masses, caustically, the extreme-leftist collective orientation has often led to extreme individualism and twisted interpersonal relationships because in order to show absolute loyalty to gain social recognition some individuals would go so far as to frame and incriminate others, including their own relatives and social contacts.

Shenren Jiaoyu ('education for sages') is another metaphor used by some educationists to refer to traditional moral education. Li and Zhong (2002) define it as an approach that takes the ethics of an 'idealised' individual, a sage, a nobleman, a virtuous person or a philanthropist as educational aims. It is based on Confucianism and serves to allow the social elite to exercise their special rights. In the 'market economy' that the country is pursuing to further develop its economy, Li and Zhong (2002) note that the fundamental code of 'not harming others to benefit self' should be promoted while such noble morals as 'always others but not the self' would have no appeal. The former represents a bottom-line moral and legal code stressed in citizenship education while the latter is a typical empty code preached in *Shenren Jiaoyu*. On a detailed reflection on the main moral concepts taught in classrooms, X.Y. Zhang (2003) states that notions such as 'others before self', 'all collectivism but no individualism' and 'selfless contribution to the country and the people' are but the utopian-style *Shengren Jiaoyu* that convinces neither teachers nor pupils in contemporary society. Promoting these 'exemplary conducts and noble characters' would, in actual fact, result in dishonesty, treachery and double-faced behaviour. Li and Zhong

(2002) and X.Y. Zhang (2003), like Wan (2003), all maintain that citizenship education which takes the dignity of all citizens as the prerequisite, integration of individuals' basic rights and obligations as the foundation and mutual legitimate bonds as the bottom line is an alternative to traditional moral education in this age of market economy and social reform. Citizenship education does not exclude moral issues but the ethics it promotes are those for ordinary citizens, not the moral standards of 'perfect' role models traditionally portrayed in textbooks. The equation of the former with the latter confuses the concept of citizenship and reduces the significance and potential strength of citizenship education.

In recent discussions, a considerable number of scholars suggest alternative pedagogies that emphasise dialogue between the educator and the educated (Shan, 2003) and that take the people involved (human beings) rather than moral codes or knowledge as the pivot or the subject in moral education (*Zhutixing Daode Jiaoyu*). Feng (2001) and Xiao (1999) maintain that any human being is a subject of their own morality and this subjectivity is the inner basis of all moral or immoral activities. Moral education therefore should be a self-constructing process in which the educator provokes subjective initiatives of the educated on the basis of democracy and equality. Pan (2004) lists four features of subjective moral education: exploratory, action-based, empathetic and experiential, the first and fourth of which are elaborated in more detail in Liu (2003). Huang (2004) sees as an inevitable trend in moral education the shift from a unidirectional indoctrination practice to a two-way, interactive approach, from knowledge orientation to experiential orientation and from externalisation of institutional inculcation to pupils' internalisation of moral codes or characters.

In summary, as we have seen, though the evolution of the concept of citizenship can be traced far back in history, the discussion of citizenship education in the sense argued for by scholars cited above is a modern phenomenon. So far there seem to be few reports documenting systematic implementation of *Gangyao* in schools. However, it seems legitimate to speculate that curricula in the name of 'civic moral education' following the terminology in *Gangyao* as a school subject may already exist in some form or are likely to come into existence soon. At this stage, therefore, academics are extremely keen on suggesting content for citizenship education. On the one hand, not surprisingly, current literature includes many discussions exclusively on how official prescriptions in *Gangyao* could be put into practice. On the other hand, it also shows little evidence to suggest that academic recommendations for citizenship education are restrained by such policy documents. In addition to the usual areas often found in conventional discourse, many formerly 'sensitive' topics have come into fairly free discussion. Individualism (He, 2001; Jin, 2000), human rights (Meng, 1999) and democracy (Pan, 2001; X. Zhang, 2003) have been touched upon even though the interpretations of these terms may differ from those dominant in the Western literature and some scholars put a modifier such as 'socialist' or 'Marxist' in front of human rights or democracy. Various models conceptualised and/or practised in other countries, such as the liberal individualistic tradition, civic republicanism and the communitarian model are reviewed and discussed, often with a view to applicability for the specific context of the country (Zhao, 2003).

Among the conceptions reviewed, multiculturalism is obviously the most examined in the recent literature. Not long ago, the concept of multiculturalism was considered by education scholars in China as relevant exclusively to minority education. Wang (1995) takes the concept developed by Western scholars such as Banks and Lynch (1986)[4] as corresponding to 'nationality education', which refers to minority education in China. In examining the literature over the past decade, Xing (2002) asserts that equating multiculturalism with minority education or taking the former as the theory or methodology for the latter is one of the major confusions in discussions of multiculturalism. Today, while how the concept should be defined and applied in the country is still often discussed in the context of minority education, there seems to be a move towards a general consensus in the academic discourse that the majority Han nationality should also be beneficiaries of multicultural education. A comparison of Wang's two papers (1995 and 2002) gives neat evidence for this move. After seven years, J. Wang (2002) refutes his own 1995 view that multicultural education should engage both minority and majority groups under the same system of general education. The traditional multicultural education (for minority groups only), which takes the mainstream culture as the core, should give way to a contemporary conception that takes into account not only the national but also ethnic and supranational dimensions. This shift of paradigm has brought about discussions on many other concepts such as multidimensional citizenship (Jin, 2000) and citizens with world visions (Li, 2001; Lu, 1999; Wan, 2003). Some effects these discussions and recommendations have on policy making and curriculum design are noted (Sun, 2003) though the overall impact on citizenship education remains to be seen.

Modes of Rationality for Citizenship Education

Over two decades ago, educational scholars and philosophers such as Giroux (1983) and Habermas (1979) reviewed various models of citizenship education and identified three approaches or modes of rationality, namely technical, hermeneutic and emancipatory. Technical rationality is found in models that emphasise transmission of knowledge and rely on inculcation of predefined beliefs, values and social behaviours that are in congruence with the established social order of a country so as to fit citizens into it. Models based on hermeneutic rationality aim to nurture individual abilities in reasoning, decision making and conflict resolution. Pedagogically, models adopting the hermeneutic rationality stress students' exploration and construction of their own knowledge of social 'objectivity' through discussions in classrooms and participation in social activities. Models adopting emancipatory rationality see as the ultimate goal the emancipation of citizens from the constraints imposed on them by social, political and economic forces. This mode emphasises dialogues in education aiming to develop critical competence in students. Of the three, the second mode covers most models conceptualised and practised in democratic societies for the obvious reason that the notion of democracy itself imposes the task of decision making on their citizens. The models based on this rationality therefore could range from the liberal individualistic tradition emphasising civil, political and social dimensions of the free and autonomous individual from Marshall (1950) to recent democratic citizenship models such as the one developed by Audigier (1998), which takes as 'core competences' for education: cognitive construction of knowledge of the principles of human rights, democratic citizenship and the objective reality; affective development concerning the choice of values such as equality, freedom and diversity; and capacities for action and participation. The emancipatory rationality, though vigorously argued for by scholars such as Freire (1972) and Giroux (1983; 1988) and more recently Guilherme (2002), is theoretically compelling and influential, though its efficacy is yet to be further proved empirically (Lo & Man, 1996).

The first mode captures many knowledge transmission and social studies models adopted in the McCarthy period and the back-to-basics movement in the USA in the 1980s (Giroux, 1983). The Chinese models of traditional political, ideological and moral indoctrination reviewed in this chapter are clearly built on knowledge transmission orientation. As shown in this chapter, they are increasingly under critical evaluation both in terms of principles and in practice. Wan (2003) states that many high achievers in 'objective' knowledge in exams of moral education are those with low morality because knowledge transmission fails to enable them to internalise the conditioned values.

Recent development in conceptualising citizenship adds a fourth mode of rationality, that is, *interculturality*, whose axioms and features are given in the Appendix in this book. In examining official positions and civic moral education models adopted in China against this rationality we may conclude that traditional Chinese conception and practice hardly demonstrate any of the characteristics and axioms of intercultural rationality defined here. However, the academic discourse by education researchers, students and policy makers such as Jin (2000), Li and Zhong (2002), Lu (1999), Wan (2003), J. Wang (1995; 2002) and Zhao (2003) gives strong evidence of awareness of many axioms presented in this book. They critically analyse diverse conceptions developed both nationally and internationally, reflect on them on the basis of the social, political and historical context and act upon their reflection by reconceptualising citizenship and pedagogy of citizenship education. Some have taken a step further by experimenting with new ideas and pedagogies (Lu, 2003). Characteristics of intercultural citizenship education presented here such as comparative orientation, cognitive, affective and behavioural development with a world view, national identities, and multiculturalism or pluralism (as opposed to relativism) seem to keep flowing into the discourse of academic debate. The engagement of the Chinese scholars, policy makers and students in the contestation of the elusive concepts is itself clearly an intercultural citizenship experience – a 'democratic, social and political activity' – that confronts traditional values and judgements and contests conventional models of moral education.

With the intercultural rationality, approaches to citizenship education are looked at from a multidimensional point of view taking into account not only learning outcomes and teaching methodology but also activities of and relationships (or conflicts) between all stakeholders in education. In a country like China with a history of thousands of years, it is usually difficult for one to discern a change of rationality as its traditional values, beliefs and practices are deeply entrenched in the educational and political culture. The definitive outcome of general education may still be to cultivate the 'socialist person' to 'serve socialism and the people' (Shu & Tang, 2003), yet there is a rapid increase in the academic discourse on citizenship education that seeks change. Intercultural activities involving many social groups including educators and pupils have become increasingly frequent. The more these activities maintain their momentum, the more intercultural citizenship experience is facilitated and individuals transformed. This new mode of rationality, therefore, provides us with a useful tool for analysing and reflecting on citizenship and, more importantly, encourages engagement of all people in inter-cultural or intersocial group dialogues and interactions.

Notes

1. The latest Education Law of the People's Republic of China was adopted in 1995. Article 5 states that 'Education must serve the socialist modernization drive and must be combined with production and physical labor in order to train for the socialist cause builders and successors who are developed in an all-around way-morally, intellectually and physically.' (*The Education Law of the People's Republic of China*, 1995).
2. In a widely-cited speech on the aim of general education by Jiang Zeming (2002: 265), the term *guoming* is used, together with *renming*, while *gongming* is not.
3. Some scholars, such as Wan (2003), refuse to mix these types of education as they argue that the aim of developing qualities of ordinary citizens (*Putong Gongmin Zhizhi*) is incorporated in none of them. Most other scholars tend to equate them to citizenship education (Shan, 2003; Yang, 2001) for the obvious reason that morality, patriotism, collectivism and political/ideological orientation are widely perceived in formal discourse as the main aims of socialist citizenship and this perception is evident in *gangyao*. I follow the view of the majority here because future citizenship education is likely to continue to be equated to moral, political/ideological education in the literature. An understanding of how traditional moral and ideological education is conducted is therefore important for this study.
4. Many of the works by J.A. Banks and J. Lynch have been translated into Chinese, including this one coauthored by the two scholars.

Part 3
Intercultural Citizenship

Chapter 6
Developing a Concept of Intercultural Citizenship

MICHAEL BYRAM

Introduction

One purpose of this chapter is to consider if and how the aims and objectives of teaching for intercultural communicative competence may be complementary to those of education for democratic citizenship and, secondly, what implications this might have for foreign-language teaching. The theoretical base for this lies in the concepts of intercultural competence and citizenship and in their potential complementarity. I will discuss this potential relationship in terms of teaching objectives, and illustrate it by reference to a framework for the planning of teaching.

A second, more ambitious, purpose is to consider if and how citizenship in a nation-state is compatible with international citizenship, and to suggest that 'intercultural citizenship' is a useful concept for relating national and international citizenship, realisable in the practice of education for citizenship.

National Identity, Language and Citizenship Education

Much of the thinking about education for citizenship is focused upon the nation-state. For example, in a recent book, *Citizenship Education in Asia and the Pacific: Concepts and Issues* (2004), edited by W.O. Lee *et al.*, the authors of papers tend to assume that citizenship education is an aspect of education in the nation-state and for the nation-state. Kennedy (2004: 17) suggests that one significant role of citizenship education is in buttressing 'the nation-state against fundamentalist extremism'. This kind of thinking corresponds to Anderson's (1991) well known notion of the nation as an imagined community. Anderson points to the significance of language and argues that the close relationship between language and nation was promoted from a European perspective, and was part of the 'model' of the nation-state that was borrowed – or as he says, 'pirated' – in many parts of the world. By referring not simply to language but to 'print-language' and the power of newspapers and books to create a sense of community, Anderson also emphasises the significance of literacy. A nation-state is thus *inter alia* a community of communication that needs a shared language, and usually this shared language is what is designated as the national language.[1] Thus linguistic identity and national identity are closely connected, at least in the context of a formal, institutionalised community of communication.

On the other hand, there are other levels of community within a nation-state that are not necessarily formalised within and by the institutions of that nation-state. The organisations and institutions of civil society have differing degrees of formality and, where there is freedom of speech, these communities of communication can challenge the official discourses of the state (Kennedy & Fairbrother, 2004: 296). Nonetheless, such discourses are likely to be conducted through the same national, officially recognised language, or in a variety of it, and again we see the significance of the national language and the reinforcement of the relationship between the national language and national identity.

The question then arises as to what level of competence is expected of people who wish to be part of a national community. The assumption in many cases is that the norm is the 'native speaker'. This is made explicit whenever there are incomers to the community because they are expected to meet minimum requirements and attempt to develop competence that can be compared with the native speaker. In Latvia, for example, there have been standards set for the Russian-speaking minorities and for those of other languages who, after independence, wished to remain in the country and gain citizenship, and the issue of a minimum-language competence has also been debated in the UK and the USA. Thus, what we have is a powerful polity, the nation-state, associated with linguistic identity and competence, where an ability to read the shared texts of the community is crucial. That competence is developed in and through schooling, and is seen as a signifier of an adherence to the nation and to the norms it demands of its citizens. The attachment to language as a symbol of state and adherence to its norms is evident in all those 'letters to the editor' that link 'falling standards' in the national language, especially in spelling, with 'falling standards' in morality. The right of the nation-state to expect linguistic competence and linguistic identity goes unchallenged.

Uniquely, in the case of the European Union we can see nation-states gradually giving up some of their power and adopting a more international, or at least European, perspective. In such circumstances, there is encouragement for other languages to be given a status as part of the creation of identification with a community. This is made very clear in the EU's White Paper of 1995:

> Languages are also the key to knowing other people. Proficiency in languages helps to build up the feeling of being European with all its cultural wealth and diversity and of understanding between the citizens of Europe.
>
> [...] Multilingualism is part and parcel of both European identity/ citizenship and the learning society. (European Commission, 1995: 67)

This is a statement where the word 'European' could be substituted by the name of almost any nationality, and parallels with the role of language in an imagined community are clear. It is also clear that, as in the nation-state, the levels of communication are not only those which are formal and institutional, but also include those of civil society.

What makes the European example different is that it is not expected that people should be native speakers of all the languages they might acquire as part of becoming European citizens even though there are powerful forces encouraging people to acquire as high a level of competence in as wide a range of languages as possible. All the work currently being carried out in Brussels on the development of a 'Europass' for languages or in Strasbourg on a 'European Language Portfolio' is a sign of the recognition by European authorities, and the national authorities which support them, that plurilingual competence of some kind is crucial. The success of a European imagined community of communication presupposes plurilingual competence so that discourses at a formal level and in civil society can be extended beyond the national frontiers to European level. Thus, the assumption that native-speaker competence is part of identification with a polity is questioned, and replaced by plurilingual competence.

The alternative to plurilingualism is to create a shared lingua franca – which at this point in history could only be English – but this is not politically acceptable as it would lead to accusations of linguistic imperialism; nor would it be desirable. Transnational discourses cannot rely on a single, taken-for-granted, shared language and its common meanings. Essentially discourse is not simply a matter of establishing an agreement on and/or an exchange of information through a lingua franca, for example. The issues that arise in social discourse are affected by contemporary and historical nuances and values, and the relationship between language and thought, between language and world-view is crucial. Cross-linguistic and cross-cultural interaction is far more complex and difficult than mere communication of information.

In summary, within the contemporary nation-state, whether at the level of state-supported discourses in formal institutions, or in civil society, the use of one or more shared language(s) and a shared set of beliefs, values and behaviours reinforces the sense of community and belonging, belonging to a nation-state through national identity and national language(s). Where such discourses are pursued transnationally, as is increasingly the case in the European context, the relationships that have to be established between identity and language are similar, as are issues of shared beliefs, values and behaviour, on the basis of which communication and the creation of a shared community might be founded. They are parallel but different, and it is therefore important, before pursuing the general argument about the relationship between citizenship and education, to consider linguistic and cultural relativity as a possible barrier to transnational communication.

Conceptual and Linguistic Relativism

It is not difficult to demonstrate that a public debate in which people of different languages are participating raises linguistic and conceptual complexities that cannot be overlooked. For example, the word 'citizen' itself can be considered. By using a French–English bilingual dictionary (Robert Collins Second Edition, 1987), the English 'citizen' is easily equated with the French 'citoyen'. Nonetheless there are variants: *town*, habitant; *state*, citoyen; *admin.*, ressortissant; *hist.*, bourgeois; (townsman) citadin.

If we turn to German, the case appears to be similar: 'Bürger; (of a state) (Staats)bürger' (Duden: das grosse Wörterbuch der deutschen Sprache, 1976).

However, when, in 1999, a Council of Europe conference entitled 'Linguistic diversity for democratic citizenship in Europe'/'La diversité linguistique en faveur de la citoyenneté démocratique en Europe' took place in Austria, the collocation of 'demokratisch' and 'Bürger' in German was not acceptable to Austrian–German speakers and the title in German became 'Sprachliche Vielfalt für ein Europa der Bürger' ('Linguistic Diversity for a Europe of Citizens'). Collocations and connotations are indications of semantic representations that are different in German from English or French, and in Polish, as Walat shows later in this volume.

As a further example, take the same words in Norwegian:

> At the conceptual level, the English words 'citizen' and 'civic' lack good synonyms in the Norwegian language. The most common

translation *borger*, denotes meanings like 'city dweller', bourgeois (as opposed to 'peasant' or 'worker') and 'politically conservative'. To overcome these problems the word *medborger* (co-citizen) seems to be gaining ground. To the extent that *medborger* colours the understanding of the concept, it probably gives more attention to the relational or collective elements. (Skeie, 2003: 55)

The author goes on to say that 'to an international readership it may seem somewhat narrow-minded to go into linguistic details', but they do reflect historical developments and cultural values. Far from being narrow-minded, the case also reveals potential problems in public debate. Even if, as seems to be the case here, a speaker of Norwegian does not expect their interlocutors to understand Norwegian connotations and collocations – a typical position, unfortunately, for speakers of less widely taught and spoken languages – the unspoken assumption that if everyone was to speak English as a lingua franca, mutual comprehension would follow, is unlikely to be true. Scholars such as Skeie, who cites Marshall and is familiar with anglophone literature and the British collocations and connotations of 'citizen', are not representative of other Norwegians and other users of English as a lingua franca. The latter would be unlikely to adopt those connotations and collocations when speaking English – however great their grammatical and phonetic proficiency. Some would not even wish to do so because of the hegemonic implications of adopting the language of the powerful, and in fact what seems to happen in lingua *franca* communication is that interlocutors introduce their own understandings into the language they are using as a lingua franca (Meierkord, 2002).

It is at this point that the concept of mediation is important. Given problems of translation there is a need for interpretation and mediation that presuppose an intercultural communicative competence and a social position of the language learner/mediator that permits them to interact with speakers of other languages on equal terms.[2]

The preliminary conclusion from these examples is that there can be considerable difficulty in understanding the word 'citizen' if one speaks Norwegian, that the concept of 'democratic citizenship' cannot be fully understood by a speaker of German, that a speaker of French has a number of options, which present difficulties of translation, and that a speaker of English would have difficulty with *medborger*, *Bürger* and *citoyen*.[3]

This quickly leads to the position of linguistic relativism, attributed in the German-speaking world to Humboldt and in the anglophone world to Whorf and Sapir. This view, that language determines and limits thought, has been much debated and often ridiculed. There is, however, some empirical work that supports it. Levinson (1997) argues that semantic representations in language are not homomorphic with conceptual representations. They are in some proximity to each other and conceptual representations are influenced by semantic representations. If this were not the case 'memories will be unretrievable or uncodable in language, and the speaker will have nothing to talk about' (Levinson, 1997: 39). He draws on empirical work with speakers of a language which does not conceptualise space egocentrically, that is, in relation to the person, using 'left', 'right', 'in front', 'behind' and so on, but absolutely in relation to the topography of their environment 'north of', 'south of' and so on. His argument is that if people had conceptual representations in terms of absolute positions and a language that used egocentric representations then there would be no intertranslatability between the conceptual and linguistic systems for the individual who would have 'nothing to talk about'.

Levinson does not address the question of intertranslatability between individuals, that is, the ability of a 'left/right'-language speaker to understand a speaker of a 'north/south' language. Yet, his paper is only comprehensible for a speaker of English (and other 'left/right' languages) because intertranslatability is possible. The translation is not at word level but at the level of explanation or mediation. Levinson explains how 'north/south'-language speakers visualise and conceptualise spatial relationships and gives examples to aid comprehension. By doing so, he implicitly refutes the strong relativist view which argues that comprehension of another language and thought is impossible because we cannot escape our own language and thought. It is evident from the way in which the explanation is written that it is not easy to explain and understand the other system of spatial description, but that it is possible.

Levinson does not give the actual words of the language he describes, a dialect of Tzeltal spoken in Chiapas, Mexico, but students of that language would have to deal with the words themselves and use them to represent their own experience. They would have to acquire new conceptual representations with new semantic representations. The implications of such phenomena for language learners have been discussed by Bredella (2001), who argues that, with sufficient explanation and effort, learners can acquire an understanding of the language and representations of other people, and illustrates this from his classes on the American Civil Rights Movement. He shows that his university students, despite their own scepticism, could to some extent 'get inside' the concepts and beliefs of Civil Rights activists.

A similar position is taken by Winch in his discussion on the ability of someone from a European–American society, with a conceptual world based on the rationality of the natural sciences, to understand the rationality of witchcraft among the Azande in Sudan.[4] He argues that in order to understand that rationality and its intelligibility 'we have to create a new unity for the concept of intelligibility, having a certain relation to our old one and perhaps requiring a considerable realignment of our categories' (Winch, 1964: 317).

The psychological analysis of this process of realignment is not within Winch's or Bredella's scope in their papers, nor can it be pursued here.[5] It is, nonetheless, an important issue if we are to develop pedagogical strategies for helping, for example, Norwegian speakers to understand and use the word 'citizen', English speakers to understand 'medborger', and German speakers to understand and use the collocation 'democratic citizenship' or 'citoyenneté démocratique'.

Communication in a Transnational Civil Society

The significance of issues in translating the concept of citizenship becomes clear in a concept of society presented by Habermas. For Habermas, a model that could replace outdated concepts of 'the classic republican idea of the self-conscious political integration of a community of free and equal persons' is a model dependent on communication flows:

> a model of deliberative democracy, that no longer hinges on the assumption of macro-subjects like the 'people' or 'the' community but on anonymously interlinked discourses or flows of information. (Habermas, 1994: 32)

This applies to the evolution of the nation-state, but even more to the evolution of democratic processes in a transnational context. Communication flows and the 'informal networks of public communication' at a transnational level presuppose favourable conditions for mutual understanding.

If, despite the problems of relativity, there is in principle a possibility of mutual understanding, then there is the possibility of a community of communication that is international. Parallels with the nation-state would then suggest that a community of practice in an international civil society is possible, that would include a community of citizenship and political practice. The question then arises as to whether a common set of values can be established as the basis for such political practice.

The most striking and demanding test of this possibility is currently found in the contrast between Western (that is, European and American) and Asian (especially East Asian) philosophers of 'education for citizenship' and their respective concepts of democracy and the relationship of the individual to groups to which they belong, in particular the nation (see Feng, this volume).

One approach to the question of contrast and difference is to attempt to establish a common core of citizenship education as Kennedy proposes (2004). In this argument, citizenship education is modelled on that of the nation-state and the purpose of a common basis is to ensure that different nation-states can support each other in maintaining their existing position in the world. An alternative view would be to facilitate cooperation at the level of civil society where an international comity might evolve which would counterbalance what Dewey (1916/1985: 87) called the anti-democratic tendencies of any closed group, including the nation-state. Furthermore, the assumption that international cooperation and comity in civil society has to be based on common values – a common core for citizenship education – is not a necessary conclusion. Indeed, if this were the case, then the possibility of an international civil society would be in doubt.

The issue is not whether successful communication and cooperation can be based only on the shared meanings in a shared language, as is the case of discourse in the nation-state, but whether an alternative is available. In other words, rather than seeking common meanings and a common core in civil society communication, for example through a uniform concept of the citizen, we should be looking for a means of communicating across national boundaries whilst acknowledging linguistic and cultural relativity. The theory of intercultural competence proposes such an alternative and can be a complement to education for citizenship and education for political action.

A Model for Intercultural Competence

I have proposed a model for intercultural (communicative) competence on a number of occasions, and it has been used for planning teaching, notably in some of the material collected in Byram *et al.* (2001). The model is a prescriptive, ideal model from which objectives for foreign-language teaching and learning can be derived. It differs from a descriptive model of being bicultural (see Byram, 2003), and it proposes an integration of linguistic/communicative objectives with intercultural competence objectives. It is thus a model of intercultural communicative competence, and not just a model of intercultural competence. Importantly, it includes the concept of critical cultural awareness:

> an ability to evaluate critically and on the basis of explicit criteria perspectives, practices and products in one's own and other cultures and countries. (Byram, 1997: 53)

What is at stake is the ability to decentre from one's own culture and its practices and products and to gain insight into another. With the help of a comparative juxtaposition, one is able to apprehend what might otherwise be too familiar in one's own culture or too strange in another. One can then make judgements based on clearly articulated and justified criteria: judgements that will be both negative and positive about one's own and other cultures. Criteria must be articulated and justified. Justification may be on rational grounds or as an act of faith, but without justification and explicitness, judgement descends into prejudice, and relativism, as will be argued below. This competence is not a *sine qua non* of intercultural communication, but is an educational objective, that is, an objective that is to be pursued where the teacher of language and culture takes responsibility for the education of pupils and not just the development of their communication skills. It is this aspect of the model that is to be compared with models for political education and education for citizenship. This model is represented in Figure 6.1.

Critical Cultural Awareness and Political/Citizenship Education

The phrase 'political education' probably needs 'scare' quotation marks for many nervous anglophone readers. It has negative connotations associated with indoctrination and there is little or no tradition of academic analysis or of the education of teachers in the field of political education. In England 'education for citizenship' in schools is a recent innovation that has its roots in rather undefined notions of 'personal and social education', and 'civic education', the latter having disappeared from curricula in the UK many years ago. In the USA there was a focus on developing 'National Standards for Civics and Government' in the 1990s, with a publication in 2003 of its second edition (see Himmelmann, this volume).

On the other hand, attention to 'political education' (*politische Bildung*) has been evident in Germany since the end of the Second World War and two writers from that tradition reflect this approach. Gagel defines two dimensions to *politischer Unterricht* (political teaching and learning): first, a social-science education dimension, with a focus on epistemology and

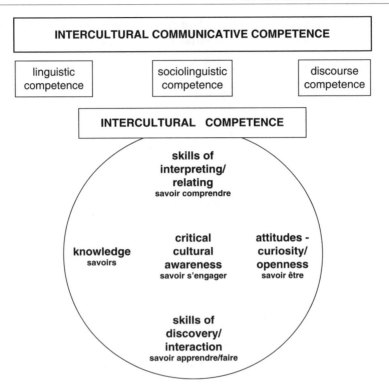

Figure 6.1 The components of intercultural communicative competence

a cognitive orientation leading to the acquisition of knowledge that has practical significance for daily life; and, second, the 'political education' dimension (in a narrower sense) with a focus on behaviour and an evaluative orientation to raise awareness of, or transmit, characteristics of 'correct' behaviour in public political life. He thus identifies three aims for political education:

> Learning to consider personal involvement in political action as desirable.
> Learning to recognise democratic forms of action as values (and only democratic forms); these can be called democratic 'virtues'.
> Acquiring interest in public affairs, being prepared to be interested in political resolutions of social problems.

He summarises them by drawing attention to a combined emphasis on cognitive, evaluative and behavioural dimensions: 'political education helps the individual towards an evaluative orientation in their environment and makes them capable of democratic behaviour' (Gagel, 2000: 24, my translation). These three elements of *politische Bildung* are, as Himmelmann notes (2003, unpublished ms), also to be found in documents written for the Council of Europe as part of the response to the call by all Heads of State and Governments of the member states to prioritise 'education for democratic citizenship'. This call came at the end of a Council of Europe meeting in 1997. It may be due to the end of opposing forces and the stimulation of communism in Europe (and the USA) that politicians became concerned to promote an interest in democratic purposes and processes for fear of growing apathy among their electorates. It may be that, in Europe, there appeared to be a need to educate whole populations about the meaning of democracy, as many people had grown up without access to democratic processes.

Whatever its origins, it is evident from writers such as Gagel, Himmelmann, and authors of the Council of Europe, that democracy and education for democratic citizenship are of unquestionable value. The only question is how to ensure that people understand and use their opportunities to behave democratically in public life. This assumption may be appropriate for North American and European societies, the societies for which these scholars are writing. American and European politicians also assume that democracy is the only form of politics that is valuable, to the extent that they are prepared to impose it on other countries. One of the issues that will arise from taking an intercultural perspective on citizenship is that even these assumptions should be (and are being) questioned.

Before considering the intercultural dimension, however, it will be useful to look in more detail at the three elements of *politische Bildung*: cognitive, evaluative and behavioural, which can be also formulated as epistemological, affective/moral and active orientations. Himmelmann (2003), who prefers to refer to *Demokratie lernen* (learning democracy) instead of *politische Bildung*, prioritises 'affective/moral attitudes' because without a will or disposition to achieve common purposes, there can be no acquisition of knowledge or active engagement in democratic processes. This can also be argued with respect to intercultural competence, as will be shown below.

Himmelmann is concerned in his paper to define 'standards' or agreed outcomes for political education, and his perspective derives from Audigier's (1998) paper for the Council of Europe, which provides the following list of affective/moral attitudes:

(1) recognition of the principles of universality, interdependence and indivisibility of basic rights and freedoms;
(2) respect for the value, the dignity and the freedom of every individual person;
(3) acceptance of the rule of law, search for justice, recognition of equality and equal treatment in a world full of differences;
(4) recognition of the importance of peace, absence of violence, and the participatory and constructive resolution of social conflicts and problems;
(5) trust in democratic principles, institutions and modes of action and valorisation of participatory citizenship;
(6) recognition of pluralism in life and in society, respect for foreign cultures and their contribution to human development;
(7) valorisation of mutuality, cooperation, trust and solidarity and the struggle against racism, prejudices and discrimination;
(8) taking action in favour of the principles of sustainable development as a balance between societal and economic growth and the protection of the environment.

The list reveals the principles and values that Himmelmann, and others, consider to be fundamental. It is also evident from this list that his attitudes or commitments have to have an object towards which they are directed. These same principles and values are also present in his second list of the elements of general cognitive capacity to:

(1) recognise (repeating and describing) facts, a statement, a problem, a situation, a conflict;
(2) differentiate (and compare) statements, assertions or facts according to different interests, needs or perspectives;
(3) discuss (and explain) different statements in a context, and develop further points of view;
(4) investigate (and explain) origins, background or history;
(5) critique (judge and evaluate) a position or perspective with respect to its consequences, its significance for the future and its capacity for resolving problems;
(6) argue (and take a viewpoint) for or against a position; according to one's own explicit criteria;
(7) justify one's own position from a legal and moral perspective and evaluate possibilities of action;
(8) reflect on (and discuss) normative issues according to criteria of human rights, democracy, a state ruled by law or moral beliefs; judge conflicts in decision and values.

Himmelmann derives this list from the USA's National Standards for Civics and Government. He labels this list 'knowledge' and he also has a separate list for the suggested contents of political education curricula of which learners would be expected to have knowledge. The first list is thus a definition of procedural knowledge ('knowing how') and the list of contents is knowledge about ('knowing that').

The third, behavioural, element of political education is again derived from the activities of the Council of Europe, which partly overlap with the cognitive capacities in the second list. This final list is labelled 'practical–instrumental capacities or skills and strategies':

(1) grasp and take seriously the opinions and arguments of others, recognise those who have other opinions as people, be able to put oneself in the position of others, accept criticism and listen;

(2) make one's own opinions (needs, interests, feelings, values) clear, speak coherently, explain clearly;

(3) abandon every kind of violence, humiliation, insult (expressions of power), etc.;

(4) take account of those who are weaker, reduce discrimination, integrate outsiders;

(5) organise group work, cooperate in the distribution of work, take on tasks, trustworthiness, perseverance, care and conscientiousness;

(6) tolerate plurality, divergences, differences, recognise conflicts, as far as possible create balance, and resolve in socially acceptable ways, accept mistakes and differences;

(7) find compromises, seek consensus, accept majority decisions, tolerate minorities, promote encouragement, balance rights and responsibilities, and show trust and courage;

(8) emphasise group responsibility, develop fair norms and common interests and needs, pursue common approaches to tasks.

Put together, these three lists describe the desirable outcomes from political education in terms of attitudes and capacities/skills.[6] They embody what Gagel calls the narrower sense of political education, and are complemented by the knowledge content derived from social sciences. Himmelmann lists the contents under four headings:

• life-world and creation of social relationships (democracy as a form of life);
• society, economy and law (democracy as a form of society);
• democracy as political order (democracy as form of governance);

- globalisation, international relations and organisations (democracy as a global project).

His list is assembled pragmatically from a wide range of literature on political education, curricula guidelines and textbooks. It seems to represent a common ground of consensus.

As Himmelmann points out, in Germany *politische Bildung* takes place in many parts of the curriculum and under many labels and guises. He lists 23 labels, from *politische Bildung* or *Politikunterricht*, to *Weltkunde* and *Gemeinschaftskunde*. Not surprisingly, there is no mention of language education, either national or foreign, but the definition of critical cultural awareness introduced earlier is comparable to items 5, 6 and 7 in the second list of elements of a general cognitive capacity, listed above. In the further elaboration of critical cultural awareness (Byram, 1997) the following objectives are specified for 'the intercultural speaker', that is, someone who is not attempting to imitate a native speaker of a foreign language but aiming to acquire an ability to occupy the 'space between' cultures of different groups and establish and mediate relationships between them:

Objectives (ability to):

(a) identify and interpret explicit or implicit values in documents and events in one's own and other cultures. The intercultural speaker can use a range of analytical approaches to place a document or event in context (of origins/sources, time, place, other documents or events) and to demonstrate the ideology involved.

(b) make an evaluative analysis of the documents and events which refers to an explicit perspective and criteria. The intercultural speaker is aware of their own ideological perspectives and values ('human rights', socialist, liberal, Muslim, Christian etc.) and evaluates documents or events with explicit reference to them.

(c) interact and mediate in intercultural exchanges in accordance with explicit criteria, negotiating where necessary a degree of acceptance of those exchanges by drawing upon one's knowledge, skills and attitudes. The intercultural speaker is aware of potential conflict between their own and other ideologies and is able to establish common criteria of evaluation of documents or events, and where this is not possible because of incompatibilities in belief and value systems, is able to negotiate agreement on places of conflict and acceptance of difference.

When 'critical cultural awareness' is presented as part of the whole model in the diagram above, it is focused on Otherness incorporated in another language, and access to other beliefs, values and behaviours is through another language. However, with some with minor changes – above all by substituting 'social group' for 'country' – the description of the elements of intercultural competence could provide objectives for an education system that had an explicit purpose of ensuring social cohesion among disparate groups within one nation-state, where everyone can communicate through a national language. These could, therefore, be posited as some of the objectives for national-language teachers and/or other teachers in a state/public school, including teachers of political education/*politische Bildung* in any of its guises.

The emphasis on the centrality of critical cultural awareness is similar to Gagel's suggestion that the central, unifying purpose of *politische Bildung* (political education in the narrower sense) and *sozialwissenschaftliche Bildung* (social science education more generally) is the concept of *politisches Bewusstsein* (political awareness) defined as critical awareness, independent judgement and political engagement. The precondition for political engagement is that the citizen becomes aware of the relationship between the life of the individual and social processes and structures. Political awareness is formed through the recognition of one's own interests and through the experience of social conflicts and relationships of governance. The politically aware and informed person should not be a passive object of politics, but as a subject should participate in politics (Gagel, 2000: 27). Gagel draws attention to the concept of *engagement* (a loan-word from French) and this corresponds to my use of the French phrase '*savoir s'engager*' for the concept of critical cultural awareness.

It would be possible but laborious to make a close comparative analysis of the nature of political education and of education for intercultural competence. There are strong parallels, above all in the central idea of an awareness that leads to engagement, but there is also the significant difference that the model of intercultural competence becomes a model of intercultural communicative competence when it is part of foreign-language teaching and learning and when the objectives include the acquisition of linguistic, sociolinguistic and discourse competence. It is through linguistic ability that people can be intercultural speakers mediating between cultures of different countries (nation-states) embodied in the (national) languages of those countries. Political/democratic education as presented by Gagel and Himmelmann seems to assume a common language among all those learning democracy. They do not address the practical linguistic skills necessary in international political engagement, even though Himmelmann's list of contents refers to globalisation and foreign cultures:

> Globalisation, international relationships and organisations (democracy as a global project)
>
> (a) international conflicts and their causes, war and peace, peace-keeping;
> (b) terrorism, new wars, humanitarian interventions;
> (c) European Union, NATO, United Nations;
> (d) variety of globalisation, international law, development politics, North–South conflict;
> (e) global environmental problems;
> (f) foreign cultures, foreign systems;
> (g) system change, system development.

A foreign-language education perspective can complement and enrich this element of 'democracy learning', as Himmelmann labels it, not only by providing the linguistic competence necessary to engage with people of other countries in democratic processes, but also, in the concept of critical cultural awareness, by introducing a process of comparison, mediation and negotiation that does not presuppose democracy as the only source of values and governance. For it is important to note that the definition of critical cultural awareness promotes the importance of individuals being aware of their own ideology – political and/or religious – and the need to be explicit about and justify one's criteria for evaluating other people's actions, or the documents and events of other cultures, as well as one's own. It also promotes the engagement of the individual with people of other ideologies, to look for common ground where possible, but also to accept difference. This includes, therefore, the acceptance of other systems of governance than democracy, and other types of democracy than that which is dominant in the European and North American thought.[7] This viewpoint raises inevitable ethical questions and the spectre of ethical relativism.

Pluralism and Relativism

The history of debates on relativism is a long one, as Berlin (1990) has shown, but Berlin makes an important distinction between relativism and pluralism and between judgement about facts and judgement about values, which is useful for the issues raised here.

Let us take the former of these first. Winch, in his discussion of how Evans-Pritchard analysed the rationality of the Azande, points out that

Evans-Pritchard appears to present witchcraft rationality and scientific rationality as of equal, relative value, and yet in the final analysis suggests that the rationality of witchcraft is mistaken, and makes errors in its analysis of the world that can be detected with the aid of the superior rationality of science. This is Berlin's 'judgement of facts'.

Putting aside the question of whether Evans Pritchard is right – Winch says he is not – we can now turn to Berlin to distinguish this kind of judgement from judgement about values. In the following statement, Berlin's emphasis on imaginative insight and *'entrare'* is what I would expect to be the aim of pedagogy. His point is that one can enter into the other's judgement about facts – and accept the judgement to be correct – without accepting their judgement about values:

> Members of one culture can, by the force of imaginative insight, understand (what Vico called *entrare*) the values, the ideals, the form of life of another culture or society, even those remote in time or space. They may find these values unacceptable, but if they open their minds sufficiently they can grasp how one might be a full human being, with whom one could communicate, and at the same time live in the light of values widely different from one's own, but which nevertheless one can see to be values, ends of life, by the realisation of which men could be fulfilled. (Berlin, 1990: 10)

Berlin thus makes a distinction between understanding and condoning. This, he says, is pluralism not relativism, for relativism, he seems to suggest, is trivial:

> 'I prefer coffee, you prefer champagne. We have different tastes. There is no more to be said.' That's relativism. (Berlin, 1990: 11)

A relativist view of values would preclude any further discussion and any further communication. Berlin's description of pluralism, however, keeps the possibility of communication open. He goes on to make a further distinction between those values which one can condone and those which are 'beyond the pale' of human reason and value, beyond what it is to be human. In such a case, one does not condone but condemns. Of course, the definition of what is 'beyond the pale' is a difficult one, but an important starting point for the discussion would be the Universal Declaration of Human Rights.[8]

There is another point raised in Berlin's statement that is important to us, namely the assertion that one can communicate with other people of a different 'form of life'. This latter phrase may be an allusion to

Wittgenstein's phrase (below), which, as Fleming (2003: 96) points out, ties language and cultural contexts inextricably together:

> Here the term 'language game' is meant to bring into prominence the fact that the speaking of language is part of an activity of a form of life.

And:

> 'So you are saying that human agreement decides what is true and what is false?' – It is what human beings say that is true and false; and they agree in the language they use. That is not agreement in opinions but in form of life. (Wittgenstein, 1953: 11 and 88)

This means then that in order to grasp another form of life it is necessary to speak the language in which that form of life is embodied. This does not mean condoning the values of other forms of life and it does not exclude the possibility of condemning them as 'beyond the pale'. Instead it is a reinforcement of the importance of 'grasping' the language not just 'by force of imaginative insight' but by work and effort.

Fleming pursues the point and, quoting Lurie, argues that the means by which the process of acquiring concepts takes place is not by abstract powers of the intellect but by adopting shared responses, developing common judgements in specific contexts:

> It suggests that exploration of interculturalism is likely to require more than intellectual enquiry, reasoned argument and acquisition of knowledge. Drama can provide concrete contexts and effective engagement for the participants and by its very nature can be seen as a form of intercultural education. (Fleming, 2003: 97)

Exploration through drama would involve the exploration of other people's rationality, of the rationality of witchcraft and of science, without a judgement that one is more 'correct' than the other through the suspension of disbelief which drama – and other intercultural pedagogy – allows.[9] And then it would be possible to discuss how drama can and should help people to explore, not only other people's values (understanding but not condoning them), but also those values which are 'beyond the pale' (understanding and condemning them). Whatever the answer to the question of exploration of cultures that are 'beyond the pale', it is clear that the pedagogy of intercultural education should take Berlin's distinctions between judgements of fact and value and between relativism and pluralism seriously.

Conclusion – Towards a Concept of Intercultural Citizenship

Citizenship is often linked only to the nation-state, being a citizen of a particular state and sharing the form of life promoted by that state, through its education system and other modes of socialisation. Citizenship can also involve challenging that form of life and the values it embodies through engagement in the life of civil society. Being and acting as a citizen of a particular state and its form of life depends on a shared language and shared language games, to follow Wittgenstein. Education for citizenship, or 'learning democracy', to use Himmelmann's phrase, prepares young people for this state of affairs.

However, in a world where states are economically and politically interdependent, education for citizenship has to take a wider perspective, involving engagement with people of other forms of life or cultures, and with their language and language games. Language teaching has a part to play in this but must go beyond the assumption that linguistic competence is sufficient, and must take intercultural competence as one of its aims. Intercultural competence includes the ability to compare and make judgements and in this respect language teachers and those who teach citizenship education are pursuing the same goals. Learners must be able to 'enter' into the form of life of other people, to understand but not necessarily accept their values, whilst always being aware that some values are 'beyond the pale' of being human and have to be condemned.

Education for citizenship leads to engagement and action, and education for intercultural citizenship should equally involve learners in engagement and action, at an international level as well as at a local, regional or national level. Learners can engage in political and civil society at all these levels, provided that they have the ability to engage in the language games and forms of life at all of those levels. Education for intercultural citizenship thus needs to bring together the hitherto separate concerns of citizenship and language teachers, and future work is needed to explore the practice of both to find common ground and new approaches.

Notes

1. There are, of course, many exceptions to this ideal-typical model, not least in Europe where the model originated. Where such exceptions exist, for example in Belgium or Switzerland, the ways in which a single-language state exists are reproduced in the various subnational sectors of the state.
2. The discussion of the mediator as social actor in the European context has been pursued on several occasions by Zarate, for example in 2003 and 2004.

3. It is evident that, if these difficulties arise within the European context and among European languages, they are likely to be even more complex in a European–Asian interchange. Feng's discussion of the concepts in Chinese makes this clear (see this volume).
4. The question of competing rationalities is discussed by Lloyd who points out that early scientists of the modern era often managed to subscribe to two rationalities:

> In the form of divination, prediction figures among what used to be called the pseudo-sciences. In the early days of the history of science, in the middle of the nineteenth century, they were always an occasion of embarrassment. [...] Astrology, alchemy, physiognomy, later phrenology, all had to be dismissed as essentially deluded. The historian of science was not to be distracted by their presence in the same periods, even in the very same authors, as those he or she was interested in, except insofar as he or she had a duty to point out how mistaken the pseudo-sciences were. (...) from the 1950s on, it was remarked that techniques of divination had their own internal coherence and obeyed certain rules, and on that score and by that criterion do not fail to be rational. (Lloyd, 2002: 15)

5. A discussion can be found in Byram (1989) and Lantolf (2000).
6. The element of intercultural competence that is not strongly present in Himmelmann's three lists, namely 'skills of discovery', is, nonetheless, found in his extension of lists of attitudes, knowledge and behaviour to include a list of 'competences in methods' (*Methodenkompetenzen*) that are modes of democratic action, for example, in practical democracy in a school.
7. It suggests, therefore, that even within a framework of education for democracy it is more important to be able to discuss different concepts of democracy – Asian and Western, for example, as suggested in the work of W.O. Lee and colleagues – rather than to seek a 'common core of citizenship education' as Kennedy (2004) suggests.
8. Midgley argues that the social contract 'myth' from the Enlightenment, though important at the time, presents a concept of society (and I would add, citizenship) which is inimical to the principles of human rights:

> Some political theorists (...) claim that we cannot have duties to people outside our own nation-state because they are not contractors in our society and *rights* (they say) arise only from contract. (...) But its (the social contract myth) limitations are that it leaves no room for duties to outsiders. This brings it into conflict with another central Enlightenment idea, namely, the unity of all humanity.

She then suggests that this idea is fundamental to human rights, which offers a means of discussing across cultures:

> This kind of belief is not, I think, confined to the West. Oppressed people in all kinds of countries now appeal to it. And in general they don't seem to be using it merely as a foreign language, but as a kind of intercultural dialect that everybody understands. It helps us to pick out the distant matters that really do call for our intervention, despite the gulfs between our societies. (Midgley, 2003: 8–9)

Her use of 'foreign language' and 'intercultural dialect' show that what she is saying is related to our concern with intercultural communication, language and citizenship.

9. Spiro (1984: 342–343) argues that it is possible to distinguish degrees of rationality and, if something is deemed to be irrational, to make a judgement:

> Hence by the two criteria that I suggested for the assessment of irrationality – there may be others – we may conclude this section by drawing the following – anti-relativistic – conclusions. (1) The alternative cultural propositions comprising different cultural systems can be compared on a scale of rationality. (2) On such a scale, many cultural propositions are cultural frames – non-rational – and are therefore merely 'different' from each other. (3) Many cultural propositions that are seemingly non-rational, and are so viewed by cultural relativists, can be assessed by this scale as irrational, and they may therefore be judged as either 'better' or 'worse' than their cross-cultural alternatives. (4) If total cultural systems differ in the extent to which they comprise irrational propositions, by such a scale cultural systems can be similarly judged to be 'better' or 'worse'.

Chapter 7

The Concept of 'Intercultural Citizenship': Lessons from Fiction and Art

MIKE FLEMING

Citizenship and Moral Values

Any conception of citizenship education that goes beyond the mere acquisition of information must include questions related to moral values. This seems to be widely recognised. In the Crick report (1998: 10), which provided the basis for citizenship education in the National Curriculum in the UK, three strands were identified: social and moral responsibility, community involvement and political literacy. The report suggests that 'guidance on moral values and personal development are essential preconditions of citizenship' (p. 11). The strand identified as 'community involvement' is clearly related to values in that it embodies beliefs about what is thought to be an appropriate form of behaviour in society. The acquisition of political literacy is defined as 'pupils learning to make themselves effective in public life through knowledge, skills and *values*' (p. 41) (my italics). Before the publication of the Crick Report, a European conference, held in 1992, identified the main areas desirable for education for democratic citizenship as: knowledge (of a society and how it works – political, legal and financial institutions and processes); skills (for example, how to debate); values or ethics and self-esteem (developing confidence in their own worth and opinions) (Edwards *et al.*, 1992: 15).

Although Himmelmann's chapter (this volume) points out that there is little attention given to 'affective, ethical and moral commitment' in the case of German 'political education', this is explained in a historical context:

> This may be explained by the German experience that 'political' education in Germany since the 19th century has gone through several stages of highly patriotic, state-centred, idealistic and normative-ideological, even race-centred teaching. (p. 79)

130

This statement is an important reminder that questions of value, if taken seriously, are unlikely to be uncontested and uncontroversial.

Outside Europe, citizenship is linked even more closely with moral values. As Lee (2001: 7) states, 'Rather than talk about politics, citizenship education in the East talks about morality. "Civics" always goes with "morals" in the east; thus civic and moral education is a term more common than civics education or citizenship education in Asian countries.' Feng's account (this volume) of citizenship education in China points out that 'citizenship education has been traditionally conducted in the form of moral education, and political or ideological education'. Likewise, Parmenter's account (this volume) highlights the fact that values feature prominently in citizenship education in Japan.

Given that questions of value are so strongly embedded in the idea of citizenship, it is not surprising that writing on the subject frequently acknowledges tensions and ambiguities between competing concepts. This is far less the case in official policy documents in the UK, where citizenship education is often made to sound straightforward. The Crick report (1998: 56) placed considerable emphasis on the need for citizenship education to embrace the discussion of controversial issues, commenting that 'Education should not attempt to shelter our nation's children from even the harsher controversies of adult life, but prepare them to deal with such controversies knowledgeably, sensibly, tolerantly and modestly'. In the National Curriculum itself, however, specific reference to 'controversial issues' is lost. Secondary age children must acquire 'knowledge and understanding about becoming informed citizens' and develop skills of 'enquiry and communication' as well as skills of 'participation and responsible action'. Questions of value have not disappeared entirely as they are implicit in the idea of 'responsible action', but what has disappeared is any specific reference to controversy. Byram (2002: 47) has commented that contemporary terminology of 'skills' and 'competences' tends to hide the fact that 'all education is imbued with social, political and moral values'. Challenging questions of value are unavoidable when trying to resolve the tension between such apparently dichotomous concepts in relation to citizenship as:

- subject–citizen (Wringe, 1992: 31)
- classical liberalism–civic republicanism (Lockyer *et al.*, 2004)
- individualism–collectivism (Lee, 2001)
- constructivism–reconstructivism (Parry, 2004: 30)
- nationalism–internationalism

Wringe (1992: 29) suggests that the identification of key elements in citizenship (such as appreciating the rule of democracy, balancing rights and duties) may evoke either the notion of 'critical independent-minded, socially effective citizens' or of 'docile conforming subjects'. He points to the ambiguity of the term 'active citizenship', which may be confined to taking part in voluntary service alongside valuing democracy and having respect for the law. The inclusion however of the development of powers of critical reflection could lead to a rather different idea of what the term 'active citizenship' entails. Wringe's focus on the ambiguity of terms highlights the difficulty in forming a common understanding of what 'citizenship' means. This becomes very evident when one looks at the terms used to mean 'citizenship' in different languages (see chapters by Byram and Himmelmann in this volume), but the fact that there is no common agreement on what citizenship means within one language is less obvious.

Lockyer *et al.* (2004: 2) sees the core of classical liberalism as being grounded in the 'protection and promotion of equal individual rights'; democratic choice largely has value in preventing government from abusing power. This view seems to be neutral between competing ways of life; it matters only that 'they are freely chosen and, as far as possible, open to all'. Civic republicanism, by contrast, subscribes to a notion of 'civic virtue' where 'human beings are deemed only to have their potential fulfilled as citizens serving the common good', and identifying with the ends and purposes of their 'civic communities' or 'nation states'. There are parallels here with the distinction between individualism and collectivism. A constructive citizen education seeks to promote society's needs according to existing priorities, whereas reconstructive education aims 'to effect a transformation of the belief systems of its subjects' (Parry, 2004).

The tension between these concepts is also reflected in the contrast between a national and international conception of citizenship. A superficial view might associate national citizenship with narrow insularity and international citizenship with openness to others. However this kind of polarity draws the distinctions too crudely. As Enslin and White (2003: 114) have observed, although the term 'nationalism' is sometimes associated with 'chauvinism, xenophobia, and militarism, as well as irrational mythologizing of historical origins and events', the concept can be used without such aggressive overtones. It can be argued that people need a sense of belonging to a community that contributes to their sense of identity and difference from others. On this view 'citizenship and nationality complement each other; citizens need a shared national identity to hold them together and provide them with a sense of community.' (Enslin & White, 2003: 114). White (1996) distinguishes between the concept of 'nationalistic sentiment' with its negative connotations, and the more positive idea of 'national sentiment'. He makes the point that 'love of one's nation does not necessarily bring with it a belief in the superiority of one's own nation over other nations.' It would be wrong then to seek to appropriate values such as tolerance and respect for others as being exclusively the preserve of an international conception of citizenship. It would also be wrong to assume that the concept of national citizenship is straightforward:

> Citizenship, in a legal sense, is anchored in the rights and responsibilities deriving from sovereign nation states. However, it also has broader meanings deriving from international law. Migration requires individuals and groups to develop multiple loyalties and identities. This reality calls into question the idea of citizenship as having a unique focus of loyalty to a particular state. (Osler & Starkey, 2003: 243)

The competing concepts have practical implications. The tension between 'subject' and 'active citizen' is embodied in the classic example of the need for a school or society to balance belief in the right to express opinions with the need to outlaw the expression of certain views. Is it right for a school in the name of 'encouraging respect for authority' to deny pupils the right to protest against a war? Should pupils be exposed to the opinion that donating to charity may contribute to social injustice by denying the state's responsibility?

We should not be surprised or unduly perturbed by these difficulties. Tensions are central to moral education, particularly when conceived not just as the following of rules but as the development of virtue, and because values are central to citizenship education such complexities are inevitable. Judging human quality is rarely straightforward, particularly when intention comes into play. With some people what appears to be generosity may be better described as self-aggrandisement. In a teaching relationship when does kindness and support become indulgence? When does toleration stray into condescension? When does respect become sycophancy? When does modesty become false modesty? The concept of goodness is not straightforward even though it is often used as if its meaning is uncontested. This is revealed by the way we use language. As Eaton (2001: 58) points out, we have the notion of being 'too good'. This idea is embodied in the character of 'goody two shoes': 'it is usually applied to someone who is shallow, mindlessly follows conventional moral rules just for the sake of following them, has no fun, seeks approval from authority figures, and is generally self-righteous and boring'. We might translate this description into some conceptions of the 'good citizen'. If the development of moral virtue is more complex than is often assumed, where do we turn to have our moral discernment and sensibility sharpened, to help us become more informed and insightful, to become educated? Many writers (for example, Nussbaum, Taylor, Eaton, Levinson, Carey) would suggest that art and particularly fiction has a key role to play.

Citizenship and Narrative Fiction

A simple syllogism that links citizenship with moral education, and moral education in turn with fiction, is enough to argue that the teaching of citizenship can be enhanced by studying plays, novels and films because so many of them provide a general insight into the development of moral virtue. This view is compatible with a number of literary theoretical traditions although it would be excluded by narrow structuralist or formalist approaches. It is important here to distinguish the use of literature to 'moralise', to promote a specific code of practice or ethical system from the recognition that engagement with literature has the potential to sharpen awareness of moral issues and nuances. In the novels of Jane Austen, for example, a recurring theme is that people who are superficially attractive and charismatic can turn out to be much less morally worthy than the person who is unassuming and neglected. Art, particularly fiction, can sharpen our moral discernment and sensibility. It is possible to go further however and suggest that works of fiction may be chosen that embody citizenship themes more explicitly. This includes many of the books studied in schools.

Golding's *Lord of Flies* tells the story of a group of boys who crash on an island and struggle to create a society through the election of a ruler and the creation of their own laws. In Arthur Miller's play *All My Sons* the protagonist allows faulty aeroplane parts to be released from his factory during the war and in the process causes many deaths. As such it can be seen as a work about the responsibility of the citizen to the wider community. Novels that provide a vision of a nightmarish future such as Orwell's *1984* prompt reflection on the value and fragility of democracy and *Animal Farm*, of course, invites us to examine specific political systems. Less well known is Ira Levin's *This Perfect Day*, which provides an account of a perfect society that is achieved at the expense of individual liberty – the citizens are given drugs to suppress their natural appetites. There are parallels with Bradbury's *Fahrenheit 451* in which firemen are used not to put out fires but to burn books because they bring unhappiness. As one of the characters declares, 'We stand against the small tide of those who want to make everyone unhappy with conflicting theory and thought.'

Williams (2002: 164) uses the example of Frank O'Connor's short story 'Guests of the Nation' as one that shows the dangers of nationalism. It reveals 'how excessive national sentiment can be destructive of the ties that bind us to other human beings.' Classical Greek plays provide a direct insight into historical ideas about the rights and duties of a citizen as well as addressing specific themes related to the exercise of power. Sophocles' *Antigone* explores within a specific historic and cultural context what it means to be a good or bad citizen and whether it is right to break a country's laws because of a more transcendent notion of moral duty. Many of Brecht's plays and novels by writers such as Émile Zola explore themes of power in relation to the individual and society. The same is true of Shakespeare's plays. With younger children the story of *The Pied Piper* reflects the rights of citizens to protest (in this case about an infestation of rats) and highlights the responsibilities of elected officials to work in the interest of the community and tell the truth.

Films which can be examined for a perspective on citizenship include *The Godfather II*. This film shows how organised crime had its origins in the needs for immigrants to protect themselves. *Citizen Kane* is usually interpreted as a film about an individual but the character is explored against a background of aspirations associated with the 'American dream'.

According to Nussbaum (1997: 88), 'narrative art has the power to make us see the lives of others "with more than a casual tourist's interests" with involvement and sympathetic understanding.'

Art and Aesthetics

I have suggested that fiction is a valuable resource for teaching citizenship. However, it is important to note that in the fields of art and aesthetics, there is a long and established tradition that objects to the use of art to serve such extrinsic and instrumental ends. This tradition is variously described as 'formalism', 'aestheticism' or 'art for art's sake' and encapsulates the view that art should be valued for itself alone. The most extreme formulation came from Bell:

> to appreciate a work of art we need bring with us nothing from life, no knowledge of its ideas and affairs, no familiarity with its

emotions. Art transports us from the world of man's activity to a world of aesthetic exaltation. For a moment we are shut off from human interests; our anticipations and memories are arrested; we are lifted above the stream of life. (Bell, in Hospers, 1982: 91)

This view has its roots in Kantian aesthetics. Kant's concept of 'disinterestedness' is interpreted as being largely about 'distance' in relation to the perception of art and the exclusion of extraneous factors. The concept has several strands but Lyas (1997: 28) provides some concrete examples to convey the central element of the idea. We are to imagine four people coming out of a theatre after watching a play, each reacting differently to the performance. One is smiling because he invested in the play, one because his daughter was acting in it, one because his boss saw him there and another because he enjoyed the play. It is the latter response that can be termed aesthetic and therefore disinterested. This does not mean that the aesthetic response is uninterested 'or that those who respond disinterestedly sat there passively (or distanced). Rather, they had no personal stake in the fate of the play.' (Lyas, 1997: 28).

The concept of disinterestedness is associated with a response that emphasises the appreciation of form and beauty exclusively in relation to art. Eaton (2001: 57) has described this view as 'separatist' (as opposed to inclusive) because it separates the aesthetic from all other ends and activities.

Formalists insist that only such features as colour, shape, line or volume in painting, rhyme, rhythm, or metaphoric images in poetry, and so on for the other arts are the proper focus of aesthetic attention and the true cause of genuine aesthetic response. (Eaton, 2001: 58)

We can characterise the two positions broadly in the following way:

Inclusive	*Separatist*
art in sociocultural context	art for art's sake
as means to different ends	art as an end in itself
includes moral content	formalism
	disinterestedness

Faced with these contrasting concepts, different responses are possible. One is to highlight the differences between art forms and question the tendency to treat all art forms as the same. From this viewpoint formalism would be seen as a theory more relevant to music and abstract painting: to deny the moral lessons of fiction, it could be argued, is to miss one of its key elements and to extend a formalist perspective to literature is misguided. That argument has some force in that there are differences between different art forms, but we do use the generic term 'art' for a reason and simply dissolving the dichotomy in this way is to sidestep rather than confront it.

Another response is to suggest that formalism, particularly as advanced by Bell, who was writing in 1913, is an outmoded view that belongs to a bygone era. His intention was to defend the Impressionist Movement in a world that did not understand it. In aesthetic theory different forms of expression theories (Tolstoy, Collingwood, Croce) which take the view that it is emotion which is central in the creation and appreciation of art have since been more influential.

However, in the case of literary theory, the separatist approach persisted in the 'practical criticism' or 'new critical' approach to the study of text. Here the emphasis was on the words on the page rather than on the context in which they were created. The literary work became an 'object in itself' severed from both author and reader (Eagleton, 1983). Since the 1960s, theoretical perspectives have been developing to replace and to restore the importance of historical and social context and perspectives in responding to literature.

Despite these developments both in aesthetic theory and literary criticism, the separatist view cannot be dismissed simply as an anachronism because it is still advanced by some contemporary theorists. Gingell (2000), for example, has recently pointed out the dangers in judging art in terms of the contribution it makes to our moral lives. On that basis we get a distorted, reductive view of the arts and miss the appeal of certain art forms: to worry about the 'message' of a Ming vase 'is to miss its aesthetic point'.

The separatist view is important to consider because it is still, for many people, the popular view of art. The term 'aesthetic' can suggest either elitism, in the case of so-called 'high' art, or 'mere' entertainment. It is associated with the unworldly and sometimes contrasted with politics:

> there will always be a portion of the population who have little desire to be politically active. Some people will find their greatest joy in other areas of life, including the family, the arts or religion. (Kymlicka, in Lockyer *et al.*, 2004: 50)

The summary of the two positions then can be extended to consider the limitations of each:

Inclusive	*Separatist*
art in sociocultural context	art for art's sake
as means to different ends	art as an end in itself
includes moral content	formalism
	disinterestedness
emphasises content at the expense of form	elitist
reductive	remote
didactic	role of art diminished to 'entertainment'

As is so often the case when dichotomous concepts are identified, it is more illuminating to see them in a dialectical rather than oppositional sense. The inclusive view reminds us that art belongs to a social, historical and cultural context and is best seen as an integral element of the life of a community. The value of the separatist argument is that it reminds us that the aesthetic element is important in our response to art. There is after all something reductive about abstracting from literature its moral message in propositional form. As Gribble (1983: 158) has said, 'To tear the thought out of the delicate organic structure of a work of literature destroys it.'

It is helpful to distinguish two uses of the term 'form'. One refers to the style or structure of a work of art (colour, rhythm, shape). The other, a more essentialist usage, refers to some general notion of the defining characteristics of art itself. The formal elements of a particular work are important in determining its emotional impact and in contributing to an individual work's subtlety and complexity. We can return to some of the examples given earlier. The novel *Lord of the Flies* is about an attempt to establish a law-abiding society on an island. The two boys, Jack and Ralph, who compete for leadership are different personalities with different priorities and values. The symbolism in the novel (the boys kill a pig and mount its head on a stick, which becomes a form of totem) raises questions about human nature and the nature of evil. The issue of the establishment of law and order is set against a wider universal concern about human nature.

Miller's play *All My Sons* is about a particular man (Joe Keller) who allows faulty aeroplane parts to be released from his factory to avoid financial ruin. Rather than simply condemning Keller, the play reveals a more complex moral situation at work in terms of the protagonist's main motivation. Towards the end of the play Keller speaks to his son about his fatal decision:

> Chris, I did it for you, it was a chance and I took it for you. I'm sixty-one years old, when would I have another chance to make something for you? Sixty-one years old you don't get another chance do you?

As we watch the play we are not just weighing up a general moral proposition but we are watching a particular individual with certain values and priorities. Before his suicide at the end of the play, Keller comes to realise that all the boys who died because the aeroplane parts were released were his sons, hence the title of the play. In each case the art works in two directions: both inwards towards the particular and outwards towards the universal.

In the case of *All My Sons* the fiction is based on Joe Keller, who lives in a town in America with a wife called Kate and two sons Joe and Larry, one of whom is dead, as he confronts an episode from his past. That is why literature helps us to see moral questions in subtle ways; yet it does not resort to easy generalisation. As suggested above, the movement is also outwards towards the universal, developing insights into humanity in general just as Joe himself does in the play.

The second use of 'form' can be called 'essentialist', the recognition that a defining characteristic of 'art' is that it relies on human intervention and intention. That is what distinguishes 'art' from a wider concept of the 'aesthetic'. We can be moved aesthetically by natural phenomena (for example, a sunset) but we reserve the term 'art' for products made by an artist. This idea is well captured by Dewey (1934: 48):

> Suppose for the sake of illustration that a finely wrought object, one whose texture and proportions are highly pleasing in perception, has been believed to be a product of some primitive people. Then there is discovered evidence that proves it to be an accidental natural product. As an external thing, it is now precisely what it was before. Yet at once it ceases to be a work of art, and becomes a natural

'curiosity'. It now belongs in a museum of natural history, not in a museum of art.

The relationship between 'ethics' and 'aesthetics' can be perceived not just in relation to the moral content of specific works of art but can draw attention to what Tilgham (1991) calls the 'humanity' in art. Art 'selects an object, a scene, a situation, and makes that object stand still to be contemplated.' Art, according to Schopenhauer, 'plucks the object of its contemplation from the stream of the world's course, and holds it isolated before us.' There is a sense in which the separatist view is outmoded because we know that the meaning of particular art forms cannot be abstracted from their historical and cultural contexts. There is also a valuable insight to be had from the separatist view that is worth retaining; the one essential distinguishing feature of all art is that it is intentionally made by human beings. Art, by definition, does not occur naturally; it is human intervention that uses form to shape meaning. It is possible to use a natural object such as a stone to create art but it crucially needs a human being to place a metaphorical frame around the object to transform it into a work of art. All art, no matter how differently it manifests itself in different cultures, can be said to draw attention to a concept of a universal and transcendent common humanity but, crucially, it always depends upon the particular and the concrete.

Citizenship and Interculturalism

How then does this discussion of ethics and aesthetics relate to the theme of citizenship? There are two aspects to the argument. The first is that narrative fiction is an important potential resource in teaching citizenship not just because it sometimes deals in topics that happen to be relevant but because, at its best, it engages us emotionally and confronts life in all its moral complexity. The second aspect of the argument has to do with parallels that can be drawn between art and the intercultural dimensions of citizenship. It was suggested earlier that a concept of international citizenship could be seen as naive if it *merely* refers to the need to rise above and beyond national citizenship and assert some sort of transcendent belonging to a world community. The concept of intercultural citizenship can be used as a more sophisticated formulation which, like art, embraces the particular as well as the universal; it does not deny the significance of belonging to particular local and national communities but suggests a higher degree of awareness of the contingency of those allegiances. Just as art is distinct from nature, an intercultural perspective is conscious of the constructed and dynamic nature of the way communities are formulated.

An intercultural perspective on citizenship also recognises the potential limitations of a narrow concept of national citizenship. National citizenship may be in danger of taking too much for granted, may not be sufficiently questioning and aware of differences or else it may promote a 'respect for differences' that is tokenistic.

The liberal principle of respect for difference then comes to be seen as a political gesture, based on assumptions that impose a subtle hegemony on nondominant cultures as a token, failing to respond fully to the quality and extent of their Otherness. Liberal respect for difference can thus maintain societies in which forms of behaviour or values are sanctioned or promoted in contradiction to the beliefs of nondominant groups (Dhillon & Halstead, 2003: 154).

It was suggested, at the start of this chapter, that moral issues are unavoidable in the teaching of 'citizenship'. One key moral issue addresses differences both within and between nations. As suggested above, an intercultural concept of citizenship, like art, must work in two directions towards both the particular and universal. This does not mean necessarily avoiding the promotion of particular forms of national allegiance and sentiment but it does mean being sensitive to the appropriateness of such values in particular contexts. An intercultural conception of citizenship will seek to promote a high degree of meta-awareness of identity and of the fact that values sometimes conflict. It is therefore appropriate to use the study of literature when teaching citizenship because easy and formulaic solutions are avoided and moral questions are identified and posed.

International citizenship, if it is only conceived in very general terms as a concept, may become, in its implementation, little more than simply asserting universal ideas such as 'recognising common humanity' as a way of smoothing over real tensions and problems. A focus on particular countries and political systems, on the other hand, with an intercultural conception of citizenship is a way of confronting difference and real issues of value. In practice this is likely to involve a comparative element in the teaching of citizenship. There is a two-way movement – towards sympathetic understanding of others and recognition of common human values but also towards a recognition of particular differences. These elements seem to come together in the concept of 'decentring': to be able to question what is often taken for granted in one's own culture. There are parallels between the concept of decentring in interculturalism and 'disinterestedness' in response to art: both relate to seeing the world in new ways, with greater intensity but also with greater understanding than was evident in traditional models.

The concept of 'disinterestedness' in its pure form is usually associated with the extreme, separatist view in aesthetics and has been described by Eagleton (2003: 134) as a 'radical political concept':

> Disinterestedness does not mean being magically absolved from interests, but recognising that some of your interests are doing an effective job to set certain of them apart for the moment. It demands imagination, sympathy and self-discipline. You do not need to rise majestically above the fray to decide that in a specific situation, somebody else's interests should be promoted over yours.

The concept of 'disinterestedness' is sometimes misinterpreted as meaning a lack of engagement or interest but it is more usefully seen as the ability to perceive without being unduly influenced by one's own distracting, practical concerns. It involves stepping outside the confines of what normally defines and constrains perception; it is, above all, an educative concept. It has parallels with 'decentring' in relation to an ability to see one's own behaviour and values from 'outside'.

I have asserted throughout this chapter that questions of value must be central to citizenship. That leads inevitably to questions of relative and absolute values, of how we decide what counts as morally right or wrong when faced by differences. Once again there are parallels here with responses to, and judgements about art. How do we resolve differences of opinion about what counts as good or worthwhile art? Does it not all come down to subjective opinion? Lyas (1997: 128) suggests that the terms 'subjectivity' and 'objectivity' are misleading here. To make a remark about whether one likes a work of art or not is to 'reach out in an effort to establish community', it is to invite discussion, to get people to see things as we do. Concepts of subjectivity and objectivity are simply unhelpful.

In a similar way ideas of 'absolute' and 'relative' values are unhelpful. Eagleton (2003: 103) suggests that the word 'absolute' adds little to the concept of 'truth'. Moral questions can only be resolved by agreement in dialogue and community not by appeals to external authority. In that sense, morality and politics are not as far apart as sometimes assumed. 'To be moved by literature is to be drawn into political sensibilities, to see the fate of others as intrinsically linked with the fate of the self' (Ward, 1999: 50).

An intercultural conception of citizenship education engages people with real moral issues and does not seek or assert easy solutions. It is likely to be more controversial and contested than simple notions of national or international citizenship. However, there is a limit to what can be said about citizenship in general terms without attention to specific contexts. It is for this reason that much of this book is devoted to an examination of citizenship in relation to the history and circumstances of particular countries.

Chapter 8

Beyond the Nation? Potential for Intercultural Citizenship Education in Japan

LYNNE PARMENTER

The aim of this chapter is to describe and analyse the present state of and potential for education for intercultural citizenship education in Japan. The focus of the chapter will be on policy and curriculum, although some reference to practice will be made where appropriate. Two main arguments underlie the chapter as a whole. The first argument is that most of the characteristics of intercultural citizenship education are present in citizenship education in Japan, when citizenship education is defined in a wide sense, and includes the acquisition of knowledge in the school curriculum, as well as the development of skills, attitudes and values through the formal and hidden curriculum, and through the experience of school itself. However, these characteristics are not applied to the intercultural sphere. The second argument is that the possibility of multiple identities beyond the nation has to be accepted, either implicitly or explicitly, before intercultural citizenship can become a possibility, and that this is not yet the case in Japanese policy and curriculum.

In order to develop these arguments, the chapter will be divided into two parts. The first part will be a descriptive analysis of present education policy and curriculum. The five areas of the curriculum most pertinent to intercultural citizenship education – social studies education, language education, moral education and special activities, integrated studies, school life and experience – will be briefly introduced and described in turn. The issue of education for minority children will also be introduced here. The second part of the chapter will be a discussion of how the characteristics outlined in the introduction to Part 2 of this book apply to the Japanese context. Throughout the chapter, the subject of discussion will be elementary (age 6–12) and junior high school (age 12–15) education. In Japan, these two phases of school constitute the nine years of compulsory education. Senior high school (age 15– 18), with a progression rate of over 95%,[1] is *de facto* compulsory, but is not officially so, and is not included in this analysis.

Description of Citizenship Education in Japan with a Focus on Interculturality

Japan's education system is characterised by a high degree of centralisation, and strict government control over the aims, content and, to some extent, methods of education. The Ministry of Education, Culture, Sports, Science and Technology (hereafter referred to as the Ministry of Education) publishes detailed education reforms approximately once a decade. There is usually a time lapse of three or four years between the publication and implementation of reforms. This period gives teachers, teacher educators, materials producers and other interested parties time to digest and adapt to the changes. During this period, textbook publishers have to write new textbooks in accordance with the reforms. These textbooks are submitted for authorisation and, if approved, can be used in schools. Once approved, associated materials, such as workbooks, teacher manuals, resource packs and audio-visual materials are produced by the publishers. School education is very much centred on the use of these approved materials and the textbook is respected as an 'authority' (Barnard, 2003: 167). In this way, central control is effectively filtered through to every classroom and student in Japan. From this perspective, an analysis of central government policy and curriculum in Japan will probably reflect more accurately what is actually happening in any individual classroom than a similar analysis in a country with a less centralised or less textbook-based system. At the same time, it should be borne in mind that policy and curriculum are the 'official' version of education in any country, and there are many points of negotiation between policy and classroom reality in Japan, as anywhere else.

Social studies education

Social studies are taught as an integrated subject from the third year of elementary school through to the end of junior high school. In the first two years of elementary school, social studies is combined with science in a subject called 'life studies', in which experiential learning is promoted. From the third year of elementary school through to the end of junior high school, it is taught separately from science. At elementary school, the curriculum is integrated, while at junior high school it is divided into three parts — geography, history and civics — which each have their own textbook and guidelines within the overall framework of the subject. The number of hours prescribed for social studies per year varies from 70 to 105 (Monbukagakusho, 2003a,b). The overall aim for social studies in elementary school is as follows:

> To develop understanding of life in society, to nurture understanding of and love for our country's land and history, and to cultivate the foundations of civic character necessary to be a creator of a democratic and peaceful nation and society, while living in international society. (Monbukagakusho, 2003a: 23)

In junior high school, the aim is similar but is developed slightly further:

> To heighten interest in society from a broad outlook, using various materials to examine multiple perspectives, to deepen understanding of and love for our country's land and history, to cultivate basic qualities as a citizen, and to nurture the foundations of civic character necessary to be a creator of a democratic and peaceful nation and society, while living in international society. (Monbukagakusho, 2003b: 16)

These aims seem directly relevant to intercultural citizenship, but the big question is how exactly the 'foundations of civic character necessary to be a creator of a democratic and peaceful nation and society, while living in international society' are defined, and how they are supposed to be developed. The Ministry of Education gives detailed guidelines on the content to be covered in order to achieve this aim, and additionally provides guidance on the attitudes to be encouraged. Although a detailed analysis is not possible here, one indicator of the government's policy can be seen in the rationale given for changes made from the previous curriculum guidelines. The basic principle of the reforms is stated as follows:

> We regard it as important to deepen understanding of and develop love for the local society and the industry, land and history of our country. Furthermore, we are aiming for [students to] deepen international understanding with self-awareness as Japanese people, and to be able to understand the role our country plays in international society. (Monbusho, 1999: 3)

This strengthened emphasis on national citizenship and identity has been developing consistently and steadily since the end of WWII (Usui & Shibata, 1999). The aim is carried through to specific aims and content related to attitudes, and brings changes such as the following, in the elementary school, sixth-grade curriculum:

> [Previous version] To develop a sentiment of valuing our country's history and traditions.
> [Current version] To try to develop a sentiment of valuing our country's history and traditions and of loving the nation.

On the other hand, the content related to sense of self in the international sphere has been articulated more concretely:

> [Previous version] To develop self-awareness as a Japanese person in international society.
> [Current version] To become aware that it is important to live together with people from the countries of the world as a Japanese person desiring peace.

Worthy of note is the fact that global citizenship, or citizenship as a 'member of international society', are not the aims, although the latter has been mentioned occasionally in recent documents and textbooks. Transnational regional citizenship (as an Asian or East Asian) does not feature either. The clearly defined, explicit aim of citizenship education within the social studies curriculum is to develop Japanese citizens with a sense of patriotism who are willing to interact cordially with people of other cultures, not to develop intercultural citizens.

Language education

Language learning is crucial to citizenship education. Traditionally, the national language has had a key role in developing a sense of national identity and citizenship (Billig, 1995: 27; Hobsbawm, 1992: 96; Smith, 2001: 5), while foreign languages have had a key role (although often unstated) in widening horizons beyond the nation, and opening up potential for an extended sense of self and belonging (Byram, 1997; Corbett, 2003). Japan is no exception, as Coulmas (2002: 203) notes in the opening sentence of a chapter on language policy in modern Japanese education: 'Japan has a tradition of considering both education and language a matter of governmental responsibility'.

In Japanese schools, Japanese, or 'national language' as the subject is called, is allocated by far the greatest number of teaching hours in both elementary and junior high school. Viewed in percentage terms, the proportion of curriculum time allocated to national language decreases gradually from 35% of total curriculum time in the first grade of elementary school to 11% of total curriculum time in the third grade of junior high school. Evened out over the nine years of compulsory education, this comes to 21% of the total curriculum time. According to the home pages of the Ministries of Education of Japan's near neighbours, this is comparable in percentage terms with Taiwan[2] and in terms of the number of actual teaching hours with South Korea, which has a lower percentage but higher number of actual teaching hours.[3]

The aims for national language (Japanese) at elementary school and junior high school are almost identical. The junior high school aim reads as follows:

> To develop the ability to express the national language properly and understand it accurately, to heighten the ability to communicate, to cultivate thinking power and imaginative power, to enrich language perception, and to deepen awareness of the national language and develop an attitude of respect for the national language. (Monbuka-gakusho, 2003b: 7)

It is in the final phrases of this quotation that the symbolic significance of the language and its function as a marker of identity (Barth, 1969) are being stressed.

The curriculum guidelines include points for attention in teaching materials (which serve as instructions to textbook publishers), and six of the eight specifications on standpoints for Japanese materials are relevant to intercultural citizenship. They are:

> Materials which serve to deepen awareness of the national language and develop an attitude of respect for the national language.
> Materials which serve to cultivate a scientific and logical outlook, and which widen perspectives.
> Materials which serve to deepen thinking about life, which cultivate rich humanity, and which develop a robust will to live.
> Materials which serve to deepen understanding of and interest in our country's culture and traditions, and which develop an attitude of respect towards the same.
> Materials which deepen international understanding from a wide perspective, which provide self-awareness as a Japanese person, and which cultivate a spirit of international cooperation. (Monbukagakusho, 2003b: 15)

As with the teaching of social studies, the main emphasis is on national citizenship and national identity, but the recommendations for materials based on a range of perspectives, developing various skills and ways of thinking, and dealing with humanity in a broad sense, are also significant.

In comparison to the 21% of classes devoted to the national language, foreign language education occupies 3.8% of total curriculum time over the period of compulsory education in Japan. Foreign language education begins at the age of 12 in junior high school, although it has become possible as part of integrated studies in elementary school since 2002. Until 2002, foreign language education at junior high school was theoretically optional, and guidelines for English, French and German were published. In practice, however, it was compulsory, and English, especially, was taught. From 2002, it became a compulsory subject, and the foreign language to be taught was specified as English.

Unlike education in social studies and Japanese, the aim for foreign language education contains few direct allusions to citizenship:

> To deepen understanding of language and culture through a foreign language, to try to develop the attitude of communicating positively, and to cultivate the basic skills of practical communication through listening, speaking and so on. (Monbukagakusho, 2003b: 90)

It is interesting to note that the previous curriculum guidelines (implemented in schools from 1993 to 2002) included 'international understanding' as part of the main aim, but this aim has been deleted from current guidelines. The reason is unclear. The objectives and content specified under the above aim are detailed outlines of grammatical structures, vocabulary and functions to be acquired in English. The issue of intercultural understanding is referred to only in the notes on materials, where the familiar refrain of 'deepen international understanding from a wide perspective with self-awareness as a Japanese person' is repeated (Monbukagakusho, 2003b: 97). In actual fact, the degree to which cultural content and the development of intercultural competence (including aspects of intercultural citizenship) are featured in English textbooks varies from publisher to publisher.

Even more salient is the fact that, in Japanese compulsory education, students have the opportunity to learn only one foreign language, English. At senior high school, a minority of students have the option of learning a second foreign language but, for the vast majority of students in Japanese schools, language education equals Japanese plus English. The implications of this narrowing of language policy for intercultural citizenship are obvious: students' language awareness tends to be limited, their developing world views are often heavily dominated by Western English-speaking cultures, especially the USA, and sense of self in the world can be quite biased.

Moral education and special activities

'Moral education' and 'special activities' are not included in the compulsory subjects of the Japanese curriculum, but one class a week (35 hours a year) is reserved for each of these elements throughout the nine years of compulsory schooling. Moral education is supposed to be carried out across the curriculum, but is formalised in one class a week. The aims for moral education in elementary and junior high school differ slightly, but are divided into the same four main areas, which are:

> matters relating primarily to the self;
> matters relating primarily to relations with other people;
> matters relating primarily to relations with nature and sublime things;
> matters relating primarily to the group and society. (Monbuka-gakusho, 2003b: 100– 101)

The last area is the one most directly related to citizenship, and at junior high school it is further divided into the following 10 objectives:

(1)   To deepen understanding of the significance of the various groups to which one belongs, and to strive to improve through self-awareness of one's role and responsibilities.

(2)   To understand the significance of laws and rules and to obey them, to know and observe one's own and others' rights and responsi-bilities, and to strive to maintain the order and discipline of society.

(3)   To heighten awareness of the sense of public duty and social solidarity, and to strive for realisation of a better society.

(4)   To value justice, to be fair and impartial to everyone, and to strive for the realisation of a society without discrimination or prejudice.

(5)   To understand the significance and honour of labour, to have a spirit of service, and to strive for the development of society and public welfare.

(6)   To deepen the sense of love and respect for parents and grand-parents, to have self-awareness as a member of the family and to construct a satisfactory family life.

(7)   To have self-awareness as a member of the class and school, to deepen the sense of respect and love for teachers and school members, and to cooperate to establish better traditions in the school.

(8) To have self-awareness as a member of the community and to love one's birthplace, to deepen a sense of respect and gratitude for ancestors who have striven for society and for elderly people, and to strive for the development of one's birthplace.
(9) To have self-awareness as a Japanese person and to love the country, to strive for the development of the nation, and to contribute to the succession of eminent traditions and the creation of new culture.
(10) To have self-awareness as a Japanese person in the world, to have an international perspective, and to contribute to world peace and the welfare of humanity. (Monbukagakusho, 2003b: 101)

One striking point is the clear promotion of a Confucian model of citizenship, emphasising continual improvement of oneself and one's group, as well as emphasising responsibilities over rights (Yao, 2000). Another point is the sphere of citizenship which is to be developed: while objectives (6) to (10) move from group to group in ever-widening circles, the final objective stops short of encouraging identity or citizenship in a transnational arena, but returns to nationality as the basis for membership and self-identification.

Like 'moral education', 'special activities' have an important citizenship role in that they are designed to promote students' abilities to work cooperatively in groups to achieve social aims. The content of 'special activities' varies from school to school and class to class, but this time in the curriculum is generally taken up with school ceremonies, school events, school trips, and planning, preparation and practice for these activities as necessary. The overall aim of 'special activities' for junior high school given by the Ministry of Education is:

> Through desirable group activities, to strive for the harmonious development of body and heart and the extension of individuality, to develop a practical, autonomous attitude of constructing a better way of life as a member of the group and society, to deepen self-awareness of the way of living as a human being, and to cultivate the ability to make the most of oneself. (Monbukagakusho, 2003b: 104)

In both 'moral education' and 'special activities', there is not the same dichotomy between self and group that often appears in Euro-American discussions of citizenship and citizenship education. 'Self' and 'group' tend to be seen as complementary, with improvement of the group or society leading to improvement of the self, and *vice versa*. Whether this is actually true in practice in Japanese classrooms is open to debate (Lewis, 1995; Okano & Tsuchiya, 1999), but as an assumption underlying

Japanese education policy and curriculum, and as a historically accepted concept, it is quite clear.

Integrated studies

An area of the curriculum newly introduced in Japanese reforms implemented from 2002 is 'integrated studies' (*sougoutekina gakushuu no jikan*). From the third grade of elementary school to the third grade of junior high school, between two and three classes a week are allocated to this area. The innovative aspect of 'integrated studies' as a policy is that the Ministry of Education does not provide detailed guidelines for the aims and content. What is provided by the Ministry of Education is an explanation of the meaning of 'integrated studies', and suggestions for what kinds of themes should be taken up therein. The basic idea is described as follows:

> In integrated studies, each school should take account of the circumstances of the local area, school and children, and should carry out cross-curricular, integrated educational activities based on original ideas according to the interests of the children. (Monbuka-gakusho, 2004: 54)

In other words, each school should decide what to do with the time. However, schools are informed that the methods of learning should involve independent learning, problem-solving, experiential and investigative learning, and volunteer activities. Four themes are given as examples for study in 'integrated studies', namely, education for international understanding, information technology, environmental studies, and welfare and health. Within 'education for international understanding', it is noted that it is possible to teach foreign language conversation, but that it should focus on familiarity with the language and with foreign lifestyles and cultures rather than the memorisation of vocabulary and grammatical structures characteristic of junior and senior high school education.

Nowhere is English specifically mentioned, but the Ministry of Education, soon after publishing these reforms, published a manual of English language activities for elementary schools. Due to this move and popular expectation, integrated studies at elementary schools have become dominated by the debate over methods of English teaching, while international understanding and the other elements of integrated studies, as well as the innovative approaches advocated for integrated studies, have been somewhat ignored.

Furthermore, it is widely expected that English will become a compulsory part of integrated studies in the next reforms. Several schools, cities and regions have already been designated as pilot areas, including one city where integrated study time is being used to teach the first-year junior high school English textbook. How the aims of integrated learning cited above will be reconciled with top-down edicts on what and how to teach remains to be seen.

As a result, although 'integrated studies' seems to offer considerable potential for intercultural citizenship, due to its flexibility and emphasis on critical thinking and active learning, it appears that this potential is not being taken up by schools and teachers, and is not yet being 'marketed' by the Ministry of Education.

School life and experience

A considerable proportion of the citizenship education that takes place in any school is not written in any policy documents or curriculum, but is found in the taken-for-granted school culture and experience, the hidden curriculum. Japan is no exception, and the daily routines, yearly routines, special events and school remit that are surprisingly common to schools throughout Japan help to shape students' ideas of themselves and of the society in which they are living.

As far as daily routines are concerned, the structure of the school day of most schools in Japan goes a long way towards instilling students with a sense of responsibility for themselves, their property and their society. This is done mostly through working groups and monitor rotas. The working groups function in various spheres of the school day. In many areas of Japan, children walk to school in neighbourhood groups, with older children supervising younger ones, and ensuring their safety. In class, students are split into *han*, or small groups, to complete tasks or discuss questions. There are further groups for cleaning the school, a task which all students and teachers participate in daily, as no cleaners are employed at most Japanese schools. From the upper years of elementary school, students also participate in Student Council committees such as the pet committee, the health committee and the broadcasting committee, ensuring the smooth running of various aspects of school life. Rotas also feature prominently, with monitors for the morning and afternoon class meetings, monitors for serving lunch, and so on. Every child is given a turn at leading a group, and being in charge of something, and every child has multiple experiences of working in peer-led groups. In this way, school life draws the child into a mesh of 'inclusive cultural citizenship' (Stevenson, 2003: 18), which forms the basis of notions of self in society.

Yearly routines and special events augment the sense of belonging in and contributing to the group, but also serve a further purpose of creating a nationally shared school culture. Students throughout Japan can recognise the significance of a culture festival or a final-year school trip, because they have all been through the same experience. Such routines and events create a link between different schools, and also between different generations, and provide shared experiences, culture and history that contribute to what it means to have been to school in Japan.

Finally, the remit of school is worthy of mention purely because it is so much wider than the remit of schools in many other countries. In Japan, it is considered perfectly natural for schools to issue letters to students and parents detailing expected behaviour in the school holidays. It is also considered natural for teachers to lecture students on their eating habits, sleeping habits, ways of spending their free time and other 'out of school' issues. Petty crime and anti-social behaviour are dealt with by schools (Yoder, 2004). Teachers are largely responsible for dealing with children who refuse to attend school. This all means that the school in Japan has a large share of responsibility in citizenship education, defined as the development and management of 'good citizens' in the community.

Education for minority children

The above sections have all applied mainly to the majority, mono-cultural Japanese children. In the final section of this first half of my chapter, I would like to briefly turn my attention to minority children. The number of foreign children in Japanese schools has risen significantly over the past ten years, as has the number of children with one Japanese and one non-Japanese parent. For these children, a more complex citizenship is an enforced reality rather than a choice, but their existence is not yet reflected in Ministry of Education policy or curriculum. The Ministry of Education has made substantial efforts in recent years to train teachers of Japanese as a foreign language, provide such teachers to schools with more than a few foreign students, and produce materials for teaching Japanese as a foreign language. They also issue annual statistics on the number of students in need of Japanese language education enrolled in state schools. However, the provision of Japanese language education is the only major recognition of minority students in Japanese education so far.

In fact, the majority of foreign and dual-culture children in Japanese schools do not need Japanese language education and do not feature in government statistics. For these children, assimilation is the norm. The assumption of homogeneity still underlies policy and curriculum, and 'self-awareness as a Japanese person in the world' is applied to the curriculum for all students. Partly due to these reasons, a significant number of non-Japanese children living in Japan do not attend school at all, but they are ignored by the Ministry of Education, because compulsory education only applies to Japanese citizens. The lack of any consideration for such children in national law, government policy and curriculum has been criticised by the United Nations (United Nations CERD, 2001) and must be a barrier to the possibility of education for intercultural citizenship for the majority.

Analysis of Education Policy and Curriculum in Japan in Relation to the Characteristics of Intercultural Citizenship Education

In this second part of the chapter, I would like to take the characteristics of intercultural citizenship education discussed earlier in this book and listed in the appendix, and analyse how they already apply and how they could apply to Japanese education.

A comparative (juxtaposition) orientation in activities of teaching and learning with critical perspective which questions assumptions

The immediate and resounding answer to the question of whether this characteristic was present in Japanese education would be 'no'. Although there is occasional mention of comparing various perspectives in the curriculum (see Section 1.1 above), there are many more forces in the opposite direction. The main forces against this characteristic are probably the structure of education policy and curriculum, the nature and importance of examinations, and classroom culture.

The structure of education policy and curriculum as a mechanism of control was described in the introduction to the first part of this chapter. One of the main purposes and outcomes of the process of detailed policy guidance and textbook authorisation system is the avoidance of such comparative orientations, critical perspectives and questioning of assumptions. The lack of comparative orientation is precisely the reason why the history textbook debate is such a long-running, highly charged issue in East Asia (Barnard, 2003). Japan, South and North Korea and

China all preserve their own version of history, which is presented to students through textbooks as 'the' true version of history. This lack of flexibility in even acknowledging alternative viewpoints of knowledge is not conducive to intercultural citizenship education.

The second force against this characteristic is probably the nature and importance of examinations. Examinations become increasingly important and increasingly frequent from junior high school onwards in Japan. Entry into senior high school and then university is highly competitive, and is based on performance in multiple-choice examinations that test factual knowledge. There are only right and wrong answers to these examinations: a question that can have two or more possible answers is considered to be a 'failure' as an examination question. Students study extremely long hours and memorise enormous amounts of factual knowledge to pass the entrance examinations for high-status senior high schools and universities, and they are not encouraged to look for alternatives, be critical or question any assumptions. Such behaviour serves absolutely no purpose in a factual multiple-choice test where only one answer can be right.

The third force against this characteristic is the classroom culture, although this is less definite than the above two forces. In many classrooms, the teacher and the textbook are the dual authorities, and students are neither expected nor allowed to be critical towards or question these authorities. However, there is more variation and more potential in this sphere. Many teachers encourage students to look at issues from alternative perspectives, and to take a critical perspective *vis-à-vis* their own ideas, if not anybody else's. As far as this particular characteristic is concerned, the classroom probably has the most potential for future development, with the elementary school and university classrooms least bound by the pressures of examinations and conformity to policy.

Becoming conscious of working with others through comparison and communication leading to multiple identities

If the emphasis is on working with others of a different group and culture through processes of comparison/juxtaposition, and on communicating in a way that emphasises the importance of learners becoming conscious of multiple identities, then it has to be said that students in Japanese schools have few opportunities to develop this characteristic. They rarely have the chance to work with others of a different culture, although such chances are increasing in many regions with the rise in immigrants.

On the other hand, attention to the basic elements of this characteristic – consciousness of working with others, comparison, communication, influencing perceptions and consciousness of multiple identities – is present in Japanese schools. As described in Part 1, consciousness of working within a group is one of the main *foci* of moral education and special activities, as well as being implicitly encouraged in the life of the school as a whole. In this process, students are supposed to reflect on their membership and role in the various groups, as well as keep harmonious relations with people in the group. They are also supposed to reflect on how the group influences them, including changes in their perceptions. In fact, the formalised version of such reflection, known as *hansei* in Japanese, is extremely common in schools, used after school events, at the end of terms, after misdemeanours and so on. The standard accepted format for *hansei* is to outline what went wrong, or your weak points, analyse how realising this has changed your perception of yourself/society, propose how to change yourself to be a better person and announce resolve to do better from now on. This is supposed to lead to self-awareness as a member of society and of various groups, which in turn may lead to the development of multiple identities.

Although the basic elements are there, they are never applied to the intercultural sphere. Policy and curriculum limitations combine with practical constraints to ensure that citizenship education is kept within the bounds of the family, school, local community and nation. Multiple identities are allowed to thrive within these bounds, but are capped as soon as the international sphere comes into play by the phrase 'with self-awareness as a Japanese person'. This caveat, which seems to come almost automatically with any mention of the international or intercultural sphere, ensures that multiple identities beyond the nation are not to be developed through the Ministry of Education policy or curriculum.

Creating a community of action and communication composed of people of different beliefs, values and behaviours without expecting harmony

Japanese schools are extremely successful in creating communities of action and communication. Some of the ways in which this is done were described above, in the section on school life and experience. Within this community, people of different beliefs, values and behaviours are incorporated to a large extent, especially at elementary schools. As Okano and Tsuchiya (1999: 58) point out:

> Primary schools maintain a cooperative, nurturing and creative learning environment, where every student is made to feel relaxed and is encouraged to find his or her own place.

One example of this inclusion is the way in which children with minor or moderate learning, social and emotional problems are included in the class. Many children who would be receiving 'special needs' education in other countries can be found in regular classes in Japanese schools. About a third of Japanese schools have a 'special class', but the numbers of students in these classes are generally low (less than 0.7% of total students). With some exceptions, students in the special class in most schools tend to be those who are excessively disruptive or violent towards other students, or who have very limited communication skills. Even these students often join the regular class for lessons in physical education, art and music. On the other hand, children with physical disabilities or other severe disabilities often have to fight for the right to attend ordinary schools, and are encouraged to attend special education schools, which cater for approximately 0.8% of the school population.[4]

An interesting point here is the parallel between students with special needs and minority students in terms of the policy of majority assimilation and minority exclusion. It is perhaps no wonder that schools, not knowing what to do with new immigrants who cannot understand Japanese, isolate them in the special class and require the special class teacher (who often has no particular 'special needs' training) to deal with them alongside students with demanding emotional and social needs. The community net is thrown as wide as possible, but those who obviously do not fit in are inevitably excluded.

It is here that this characteristic finds its limits in Japanese schools. Communities of action and communication composed of people of different beliefs, values and behaviours are created in schools, but harmony is expected. Anything that is too much of a threat to the status quo and to harmony is rejected or excluded. This is an issue that is well illustrated by the case of non-Japanese children in Japanese state schools. Third-generation Korean immigrants, as well as fluent Japanese speakers who can be and accept being assimilated into the school are accommodated, but those who cannot fit in are isolated, and those who will not fit in are often excluded. This leads to frequent efforts by non-Japanese children to hide their 'foreign' identity (especially in the case of Koreans) or to deny their difference and strive to assimilate (Murphy-Shigematsu,

2004). Differences of beliefs, values and behaviour within a certain range are allowed and accepted, but transgressing the boundaries of the group and threatening the ideal of the harmony of the group (even if this does not exist in reality) often leads to exclusion, representing a lack of access to 'social citizenship' (Dwyer, 2004).

Awareness of identities and opening options for social identities additional to the national and regional

This is a characteristic that Japanese education policy and curriculum unequivocally discourages. As described in the first half of this chapter, intranational regional identity is accepted and national identity is forcefully encouraged, but any identities beyond the national sphere are discouraged, with the possibility of any such identities curtailed by the recourse to national identity in the recurring phrase 'with self-awareness as a Japanese person'. Although this is official policy, this is a point that seems to be open to some negotiation by textbook publishers. In social science textbooks and English textbooks, it is possible to find occasional mention of the concept of a global citizen.

While global identity has some support, transnational regional identity is an extremely weak concept amongst students of all levels in Japanese education. According to a survey conducted in 1999, only 31% of fourth- and sixth-grade elementary school children in rural schools in Japan could even identify Japan as being located in Asia, let alone have an associated identity (Parmenter *et al.*, 2000: 137). Another survey on students' sense of self in the world, conducted with 604 university students in 2004, revealed that the average self-ratings for identity on a scale of 1 to 5 (where 1 is low and 5 is high) were as follows (Parmenter, 2004):

National identity	4.19
East Asian identity	2.71
Asian identity	2.92
Global identity	3.52

In other words, even amongst university students, awareness of transnational identities is quite low, although a sense of global identity is stronger. This is hardly surprising given the way in which inter-nationalisation is used to promote national identity throughout the education system (Parmenter, 1997), and in society at large (McVeigh, 2004). However, such emphasis in education on national citizenship at the expense of all other possible citizenships does present a barrier to the development of intercultural citizenship.

Heater (2004b: 326) draws up a cubic model of citizenship, one face of which is composed of four geographic levels: provincial/subnational; national; continental; and world. He advocates multilayered citizenship, where these levels are balanced with each other as well as balancing with the other faces of his model. Japanese education policy and curriculum, however, refuse to acknowledge, much less encourage, the continental and world levels. As these are the levels crucial to intercultural citizenship, this is a serious blow to the potential of intercultural citizenship education in Japan.

Paying equal attention to knowledge, attitudes and skills

Paying equal attention to knowledge, attitudes and skills is emphasised in Japanese policy and curriculum, especially at the elementary school level. Children are expected to acquire the knowledge they need for citizenship, but there is also an emphasis on the skills and attitudes the Ministry of Education thinks are necessary for citizenship.

The appropriateness of these skills and attitudes as well as the degree to which they facilitate or hinder intercultural and other non-national citizenships remain moot points. For example, the attitude of loving and respecting the nation and the national language that is encouraged in social sciences and national language curricula may be conducive to the development of national citizens, but may actually hinder the development of other citizenships. This is particularly true when multiple citizenships and multiple identities beyond the nation are discouraged, and the 'foreign' is perceived as a threat to the 'national'. It is also particularly true when such attitudes are to be developed in a passive rather than critical way, which is the case in Japan. It becomes dangerous when such attitudes, developed in such ways, are graded on report cards, as happened in many schools in Japan in 2002, following a Ministry of Education recommendation. The skills and attitudes required of a 'critical citizen for an intercultural world' (Guilherme, 2002) are frequently inconsistent with those required of an obedient national citizen. Although the elements of citizenship developed in the other characteristics may be transferable to intercultural citizenship, this is one case in which the effective development of this characteristic in the national sphere may actually hinder the effective development of the

characteristic in the intercultural sphere. In this respect, Hoffman's (2004) contention that, in general, an inclusive notion of citizenship is incompatible with the nation-state is valid.

Commitment to values, and awareness that values conflict but commitment to finding cooperation

As is evident from the first part of this chapter and in Fleming's chapter earlier, values feature prominently in citizenship education in Japan. From peace and democracy to respect, tolerance and hard work, students are expected to acquire and develop the values of a 'good citizen'. This emphasis on values as the core of citizenship education is common to many Asian countries and is shared by many Asian educational leaders (Lee, 2004). The majority of these values are generic values that would be seen positively in any country, and that would contribute to 'good citizenship' in any geographical sphere.

On the other hand, the issue of conflict of values does not receive much attention in Japanese policy and curriculum. There are occasional recommendations to encourage respect for other cultures and ways of living, and textbook materials do occasionally highlight alternative values and ways of thinking in their treatment of other cultures. At the same time, the issue of conflict between various values is rarely considered. From my own experience on teaching-materials-producing committees (such as junior high school textbooks and entrance examinations), such potential conflicts of values are subjects to be studiously avoided in educational materials, as they will lead to criticism from people in power. For this reason, socially sensitive and potentially controversial materials are usually also self-censored before reaching the stage of being censored by higher-level committees.

In terms of policy, curriculum and materials, then, the issue of conflict of values tends to be avoided. At the same time, though, the conflict of values and the commitment to finding cooperation is an integral part of school life. In many schools, teachers and students spend inordinate amounts of time and effort dealing with value issues. One example from my own experience is the case of a small group of junior high school boys who were found to have scribbled graffiti on an old, boarded-up shrine in a small rural town. They owned up to the offence, wrote *hansei*, apologised formally and cleaned the graffiti off the shrine. This, however, was not the end of the issue, which was taken up in assembly and in moral education classes. Students discussed why the incident had happened, with some arguing that as the shrine was falling down and boarded up, and the boys had only written on the temporary boarding, it was not such a serious offence, while others argued that all communal property should be respected. The discussion continued, with the final consensus being that the students had a responsibility to beautify the town, and then nobody would want to write graffiti. As a result, whole classes spent an afternoon clearing and cleaning the shrine and surrounding area, and there were no further graffiti incidents. Altogether, the incident occupied several school hours, but teachers were willing to give up academic subject time as they considered this to be a more important lesson in values. The emphasis in such incidents is on negotiating consensus, which can serve as a basis for cooperation.

This incident, like the majority of such incidents in Japanese schools, had no intercultural perspective, but in schools that recent immigrants attend, the same processes of lengthy reflection, discussion and consensus building regarding conflicts of values are frequently observed. It is in the classroom that teachers and students have to negotiate the gap between the homogenous, harmonious values of education policy and the diverse, potentially conflicting values of reality (Ota, 2000). However, the chance for such negotiations is limited to the immediate sphere and immediate problems and issues, and is rarely generalised beyond that sphere. As intercultural citizenship education, it is therefore available only to a limited number of students, and is dependent on (often negative) immediate necessity.

Conclusion

To end, I would like to return to the two arguments outlined in the first paragraph of this chapter. The first argument was that most of the characteristics of intercultural citizenship education are present in citizenship education in Japan, but they are not applied to the intercultural sphere. As shown throughout the chapter, the characteristics of working with others through comparison and communication, creating a community of action and communication composed of people of different values and behaviours, awareness of identities and commitment to values and to finding cooperation are encouraged in various spheres of Japanese education. These characteristics tend to be promoted at various levels up to the national level, but not beyond. However, it could be argued that all these characteristics would be relatively easily transferable to the intercultural sphere, either at policy level (by changing education policy and curriculum) or at individual level (which does actually happen in some cases). One of the characteristics – paying equal attention to knowledge, skills and attitudes – is encouraged in Japanese education but, in this case, transfer would probably be negative rather than positive. Two of the characteristics – a comparative orientation with a critical perspective that questions assumptions, and awareness of and creation of opportunity for social identities additional to the regional and national – are not encouraged at present in Japanese policy and curriculum. However, the introduction of integrated studies, where the Ministry of Education is promoting investigative learning and critical thinking, is a step towards the first of these characteristics.

The latter characteristic – social identities beyond the nation – is the one most closely connected to the second argument of this chapter, which was that the theory of multiple identities beyond the nation has to be accepted, either implicitly or explicitly, before intercultural citizenship can become a possibility. As has repeatedly been pointed out in this chapter, this is not the case in Japan. Multiple identities – as a member of the family, school, community, nation – are accepted and promoted, but once it comes to the sphere beyond the nation, the only identity that is permitted and encouraged in Japanese education policy and curriculum is identity 'as a Japanese person'. In this case, intercultural communication and exchange is, of course, possible, but intercultural citizenship is not. I would argue that the greatest potential for change in this respect is to be found in the increasing presence of non-Japanese children in Japanese schools. As the numbers of such children rise, and awareness of the issues they face becomes more widespread, the assumption of homogeneity on which Japanese policy and curriculum is based comes under threat. Once this assumption of homogeneity is broken in government policy, as it already has been to a large extent in society at large (Befu, 2001; Oguma, 1995), new assumptions will have to be made for the bases of citizenship in education policy and curriculum, and there is hope that these new assumptions will allow for a more flexible approach beyond the nation.

Notes

1. http://www.mext.go.jp/b_menu/shingi/chousa/shougai/008/toushin/030301/07.htm.
2. Taiwan school curriculum: http://140.111.1.22/english/home_policy.htm.
3. South Korea school curriculum: http://www.moe.go.kr/en/down/curriculum-3.pdf.
4. http://www.mext.go.jp/english/statist/index01.htm. Recently the law has been changed to make clear the right of children with disabilities to attend regular school, and the situation is changing slowly.

Chapter 9

Towards an Intercultural Frame of Mind: Citizenship in Poland

MARIA WALAT

Introduction

When the Council of Europe and the European Union (EU) negotiated the terms of accession with former communist countries, it was clearly stated that those countries needed to establish a civil society and exemplary democracy. The presence of civil society was considered a norm for the evaluation of a society (Sokolewicz, 1997: 119–120). Understandably, joining the EU could be seen as the final phase of the process that began in 1989, that is, the collapse of communism. However, Poland is still in its transformation period and since then it has not been able to build a civil society. There is a strong need for Citizenship Education (CE) to enhance the role and involvement of civil society in democratic processes, this being a necessary prerequisite for Polish society to become more diverse and open, and to be able to cope with pluralism in terms of culture and politics.

Concepts of 'Citizenship'

Before looking at citizenship in Poland, it will be useful to explain the concept of 'citizen' and its historical development. The Polish word *obywatel*, which is translated as 'citizen', is connected with residence. In the Middle Ages one would acquire citizenship through birth or the right of residence. With regard to the gentry, it was important to possess land, and in case of the townsfolk, property. The crown or the state was of a multiethnic character, and ethnic factors were of secondary importance as civil and political rights and liberties depended on ties within the social order, that is, its hierarchy consisting of knights, the nobility, the clergy and a burgher class. From the end of the 15th century, rights and liberties were reserved mainly for the nobility; they not only had the right to possess land, but they were obliged to protect both the land and the crown. The result was that until the end of the 18th century, civil liberties and political rights did not apply to the peasants, the townsfolk, or non-Catholics, including Jews. It was only with the Polish Constitution of 3 May 1791, the Napoleonic Code, and the independence movements of the 19th and 20th centuries that civil rights were gained by the rest of society (Sokolewicz, 1997: 107–108).

Towards European Union Citizenship

The establishment of EU citizenship involves direct links between the institutions of the union and its citizens, and their welfare, but most of all, as far as individuals are concerned, it involves responsibilities for the decisions of the civil society of the state where they reside, and responsibilities for the activities of the EU (Sokolewicz, 1997: 103). On the other hand, Konapacki argues that European citizenship is defined by national citizenship. It is not the institutionalised European community that determines it but the member states (Sokolewicz, 1997: 117). Therefore, in order for students to become familiar with EU citizenship, the Citizenship Education curriculum should emphasise the fundamental characteristics of European citizenship, such as the notions of human rights, fundamental liberties, the rule of law, the principle of subsidiarity and national identity.

Defining Citizenship

The notion of citizenship has a very wide scope and embraces a number of issues (including responsibilities, social status, attendant privileges), and thus is an intricate cultural problem (Sokolewicz, 1997: 106). The definition of 'citizenship' used for this chapter is the one which states that it is 'a frame of mind' (Thomas, 2001: 54). This particular notion denotes an individual and their perception of their political, social and cultural rights and responsibilities where the individual does not lose their national personality, culture, religion or sovereignty in a free and open Europe. This Europe is characterised by shared moral and spiritual values that result in understanding and respect, and where relations are developed between people of diverse nationalities and cultures (Thomas, 2001: 57). This understanding of citizenship can hopefully lead to crossing visible and invisible borders.

The Polish Context: Political and National Circumstances

After WWII, as a consequence of the decisions taken at Yalta, not only was Poland's sovereignty limited but the country was placed outside the

Western European domain. The collapse of communism in 1989 became the decisive point in the contemporary history of Poland as since then political, social and economic changes have been introduced. This meant the establishment of basic democratic structures and the protection of human rights, a market economy and the implementation of systematic reforms on a large scale. What is more, Poland has become active on the international scene, as in 1991 it came to be a member of the Council of Europe; in 1993 the Association Agreement with the European Union was ratified; and in 2004 eventually it became a member state of the EU. In 1996 Poland became a member of the OECD and in 1999 of the North Atlantic Treaty Organisation.

However, the collapse of communism and the elimination of the Iron Curtain brought not only freedom to Poland but also other concerns. Marion Dönhoff, who contributed remarkably to the improvement of Polish–German relations after WWII, comments on this development saying that the years of isolation resulted in a Polish

> desire to return to Europe and [...] backwardness. In the forty years of isolation and mutual recrimination, Western and Eastern Europe have grown much further apart than might be described by the concepts of democracy and dictatorship. The two systems, differing not only in their principles and ethical concepts, but also in their practical attitudes and daily life, have produced two types of man; these cannot be bent to fit one pattern simply with the help of the market economy. The Western concept of freedom does not coincide with the Eastern one. With us, freedom means the rule of the law and individual human rights; under communism, freedom means satisfaction of economic needs. (Dönhoff, 2001: 12)

This implies that for Poles to meet the EU citizenship requirements would demand, among other things, a great effort on the part of the education system.

The State of Polish Contemporary Society

When analysing contemporary Polish society, Dyczewski (1993, quoted in Grad & Kaczmarek, 1999: 101) documents a dominance of a new mass lifestyle. Among tendencies such as a lack of values and patterns of behaviour, he notices that Poles are not able to defend their point of view, or pursue individual interests and are indifferent towards spiritual cultural values. Additionally, Grad and Kaczmarek (1999: 98–99) note that in Poland, apart from the development of mass culture influenced by the USA, there has been a collapse of a 200-year-old symbolic and romantic culture that was very important in the subversion of totalitarianism.[1] What is more, Polish consciousness is characterised by being present-orientated, meaning that Poles live in the 'culture of the present'. One of the most characteristic problems that Gałaś (2000: 34) identifies concerns tradition, claiming that, as a result of postmodernism, tradition has lost its intellectual authority and its role as an orientation point for making decisions connected with value systems. This leads to losing one's cultural identity, and makes both an individual and a society susceptible to the manipulations of the mass media.

To elaborate more on the above, some of the selected issues connected with the transformation period that Poland is in now will be discussed. Citizenship Education in the Polish education system, as it will be presented later in this chapter, stresses mainly the development of students' values, attitudes and understanding connected with the standards of civil society, and therefore a brief examination of the state of civil society will be the focus of this section.

Civil society at risk

Prawelska-Skrzypek draws attention to the fact that communism in Poland meant the decline of civil society where there was no possibility for an uncontrolled organisation of people into associations or the free expression of opinions. It resulted in the strengthening of family and social bonds where different moral standards prevailed to those that were of importance in public life. The latter were contaminated by conformity, opportunism and simulated activity (Prawelska-Skrzypek, 2001: 40). In the same vein, Gliński (1999) and Sułek (2004) argue that there are no prospects for any social forces to advance the creation of civil society in Poland. Gliński (1999: 126) states that the process of shaping civil society is threatened by the fact that a considerable part of Polish society does not benefit positively in the transformation of the system because of institutional and consciousness-related remnants of communism. Sułek (2004) admits that hopes that civil society would flourish in Poland have been based on beliefs in social ideals and the high esteem Poles have of themselves in terms of good citizenship. When it comes to realities, practical issues like participation in elections show that Poles are disappointed as far as the state is concerned. This might be the result of the fact that there is no self-organising tradition in Poland but rather, as history has shown – a tradition of rebellion (Mach, 2001: 255).

With reference to more basic issues, Gliński (1999: 126) suggests that the differences within society connected with income and material deprivation[2] of a wide range of social groups do not lead to the generation of civic standards and there are no prospects that in the near future this will change. This is the result of educational and cultural negligence in Poland's communist past that verges on a pathological barrier.

Gliński (1999: 123) also stresses the fact that a number of conflicts have been exposed since 1989. These conflicts are a result of social reforms that have been introduced in a fast and costly manner, due to severe competition among various interest groups. Most of all, these developments are not favourable as far as tolerance among Polish citizens is concerned. What is worse, Polish society has still not developed institutions of a mediating and negotiating character that will be of use in cases of conflict, though a recent development is the Centre of Consultation and Dialogue established in Warsaw.

Civil society at work

Having said all this, it should not be overlooked that some aspects of civil society at work in Poland can be identified. For Gliński (1999: 119) one aspect is the activity of some local communities integrated around a well organised local government, within the nongovernmental sector. There are instances of parish communities, trade unions, workers' self-governments or political parties. The 1990s witnessed a growing respect for democratic institutions and the rule of law. This can be described as mature civic consciousness of a 'declarative' character, meaning that respect for the rule of law and democracy became a value that has been acknowledged although not always put into practice (Gliński, 1999: 121). Moreover, the process of the development of civil society and the related phenomenon of civic consciousness and culture are of the 'long duration' type (Braudel, cited in Glinski, 1999: 120).

Furthermore, Mach (2001: 249) draws attention to the fact that pluralism, which is fundamental to the concept of civil society, has begun to take shape in Poland. Poles are beginning to ask themselves questions connected with their relationships with other nations, and with ethnic groups inside and outside the country. The notion of a homogenous society[3] promoted by the communist government and seen as its major strength was questioned after the collapse of communism. Mach (2001: 247) claims that divisions that were hidden during the 50 years of communist rule have become visible. The pluralistic society that has begun to emerge stresses phenomena such as 'the progress in ideological, religious and political pluralism, the divisions in the sphere of economic interests, the emergence of different subcultures or the rediscovery of regional and ethnic differences'. In this process, the imposed unity has been rejected, leading to the opening up of social communication, stressing economic interests, rejection of a controlled market, and promoting new ideas and lifestyles. This involves, according to Mach, not only the participation of individuals and groups in social life, but also their right to join together and to articulate their diverse views of the world. This process has been observed in Western Europe and the USA for many years but Poland, being in its transitional stage, has only begun to witness this trend.

The values crisis

Within this general perspective, the period of transformation has revealed social problems connected with a crisis in the values of confidence, loyalty and solidarity. Drawing on Sztompka (1997), Prawelska-Skrzypek (2001: 40) refers to this as the 'moral atrophy bonds' and explains it as follows:

(1) The crisis in confidence not only towards other individuals but also towards institutions is connected among other things with unemployment and criminality. According to Prawelska-Skrzypek (2001: 41), unemployment varies from 30% in the Northern regions in the areas of former state farms to less than 4% in urban agglomerations. This continual unemployment leads to the marginalisation of large social groups, visible especially in rural areas where passive and demanding attitudes prevail.
(2) The crisis in loyalty is perceived as a reaction to distrust and cynicism leads to a culture of manipulation, which results in the rise of cliques or groupings that then prevail in the field of politics.
(3) The crisis in solidarity can be understood as a lack of existential safety, which leads to a culture of indifference. The market economy has led among other things to stratification by financial status, especially visible in the rural areas, whereas in large cities spatial segregation becomes noticeable in old, neglected quarters, contributing to the progressive process of deprivation (Prawelska-Skrzypek, 2001: 42).

Poland's social problems thus stimulate actions that are either of a normative or spontaneous character. Normative activity comes from groups whose existence has been threatened as a result of economic changes, such as miners, who would claim special privileges. Regulations that lead to the efficiency and transparency in the functioning of public administration are also normative in character.

Activities of a spontaneous character are taken up by groups of citizens or social organisations that were unknown during the communist era. They aim at defence of interests and ideas or they support institutions or certain undertakings. For example, according to Prawelska-Skrzypek (2001: 42) the number of nongovernmental organisations has grown from the 1990s up to 40,000. Moreover, she notices that an increased demand for education both at secondary and tertiary level is also spontaneous. Communist propaganda maintained that education was accessible to all but the percentage of population with university education was only 7%, whereas, after 1990, a rapid rise in young people and adults who wish to pursue their education at various levels has been recorded. This is partly due to the demands of the labour market, where there are better job opportunities for well qualified workers.

As a consequence of the problems described above, there is little doubt that membership in the EU, together with the articulation of European citizenship and its scope in the Maastricht Treaty, will certainly be conducive to the formation of higher civic standards and attitudes in Poland. However, cultural, mental constraints and the raising of awareness among various representatives of nations cannot be ordained by decree (Pawełczyk, 2001: 44). Although European history brought a number of events that might be said to have generated national prejudices, the post-war period offered a number of opportunities to overcome them, but Poland suffered a delay in access to these opportunities for 50 years. A question that can be posed is whether teachers of Citizenship Education in Poland who are part of this particular past can encourage the development of an open identity in young people who in turn are to become active, intercultural citizens and prepare their students to cross existing boundaries.

The System of Public Education

The Polish education system before school reforms of the 1960s was, generally speaking, divided into seven-year primary and four-year secondary schools. The Act of 1961 established grounds for reforms in the education system – the major innovation being eight years of compulsory primary education. With the political transformation of 1989, new legislation established the ground for reforms in school education, which resulted in new school structures, innovations in the curricula and the grading system and requirements made of students. The new legislation also allowed for non-state schools to be established.

The Structure of Schooling

Since the reform, compulsory education begins at the age of six in 'Form 0' and continues for six years at primary school and then for three more years at a new lower-level secondary school, called *gymnasium*. The admission requirement for *gymnasia* is the primary-school-leaving certificate, which now includes results both of final internal evaluation and the external standardised test. In the final year of the *gymnasium*, a compulsory external, standardised examination is taken by all pupils. On the basis of the results of this examination, students choose their upper secondary school. These schools prepare pupils to take the final *matura* examination from 2005 and 2006, which consists of an oral examination at the candidate's school, and an external written paper, marked by an external board of examiners.

The results of the *matura* examination are decisive for admission to tertiary education establishments, although it is at the discretion of those institutions of higher learning whether they set their own admission standards or not. There are also postsecondary schools, which provide a vocational qualification diploma for secondary education graduates.

The Core Curriculum

The actual level of expected educational attainment is determined most of all by the core curriculum and, depending on it, the curricula and course books, as well as evaluation and examination systems. Core curricula for general and specialist vocational education define the main school curricula activities, which must be completely incorporated in the teaching schedules and in all elements of evaluation (especially in requirements of standards and syllabuses). They formulate the school curriculum, and they make it possible to describe a national teaching programme by defining what is common for the whole country. The core curriculum has to be respected by every school. At the same time the teachers can follow one of the selected programmes from a set of those approved for use in schools by the Ministry of Education. They indicate how educational tasks set in the core curriculum could be realised. The teachers are also entitled to prepare their own programme, which must meet criteria described in an appropriate act, choose their own methods of instruction, as well as use various textbooks from a list approved by the Ministry.

The Social Science Curriculum

The social science curriculum is the place where education for citizenship is most likely to be located and this is where we begin. In Primary Stage 1 (Forms 1–111) teaching is designed to ensure smooth transition from preschool to school education. It is arranged on an integrated basis. As in all parts of the core curriculum, teaching programmes are defined within four dimensions: Educational Goals, School Tasks, Teaching Contents and Achievements. Civic education is not articulated clearly at this stage but General Educational goals of the primary school point to the objectives that can be considered as crucial to Citizenship Education when its elements are introduced. They are presented in the comments on the social science curriculum below.

In Primary Stage 2 (Forms 1V–V1) separate subjects like Polish language, history and civics, a modern foreign language or mathematics are taught, in addition to which 'educational paths' are introduced. The school head is responsible for the inclusion of these paths in the curricula implemented by particular teachers. Among the educational paths there is the 'education for society' path. It comprises education for family life, cultural heritage of the region and 'patriotic and civic education'. This means that 'patriotic and civic education' at Stage Two is not taught as an independent subject but is only one of the components of the 'education for society' path.

However, Educational Goals, School Tasks, Teaching Contents and Achievements for 'patriotic and civic education' are specified in the core curriculum. Educational Goals aim mainly at the development of ties with the homeland and civic standards of conduct. School Tasks emphasise ties with national celebrations, institutions or thus preparing pupils for active participation in public life. Teaching contents should instil in young people matters connected with national character like symbols or great Poles, but also emphasise issues like the structure of social life on the axis of 'individual–society–nation–state' and, connected with this, rights and duties. 'Achievements' relate to abilities such as making decisions concerning the group or conducting elections to school government, but they also entail knowledge of the system of social assistance for handicapped people. Attempts should be made to define civic and patriotic attitudes.

Citizenship Education is therefore not taught at Stages One and Two of primary school as a single subject but rather elements of Citizenship Education are specified either in general educational goals or in the 'education for society' path within patriotic and civic education and are to permeate other school subjects. It can be said that the focus is on the individual and the development of a sense of belonging to the school, local, regional and national community. It is both the school head and teachers' responsibility whether general educational goals are realised and whether they develop habits of social life, the awareness of one's self, family, social, cultural, technical and natural environment, strengthen the sense of cultural, historical, ethnic and national identity, emphasise family ties, take into account individual needs and ensure equal opportunities, create conditions supporting the development of self-dependence, sense of duty, responsibility for one's self and the nearest surroundings, and create conditions supporting individual and group actions, undertaken on behalf of others.

In the *gymnasium* (lower secondary school) teaching is arranged in subjects, taught by specialist teachers. However, beside separate subjects, the 'educational paths' called 'European education' and 'Polish culture in the context of Mediterranean civilisation' are introduced. There is a compulsory subject, 'civic education', which consists of three modules, one of them being 'citizenship education'. Educational Goals continue with what it is hoped has been developed at Primary Stages One and Two, that is, strengthen the sense of belonging to the Polish state and nation and to the local community, and awareness of one's rights and obligations. What has been added at this stage is an understanding of political, economic and social events. School Tasks stress attitudes that at this level become a requirement of proper behaviour at school and state ceremonies. They are connected with offering help in recognising one's rights and duties or showing practical aspects of implementation of democratic procedures in school community. School Tasks also develop a sense of responsibility not only for oneself but others, too.

Teaching Contents focus on national issues like the political system, the Polish Republic Constitution or political parties, but also on the local or school governance or civil service. Teaching Contents include the human being as a social individual with his/her indispensable human rights and stress national identity. Within 'Achievements' the *gymnasium* should allow pupils to use their acquired knowledge by being able to comment on public life, to recognise their rights and duties, to participate in a discussion and to not only present but defend a viewpoint. They are also expected to consider the argument of those who are in opposition, to cooperate in a group and share tasks, and finally, to accede to the requirements of democratic procedures.

Among compulsory subjects taught at the *lyceum* (upper secondary school) is civic education ('knowledge about society' in Polish) taught two hours per week. The set Educational Goals stress achieving social activity that is based on respect of one's own country and its law and developing responsibility for the society and the country. Other Educational Goals aim at advancing social and civic virtues, responsibility for the common good and for example the capacity to use the regulations of law. The Schools Tasks are, among others, to support school government or create conditions that would enable students to exchange their views.

The Teaching Content comprises four modules: Society; Politics; Law; and Poland, Europe, the World. The contents of the first module, Society, aim at preparing an individual to actively participate in the life of society and be able to fulfil a number of roles. This is the reason why they focus on the structure of social life, models of civic action or social life ethics. The next module focuses on aspects connected with politics at various levels. It has been implied that knowledge of the theory of politics will lead to civic activity and therefore, the following topic areas are introduced, for example, citizen and authority in totalitarian, authoritarian and democratic systems, fundamental rules of ancient democracy or Christian roots of democracy. The Law module provides students with indispensable knowledge related to different aspects of law with the intention that students will be able to act according to it in future. They learn about various types of law, for example European or natural law, or about human rights by studying primary sources or legal acts. The fourth module, Poland, Europe, the World, comprises contents that concentrate on international matters related to international order, conflicts, security systems or European integration.

Intercultural Citizenship in the Core Curriculum

In the following section I will analyse the curriculum described above, using the axioms and characteristics of intercultural citizenship introduced earlier in this volume and listed in the appendix. The procedure taken will be to identify to what extent the characteristics of intercultural citizenship can be found in the Core Curriculum (CC), its Educational Goals (EG), School Tasks (ST), Teaching Contents (TC) and Achievements (As) in Primary (P), Gymnasium (G) and Lyceum (L). The main approach will be to represent the locations in the curriculum where there is potential for the axioms and characteristics to be realised. These will be summarised without detailed quotations from the documents but first I will present some examples with quotations to indicate the underlying process.

In a first example I will take the following extract from the description of the axioms:

> intercultural citizenship education involves
> - Creating learning/change in the individual: cognitive, attitudinal, behavioural change; change in self-perception/spirituality; change in relationships with Others, that is, people of a different social group; change which is based in the particular but is related to the universal.

In the analysis the following entries were identified that matched the above axiom:

> GEG 8. Developing the child's ability in understanding of oneself and family environment, social, cultural, technical and natural environments available in experience. P
> TC 44. Variety of heritage and research in cultural sphere. P I–III
> TC 47. Understanding, acceptance and tolerance to others in artistic expression. P I–III
> EG 1. Developing ties with the homeland and civic awareness. P IV–VI
> EG 3. Developing respect towards one's own state. P IV–VI
> EG 4. Understanding important events of social, political and economic life in the country and in the world. G
> EG 5. Deepening the respect for one's own country. G
> TC 1. European integration, Poland in Europe. L
> TC 2. International order – conflicts and security systems. L
> TC (*PEW*) 3. Problems of the modern world. L

As a second example, I take the following from the list of characteristics:

> all of the above with a conscious commitment to values (i.e. rejecting relativism), being aware that values sometimes conflict and are

differently interpreted, but being committed, as citizens in a community, to finding a cooperation.

In the analysis the following entries were identified that matched the above

> ST 1. Bringing students' attention to communities such as: family, local environment and homeland, as ones that can enrich their lives, and that everyone has duties towards these communities. P I–III
>
> EG 2. Developing respect towards prosocial attitudes and common goodness. P IV–VI
>
> TC 10. Values and norms of social life. Categories of common goodness. Patriotism. Social culture. P IV–VI
>
> As 8. Attempts at defining modern civic and patriotic attitudes. P IV–VI
>
> TC 12. Indispensable character of human rights, their catalogue and protection system. G
>
> TC 13. Ethics in public life. G
>
> EG 2. Developing social and civic virtues, patriotism and responsibility for common goodness. L
>
> EG 3. Improvement of assessment skills of positions and participants of public life actions from the point of view of basic social life values. L
>
> EG 4. Understanding and gaining the ability to use regulations of law. L
>
> ST 1. Forming prosocial and civic attitudes. L
>
> ST 2. Supporting students' engagement in individual and group actions for the common good and the benefit of others. L
>
> TC 5. Rights and duties, civic virtues, political culture. L

The results of the analysis showed that the core curriculum does not include material that corresponds to the first three axioms. Although, as suggested in the first axiom, intercultural experience may take place in the areas where ethnic minorities live and in the Eastern or Western border areas of Poland, the core does not take this into account. On the other hand, material corresponding to the following elements of the axioms and characteristics can be found (which have been labelled for use in the later table).

> Axioms
> – intercultural citizenship education involves

- (D) causing/facilitating intercultural citizenship experience, and analysis and reflection on it (and on the possibility of further social and/or political activity);
- (E) where 'political' is taken in a broad sense to mean activity that involves working with others to achieve an agreed end;
- (F) creating learning/change in the individual: cognitive, attitudinal, behavioural change; change in self-perception/spirituality; change in relationships with Others i.e. people of a different social group; change which is based in the particular but is related to the universal.

Characteristics

(1) a comparative (juxtaposition) orientation in activities of teaching and learning, e.g. juxtaposition of political processes (in the classroom, school ... country ...) and a critical perspective that questions assumptions through the process of juxtaposition;

(2) emphasis on becoming conscious of working with Others (of a different group and culture) through (a) processes of comparison/juxtaposition and (b) communication in a language (L1 or L2/3/...) that influences perceptions and emphasises the importance of learners becoming conscious of multiple identities;

(3) creating a community of action and communication that is supranational and/or composed of people of different beliefs values and behaviours that are potentially in conflict – without expecting conformity and easy, harmonious solutions;

(4) having a focus and range of action that is different from that which is available when not working with Others, where 'Others' refers to all those of whatever social group who are initially perceived as different, members of an out-group;

(5) emphasising becoming aware of one's existing identities and opening options for social identities additional to the national and regional etc. (e.g. the formation of perhaps temporary supranational group identities through interaction with Others;

(6) paying equal attention to cognition/knowledge, affect/attitude, behaviours/skill;

(7) all of the above with a conscious commitment to values (i.e. rejecting relativism), being aware that values sometimes conflict and are differently interpreted, but being committed, as citizens in a community, to finding a cooperation.

Results of the analysis of curriculum documents

The item numbers in the cells of the tables below are the reference numbers from the core curriculum. The 'Total' shows how many entries from the core curriculum matched *D E F Axioms* and *1 2 3 4 5 6 7 Characteristics*.

Primary Education Stage One (I– III)

	D	*E*	*F*	*1*	*2*	*3*	*4*	*5*	*6*	*7*
EG	–	–	–	–	2	–	4	3	–	–
ST	–	–	–	–	–	–	–	–	2	1
TC	–	–	44, 47	–	–	–	–	1, 2, 3, 5	15	–
As	–	–	–	–	–	–	–	–	–	–
Other	–	–	GEG 8	–	GEG 14	–	–	GEG 9	–	–
Total	–	–	3	–	2	–	1	6	2	1

Primary Education Stage Two (IV– VI)

	D	*E*	*F*	*1*	*2*	*3*	*4*	*5*	*6*	*7*
EG	–	–	1, 3	–	–	–	–	–	–	2
ST	–	3	–	–	–	–	–	1,2	–	–
TC	–	9	–	–	–	5,	–	1,2,3,4	15,6,7,8	10
As	7	–	–	–	2	–	3	1	2,5,6	8
Other	–	–	GEG 8	–	GEG 14	–	–	GEG 9	–	–
Total	1	2	3	–	2	1	1	8	7	3

Gymnasium Stage Three (lower secondary school)

	D	E	F	1	2	3	4	5	6	7
EG	–	–	4, 5	–	–	–	3	1, 2	–	–
ST	–	2,	–	–	–	–	3, 4	1	5	–
TC	–	6, 11	–	4, 5	–	–	–	1, 2, 3	7, 8, 9, 10, 14	12, 13
As	–	2, 3	–	4,	5, 6, 8	–	–	1,	–	
Total	–	5	2	3	3	–	3	7	6	2

Lyceum – general upper secondary school

	D	*E*	*F*	*1*	*2*	*3*	*4*	*5*	*6*	*7*
EG	–	–	–	–	–	1	–	5	–	2, 3, 4
ST	–	–	–	5	–	–	6	–	3, 4	1, 2
TC	1,2,4,1, 2, 3, 4, 5, 6	7	1, 2, 3	–	2, 4, 6, 7	3, 3, 5	6	1	–	5
As	–	6	–	1, 2	4, 5	8	7	–	3, 9	–
Total	9	2	3	3	6	5	3	2	4	6

Total number of the core curriculum entries at the primary, *gymnasium* and *lyceum* level matching *D E F Axioms* and *1 2 3 4 5 6 7 Characteristics*

	D	*E*	*F*	*1*	*2*	*3*	*4*	*5*	*6*	*7*
Total	10	9	11	6	13	6	8	23	19	12

It is worth repeating here that teaching at Stage One of primary school (I–III) is established on an integrated basis and Citizenship Education as a subject is not present. At Stage Two of primary school (IV–VI), Citizenship Education is not taught as a separate subject but 'patriotic and civic education' is one of the components of the 'education for society' path. At *gymnasium*, Stage Three, 'citizenship education' is one of the modules of a compulsory subject, 'civic education'. At the *lyceum* level there is a compulsory subject, 'civic education' (in Polish 'knowledge about society'), which can be taught both as a basic scope or an extended one and can be taken at the final new *matura* examination. Therefore, one should note here that 'citizenship education' is not a compulsory subject at any level of education but it either forms a part, a module or permeates the 'civic education' subject. I will deal with the locations in order of frequency totals.

Characteristic 5 = 23

The totals reveal that the core curriculum would certainly contribute to the awareness of pupils' existing identities of cultural, historical, ethnic and national character. This is emphasised in the Teaching Contents of the core curriculum entries at Stage Two and Stage Three of education, and to a lesser extent at Stage One. Possibly, it is assumed that at the *lyceum* level, pupils are already aware of their identities, therefore options are open for formation of new social identities.

Characteristic 6 = 19

The core curriculum also establishes grounds for gaining knowledge of the working of democracy at various levels, the school level or the local one (this can be traced especially in Teaching Contents of Stages Three and Two). It allows not only the shaping of attitudes of pupils towards their peers, teachers, school or state celebrations but also the development of skills that lead to the analysis of somebody else's viewpoint, and justification or defence of one's own position in the public forum.

Characteristic 2 = 13

Upon close reading of the core curriculum it might be deduced that it is at the *lyceum* level that students become conscious of working with others (and this does not happen at Stages One, Two or Three). They become aware of this possibility by learning about models of civic actions, application of democratic procedures or when organising actions of a civic character is emphasised. Additionally, it is hoped to establish prosocial foundations related to civil courage or solidarity. It can be hoped that by having formed and maintained proper contacts with other children, adults, handicapped people and representatives of other nations or races (Educational Goals of Stage One) young people gradually become aware of multiple identities in people.

Characteristic 7 = 12

With reference to this characteristic pupils learn about a value system of relevance to social life at both Stages One and Two of primary education, then, at the *gymnasium* level, they learn about the indispensable character of human rights, and it is hoped that within ethics they learn about the threats of relativism. But it is at the *lyceum* level that they should attain capability and understanding of a conscious commitment to civic virtues. This should take place when they become engaged either in individual or group actions with the aim of reaching a common cause. The core curriculum entries do not specify openly that values may become a cause of a conflict or can be interpreted differently by individuals but it may be assumed that within the 'forming of the prosocial attitudes' item, they are taught how to find cooperation when they become involved in actions for the benefits of others.

Axiom F = 11

Regarding this axiom, the entries identified in the core curriculum were evenly spread at all levels of education. It may be expected that being, for example, exposed to a variety of heritage and being able to understand and accept Otherness in artistic expression (as the core curriculum states) might create change in the individual at the attitudinal or spiritual level (Stage One I– III). Whereas the general educational goals of primary school are to develop in young children an ability of perceiving themselves being related not only to family but also to their social, cultural, technical and natural surroundings might lead to change in relationships with others. This is what should happen at Stages One and Two and may establish grounds for developing understanding of the character of international events that are of importance both to one's own country, Europe and the world (Teaching Contents at *lyceum*). However, to be able to generalise the particular experience and apply it to the universal would require a great engagement both on the part of the teacher and the learner.

Axiom D = 10

It is highly speculative whether an intercultural democratic experience ever takes place in the educational system in Poland, as only 10 items were identified to match both axioms and characteristics. It is noteworthy, however, that nine out of the ten entries are from the *lyceum* core curriculum. Learning about ancient democracy and the Christian roots of democracy, modern political doctrines, various types of law (including international and European ones), and then about sources, documents and procedures related to human rights, could lead to an understanding of what intercultural democratic experience might entail rather than to actual experience. This places stress on future social and political activity that *lyceum* graduates will be involved in.

Axiom E = 9

There are no entries in the core curriculum that would relate to this axiom at Stage One but it is emphasised at Stage Three and less visibly at Stage Two and *lyceum*. In fact, it is doubtful whether intercultural experience takes place at all, but this experience might be facilitated by a move away from just gaining knowledge of the state system of the Polish Republic with its organs of authority and their competencies, public administration and regional autonomy, to using this knowledge along with the recognition of one's rights, duties, civic awareness and civic virtues (especially stressed in *gymnasium*). This would establish grounds for the future working with others towards the common good. However, the core curriculum items do not refer to the skills of analysis or reflection.

Characteristic 4 = 8

This characteristic is articulated less evidently than those already mentioned and entries related to it are more pronounced at the *gymnasium* and *lyceum* level. The core curriculum refers to various actions that can be taken within the school or local community. Acquiring knowledge about forms of citizen participation in public life and being able to differentiate between the competencies of selected institutions or social organisations will establish grounds for future actions.

Characteristic 1 = 6

Characteristic 1 is not reflected at Stage One and Stage Two of education. The items that have been identified at the *gymnasium* and *lyceum* level lay the foundation for activities that create conditions for students' exchange of views when conflicting viewpoints are compared and defended, or when the understanding of problems in public life is connected not only with defining their causes and forecasting their consequences but also demanding the critical use of different sources of information. The comparative dimensions of teaching and learning are brought to the fore when the role of a citizen and public authority are studied in totalitarian, authoritarian and democratic systems. This should take place at the *gymnasium* level.

Characteristic 3 = 6

This particular characteristic is not present at Stages One and Three. At Stage Two only one entry has been identified when life in a group might be related to conflicts. The *lyceum* core curriculum attempts to bring into focus social conflicts, conflicts of values in public life, and most of all, skills of critical analysis of public debates and participants' arguments that lead to an understanding of their position.

As this chapter aims to highlight the role Citizenship Education can play in the quest for better understanding and mutual respect among Polish citizens and between all European citizens, it is important to note that the tables above clearly show that the core curriculum of Stage One of primary education and Stage Three does not lay grounds for *D* and *E Axioms*, as it does not assume that democratic experience will take place or will be facilitated. Therefore, neither analysis nor reflection on those issues can take place.

The analysis of the core curriculum reveals that Citizenship Education within the core curriculum, rather than developing critical, active citizens, transmits knowledge and basic skills that enable pupils to act as Polish nationals and in this way strengthen their national identity. This would imply that Citizenship Education does not lead to acquiring a European identity. However, it can be hoped that if young people come to understand their own society then an attempt might be made to understand that of their neighbours. Eventually, with this development, a change will take place in their socialisation in Europe. Citizenship Education, rather than reproducing patterns of previous generations, should prepare young people for this particular change that would result from the analysis and reflection on young people's examination and understanding (mainly through activities) of the relationship between the self and society. Secondly, their views on respect for diversity should be enhanced through the study of not only issues of citizenship like power, justice, rights and privileges, but also controversies connected with culturally diverse communities and issues like identity, racism, gender or economic and social inequality. Practical guidance should be offered on classroom activities connected with moral judgements about right and wrong, and discrimination and exclusion.

The curriculum should consider how to best equip young people with intercultural competencies, so as to enable them both as individuals and citizens to participate in the complex societies of the modern world. The axioms and characteristics of Intercultural Citizenship Education are our attempt to formulate a clearly defined agenda and the discussion of intercultural citizenship is recent. The core curriculum under study was devised in 2002, so it is perhaps not surprising that school curricula and the textbooks used by teachers do not meet intercultural requirements. The same applies to teachers of Citizenship Education and authors of textbooks. So far, the contents of Citizenship Education textbooks focus on knowledge that makes young people understand the way a society, a country, the world work. It is assumed that by becoming knowledgeable in these content areas, young people become fully fledged citizens, aware of their rights and duties. Whether they become intercultural citizens becomes an issue that needs further studies as interculturalism itself is not present in the core curriculum, not to mention course books. Therefore, at present much will depend on the teacher, and whether he/she himself/herself is familiar with the issues under discussion.

Openness, free ideological competition and the recognition of various minorities are fairly new phenomena in Polish culture, and therefore both the Citizenship Education teaching contents and activities should promote a positive attitude towards pluralism. Thus, there is a challenge to design a programme of activities which reflects the need to express the diversity of opinions and attitudes. Among other aspects, these activities should lead to the implementation of political concepts of the Council of Europe such as the promotion of democratic/intercultural citizenship, social cohesion, mutual understanding and respect.

European integration needs to be accompanied by a search for a middle ground between open, integrative and isolationist trends. The central issue here is the role of dialogue to overcome barriers, fears, prejudices and stereotypes. Norman Davies, while speaking at the British Council seminar on 'Exploring the impact of national identity on relationships between people from European countries, using the case study of Poland and the United Kingdom' (Warsaw, 18 March 2002), said that in order to increase intercultural understanding, the narratives connected with lesser development should be put aside as well as the division between Western and Eastern civilisation. That is why recognition and cooperation should become the most essential values to be emphasised by intercultural education (Nikitorowicz, 1999: 30).

Recommendations concerning the future of intercultural citizenship education in Poland might be as follows:

(1) The treatment of Citizenship Education should receive special recognition in Polish education where the experience of difference

and openness should be established as a central element in devising the core curriculum. There is a new educational role for Citizenship Education teachers as they have to be aware of the challenges of interculturalism.

(2) The attainment of the set objectives will depend more on the way Citizenship Education is presented than on a mere prescription of topics and themes to be studied. In determining classroom approaches, the experience of teachers will be invaluable, hence the importance of teacher training programmes with respect to Citizenship Education.

(3) It is not possible to indicate what content areas should be included in the Citizenship Education curriculum. In a changing world some topics are more readily applied than others. It is a task for teachers to select issues that would be most appropriate for their classroom situation. Therefore, the importance of the individual teacher should be acknowledged. Teachers' own expectations should be considered as the teacher should be convinced that the approach adopted is not just appropriate to the learners, but corresponds to the teacher's own expectations.

(4) As intercultural Citizenship Education challenges and reshapes learners' understanding of the world and their cultural identity, the responsibilities of the teacher should be recognised. Teacher education has to confront these implications and accommodate them with the practical and theoretical foundations for these responsibilities. This implies that teachers of Citizenship Education will need training structured differently from the present one.

(5) With respect to the content, a selection has to be made from the abundance of potential themes. It should adhere to some organising principles where the axioms and characteristics used for this analysis could be referred to. Most of all, these organising principles should be clearly articulated. The criteria for the selection and organisation will have to take account of goals learners are to achieve.

(6) To implement these proposals working groups will have to be established to outline the content of the themes, together with the knowledge, skills and understanding that learners will be expected to acquire in studying them. It has to be noted at this point that a committee of experts and practitioners has already been appointed at the Institute of Public Affairs under the guidance of Prof. Konarzewski.

(7)　More effort should be made to overcome educational constraints and to implement an intercultural perspective in all school subjects.

In conclusion, it is the belief of the author that it is the sense of openness to experience which is basic to any real intercultural development. This essential prerequisite of an intercultural frame of mind is well expressed in Soros's (2000: 2) commentary on the open society, which could be used as the starting point for future undertakings related to intercultural citizenship education: 'open society is based on the recognition that we act on the basis of imperfect understanding and our actions have unintended consequences. Perfection is beyond our reach; we must therefore content ourselves with the second best: an imperfect society that holds itself open to improvement.'. This idea of imperfection might be applied to the Polish context as it not only gives hope regarding Citizenship Education and education in general, but also the future of democracy.

Notes

1.　Grad and Kaczmarek (1999: 98–99) support this by a comment from Dahrendorf who argues that 'when totalitarian pressure gets weaker people rush to grab at the tabloids, hamburgers, dish-washing machines, shiny motorcycles, and holiday at Costa Brava. If some of the solid values were saved it would be a good idea, but it is difficult to say how to do it' (author's translation).
2.　Drawing on Tarkowska et al. (1999), Gliński (1999: 125–126) points out that, according to data, more or less 50% of Polish society live below the social minimum. The financial elite is around 2% of Polish society, whereas those who benefited financially most in the transformation belong to the group of between 15% and 25% of Poles.
3.　Mach (2001: 250–251) states that within the Marxist–Lenin philosophy, minority cultures and, connected with them, ethnic identities, belonged to the past. Hence, nothing was mentioned about them either in the media or school curricula. Minorities, however, existed and although statistically insignificant, in some parts of Poland, like Opole-Silesia, the Bialystok or Przemysl regions, they had great importance in social life. Therefore Polish history was taught at schools before 1989 from the perspective of a 'uniform nation' when 'the history of the minorities was either overlooked or disregarded – just like the history of some regions of Poland'.

Chapter 10
Citizenship Education in Spain: Aspects of Secondary Education

MARÍA del CARMEN MÉNDEZ GARCÍA

Introduction

In Spain, as in many other European nations, there is a growing tendency in education to give prominence to the present-day European context and to the international or global context of which Spain is an integral part. The education laws make explicit the necessity for young Spaniards to be aware of this relatively new European and international orientation in Spain if the new generations aspire to be successful both within and outside the country. Clear economic reasons underlie this statement, even though humanistic goals are also recognised. Promotion of democratic values, tolerance, respect and interpersonal understanding are the pillars of a multicultural Spanish society. The necessity to develop intercultural understanding in a world in which contact with peoples from other cultures is highly frequent turns out to be a similar key issue in the Spanish education laws.

Citizenship education in Spain should ideally reflect these national and international dimensions. Citizenship education is indeed linked to cross-curricular themes, such as 'civic education' or to specific courses such as 'History and Geography'. However, intercultural goals and issues are more often related to foreign-language teaching, both in the education laws and in the teaching material. There is an assumption that the idea of the European and intercultural dimensions, which are dealt with in 'History and Geography' from a clearly cognitive approach, would invariably lead to the development of highly competent inter-cultural speakers who have managed to overcome their ethnocentric and/or biased views of Otherness. The assumption on which Spanish education laws seem to rely is the fact that international contact will be successful if Spaniards apply the knowledge and skills developed during their schooling; it is the 'put-them-together-and-they-will-succeed' hypothesis. Nevertheless, becoming a real intercultural citizen requires a much more in-depth analysis of human groups, how they interact, where differences stem from, the origin of conflict, and so on. Human/ intercultural communication does not seem to be the main focus of any course in the curriculum, even though some of the goals of the foreign-language courses should, by law, help promote intercultural understanding.

The most notorious aspect seems to be the fact that national and/or regional citizenship is prioritised by the whole community (the school included) and that learners appear to develop a sense of national and/or regional identity with ease. On the other hand, the promotion of a supranational and an international citizenship seems to be mainly worked on in the school context. No doubt, this is a complex and not easy-to-achieve objective.

Taking the aforementioned context as a basis, this chapter explores whether the Spanish education system in its preuniversity cycles contemplates and promotes education for intercultural citizenship. The status of citizenship education and intercultural citizenship education in Spain will be studied here from the point of view of the education laws. The aim of this chapter is to clarify what 'citizenship education' means in Spain and how it is carried out. The possibilities promulgated by the law, both in terms of national and supranational identity, are examined and conclusions on the status of 'citizenship education' will be drawn.

The Concept of Citizenship and Citizenship Education

'Citizenship' and 'citizenship education' have recently become highly topical issues in Europe. Defining 'citizenship', however, is not without difficulty given the multiplicity of perspectives from which the concept has been approached: political, legal, educational, economical, in connection with minorities, and so on, and the different layers of citizenship discovered in contemporary European societies: local, regional, national, European, international/global.

Crick (2000a: 4; quoted by Holford & Edirisingha, 2000: 3) asserts that the notion of 'citizenship' originates in ancient Greece, where 'citizens' as individuals who 'had a legal right to have a say in the affairs of the city or state', were distinguished from 'subjects' in that '[A] subject obeys the laws and a citizen plays a part in making and changing them'. On the basis of the tradition of Marshall's 1950s classification of citizenship with three elements: civil (rights for freedom), political (rights to take part in political bodies and power) and social (rights to enjoy the benefits and social heritage of a particular society), Holford and Edirisingha (2000: 3–4) consider that current notions of citizenship are linked either to the idea of membership of a society or to the combination of rights and responsibilities. Osler and Starkey (2005)[1] make a comprehensive analysis of the concept of 'citizenship' in the tripartite classification they propose: citizenship as a feeling (the individuals' sense of belonging to a community), as a status (which confers on the individual the rights to residence, employment and vote) and as practice (active participation in the building of democratic societies). Active citizenship is a key issue in democratic societies and it requires both the individual's critical analysis of the social phenomena and their active participation, as Guilherme (2002) puts it.

The complexity underlying the term is emphasised by Breidbach (2003: 9), who agrees with Everson and Preu (1995: 47) in the sense 'that the "peoples of Europe" possess a great variety of understanding of the concept of citizenship'. Breidbach, in fact, deems that even different European institutions have emphasised different aspects of citizenship, with 'European Citizenship' based on legal institutions according to the European Union, versus The Council of Europe's insistence on education in the promotion of participatory democracy. Holford and Edirisingha (2000: 5) summarise this multiplicity of perspectives by referring to key issues at present associated with citizenship such as the ideas of identity and participation, the individual's status and feeling, the many identities of an individual and society's collective memory.

'Citizenship', therefore, needs to be understood as an all-inclusive concept in which the many identities of the individual or his/her multilayered sense of belonging plays a relevant role. The process of socialisation (Berger & Luckmann, 1966) and the transformations the person undergoes in learning how one becomes a member of different social groups, underscores the importance of education in the construction of self-identity. However, nowadays, this has turned out to be a particularly complex phenomenon because the contradictory forces towards globalisation, on the one hand, and towards local or regional identities that are currently developing on the other, demand a flexible individual who is able to feel at ease with their multiple identities: local, regional, national, European and global or cosmopolitan, as Osler and Starkey (2005) call it.

In this context, Soysal's words (1996: 23), quoted by Breidbach (2003: 10), re-examine the notion of national identity: 'In the new model, the membership of individuals is not solely based on the criteria of nationality; their membership and rights are legitimated by the global ideologies of human rights. Thus, universal personhood replaces nationhood; and universal human rights replace national rights'. European identity, on the other hand, according to Breidbach (2003), generally perceived in political terms, seems to be rather a goal than a reality, which implies that European identity is yet to be created. Indeed, it is in times of crisis when this identity seems to be clearly emerging, as the European reactions to the attacks on the trains in Madrid on 11 March 2004 demonstrated. The impact of crisis has the same effect of raising awareness of national identities, forged or given impetus in the 19th century, but questioned nowadays, as a result of the new composition of European societies with a growing number of immigrants and/or with the increasing recognition of regional specificity and regional identity. As Starkey (2002: 5) points out, 'citizenship is most commonly experienced at local levels and it exists at supranational levels.' The close relationship between local and global citizenship is likewise underlined by Guilherme (2004), who specifies that to the notion of cosmopolitanism the nuance of 'rooted cosmopolitanism' has to be added, that is to say, the same person needs to have both 'roots' and 'wings' for, as Beck (2002: 19) states, 'there is no cosmopolitanism without localism'. The paradox here is that cosmopolitan citizenship becomes a highly demanding process in the sense that it requires the individual to question and modify their national identity. Guilherme (2004) specifies that 'if national citizenship entails a sense of belonging, and therefore it is political, on the other hand, cosmopolitan citizenship, is also political precisely because it implies to untie, or at least to loosen, any previous ties'. 'Multiple citizenship' then, the presence of manifold loyalties (Donati, 1997), turns out to be paramount.

In terms of citizenship education, an interesting model emerges in its three-dimensional perspective: education 'about', 'through' or 'for' citizenship. Education 'about' citizenship represents the most traditional way of approaching the issue. It is based on exclusive attention being paid to a specific content, the formulation of education goals in terms of the knowledge students have to gain and the formulation of the assessment criteria according to the knowledge students are supposed to have achieved at the end of the course. In short, education 'about citizenship' only focuses on developing the learner's cognitive capacity. Education 'through' citizenship involves learning by doing and partici-pating. The goal is not the person's cognition but the development of the appropriate capacities and skills that they will need to become an active participant in society from a practical approach, that is to say, by taking part in the community's associations or decision-making bodies. Finally, a more global type of instruction resides in education 'for' citizenship, which is a combination of both, the cognitive and the experiential and participative approach.

Spanish Perspectives on Citizenship

Spanish scholars and Spanish institutions have not made an extensive analysis of 'citizenship' and 'citizenship education' (Flecha *et al.*, 2000: 145). The specific literature on this issue is recent and some of the studies carried out in Spain are part of international teamwork and usually within volumes that focus on international comparisons.

'Citizenship' and 'citizenship education' in Spain have to be seen in the Spanish historical context. Indeed, the transition from Franco's authoritarian regime to democracy tends to be equated with Spaniards' change of status from 'subjects' to 'citizens' (Flecha *et al.*, 2000: 147). Bruno-Jofré and Jover (2000: 3) consider the 1978 Spanish Constitution as a turning point; from then onwards 'Spanish people began to be familiar with terms such as justice, freedom, equality, political pluralism, rights of citizens, etc.'. The profound change that the national values witnessed is parallel to the rise of a European orientation in Spain, marked by Spain's joining the Council of Europe in 1977, the signature of the 'European Convention for the Protection of Human Rights and Fundamental Freedoms' and culminating in 1987 when Spain effectively joined the European Union.

Spain had been for decades a country from which people migrated to European and South and Central American countries. The moral, social, economic, political and cultural changes undergone in Spain and associated with Spain opening to Europe have been accelerated by the configuration of a Spanish society in which there is an increasing and gradually more influential population of immigrants from South and Central America, northern Africa and, recently, Eastern European countries (Bruno-Jofré & Jover, 2000: 3; Flecha *et al.*, 2000: 145–146). Bearing in mind that European citizenship is originally a political construct, the status of immigrants poses problems in terms of inclusion and exclusion.

Additionally, Bruno-Jofré and Jover (2000: 2) believe that Spanish people are aware of their multiple citizenship: 'To be a Spaniard is to be at the same time a citizen in various sites: local, autonomic, national, European, etc.' – the use of the word 'autonomic' here refers to Spain's autonomous regions or provinces. In principle, Spanish people seem to be prepared to assume their multiple identities and do not think that adopting a European or a global citizenship threatens their national, regional/autonomic or local identities. Nonetheless, the real fact is that, as shown in Figure 10.1 which is an overview of identities and identity development, not all these identities seem to be promoted on equal grounds and may not be equally 'balanced' within the individual.

Through the process of socialisation, individuals learn the practices, knowledge, beliefs, values and skills necessary to be successful citizens in their communities. Berger and Luckmann (1966: 142–182) underline the relevance of primary and secondary socialisation. They define 'primary socialisation' as the cultural foundations laid by family and relatives in the person's early childhood; a subtle, gradual, mostly unconscious sociocultural learning, but an everlasting one. 'Secondary socialisation' takes place with the school entrance and is determined by the education institutions and laws of a particular society. Both primary and secondary socialisations are determining factors in the individual's perception of reality, in their worldview, and lead to a very strong sense of belonging to the community, fostering, chiefly, the local, regional and national sides of citizenship.

Where and when are the supranational sides of citizenship favoured? Byram (1990) and Doyé (1992, 1999), on the basis of Berger and Luckmann's classification, propose the term 'tertiary socialisation' to refer to the international and/or intercultural encounter. For many people, the process of approaching Otherness begins in the foreign language class and hence the relevance of foreign language teaching in individuals' global education. Byram and Doyé assert that when people from different cultural and linguistic backgrounds interact, their systems of values and beliefs, so far taken for granted, may seem incompatible. This intercultural experience is a highly demanding process in that its success depends on the participants' degree of flexibility and the constant revision of their standpoints. At this stage, supranational identity, European or global citizenship, may begin to be developed or, in some cases, may be rejected, the feeling of national identity and/or ethnocentrism being much stronger.

The democratic orientation in Spain is evident, as the studies carried out by Morán and Benedicto (1995) and Montro *et al.* (1998) have confirmed. Bruno-Jofré and Jover (2000: 3) state that these studies also show that 'young Spaniards consider the rights related to their close needs (housing, jobs, education) more important than basic freedoms (such as religious and ideological freedoms, freedom of expression, etc.) and the right to political participation.' Spaniards' attitudes toward active citizenship, hence, seem to be in line with those of other European

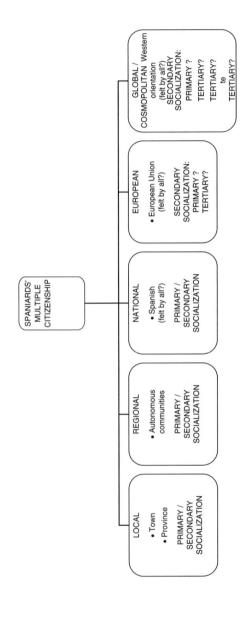

Figure 10.1 Multiple citizenship as promoted in Spain

peoples and this low involvement in social and political decisions has to be understood as a threat to European democracies, Spain included.

Citizenship Education in Spain: Identities Promoted

Initial remarks

Citizenship education in the school context has recently begun to be paid heed to in Spain. The influx of similar studies carried out in other European countries and the implementation of the curricula on the basis of the new laws issued in the 1990s, with an explicit emphasis on educational values, have definitely fostered this incipient line of research.

Naval *et al.* (2003: 1) question whether civic education in Spain has been conducted appropriately and whether Spanish education has been successful in developing participative citizens:

> The tragic sinking of the *Prestige* off the northern Spanish coast in late 2002, and the consequential devastating oil spillage, provided an excellent opportunity for such participation. While many Spanish citizens participated in the arduous clean-up task, much could have been achieved by young citizens to democratically address significant issues of environmental pollution. That they did not reflect, in part, is a lack of civic engagement of young Spanish citizens which, in turn, reflects inadequate education for democratic citizenship in Spanish schools. (my translation)

The following pages will provide an account of the status of citizenship education in Spain, its defining features, the recently issued laws on secondary education and the treatment of the matter of citizenship education in particular textbooks. This study will allow the examination of citizenship education in secondary education in Spain, with the aim of stating whether it promotes or has the potential to promote regional, national, European or global citizenship and whether an international and intercultural dimension underlies the Spanish approach to the issue of citizenship.

Education policies, values, aims and materials

Spain is said to be, from Kerr's viewpoint (1999c: 5), a country with a centralised government, which regulates education, even though the local autonomy of the different regions is also acknowledged. Indeed, in Spain the Ministry of Education issues education laws that are applicable to the whole country. Nonetheless, these laws are by nature general and their actual implementation depends on the promulgation of more

concrete laws on the part of the different autonomous federal governments, which specify the way the general framework should be applied in that particular part of Spain. Spain is divided into 17 *comunidades autónomas* (literally: 'autonomous communities') or regions and from 1981 to 2000 all of them progressively acquired specific education powers.[2] Thus, the education policies of the whole nation are based on a common core, even though the current education practices vary considerably across regions.

With respect to educational values and aims, the existence of the national and the federal authorities makes the expression of national values to be promoted very general. The formulation of the aims of education is articulated according to basic standards usually expressed in the conjugation of knowledge, attitudes or values and skills to be developed. This model of educating citizens in Spain can, hence, be understood as a basis for intercultural citizenship education (which pays equal attention to cognition, affect and behaviours/skills) that the Spanish laws already meet.

Textbooks in Spain are very closely linked to the law and to the official curricula. Textbooks have to be consistent with the relevant legislation and are generally verified by the education authorities before they can be marketed. This ensures that the core content stipulated in the laws is integrated in textbooks all over the country, irrespective of the region where they are going to be used. As all the Spanish autonomous regions have at present the power to add further contents or to add nuances to the ones stipulated by the Spanish Ministry of Education, the reality is that textbooks are finally produced for and approved by each of the autonomous regions. This implies that, as Figure 10.2 expresses, a large part of the textbook will be identical in all the regions, whereas a few additional topics will deal with specific cultural, economic, political, etc. issues of the particular autonomous region where it is going to be used.

Citizenship Education at Primary and Secondary School Level

Spanish education laws and the issue of citizenship education

The changes undergone by Spanish society in the last decades have propelled the formulation of different laws that try to make education adequate for the needs of a dynamic society. One of the most outstanding factors in the promulgation of these laws is the necessity to respond to an unprecedented global change. In this context, citizenship education has

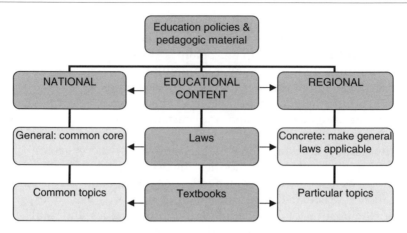

Figure 10.2 Education policies and pedagogic material

been a constituting element of the educational reforms that have taken place from 1990. In the two previous laws, it was not a matter explicitly addressed.[3]

Citizenship education is marked by Spanish membership of the European Union and the current movements of globalisation and internationalisation. According to the Law for the Quality of Education (LOCE, 2002: 45.189), which adds some nuances to the Law for the Regulation of the Spanish Educational System (LOGSE, 1990), in a 'society that tends to universalization, an open attitude, the capacity to take the initiative and creativity are fundamental values'.[4] Consequently, the attitudinal component and the promotion of active citizenship are paramount in the Spanish educational system; the relevance of personal effort and achievement is likewise highlighted as a key issue (LOCE, 2002). Nonetheless, the law seems to be naïve in this matter, as the development of an open attitude does not in itself lead to intercultural competence. Human communication, particularly between and among intercultural groups, is a complex process that requires the development of particular knowledge, attitudes and skills (Byram *et al.*, 2002).

Of the twelve principles that underlie the LOCE, three of them refer to citizenship education and the principles of democratic communities. The new law aims to favour:

(a) Equity, which guarantees equal opportunities of quality, for the full development of the personality through education, in the respect for democratic principles and fundamental rights and freedoms.

(b) Capacity to transmit values that favour personal freedom, social responsibility, cohesion and improvement of societies, and equality between the sexes, which help overcome any type of discrimination, as well as the practice of solidarity, through the impetus to pupils' and students' civic participation in active citizenship.

(c) Capacity to act as a compensating element for personal and social inequalities. (LOCE, 2002: 45.192)

In general terms, the explicit promotion of democratic values such as equality, freedom, solidarity or active citizenship are at the heart of the Spanish education system. More specific goals underlie each education stage:

- In preschool education (up to 3 years old) the most immediate goals are the discovery of the immediate environment and the norms that determine coexistence and social relationships (LOCE, 2002: 45.195).
- In infant education (ages 3–6) the specific aims are the child's physical, intellectual, affective, social and moral development (LOCE, 2002: 45.195).
- Aspects such as basic notions of the culture and coexistence are the most outstanding objectives (LOCE, 2002: 45.195) in primary education (ages 6–12).
- Citizenship education for the education of learners in the exercise of their rights and in the acknowledgement of their duties is stated, together with the transmission of basic cultural elements (LOCE, 2002: 45.196), among the goals of compulsory secondary education (ages 12–16).
- Education for democratic citizenship is made even more explicit in the postcompulsory cycle of secondary education, Bachillerato (ages 17–18), which aims at developing capacities such as 'the consolidation of the sensitivity of a responsible citizen, inspired by the values of democratic societies and human rights and committed to them' (LOCE, 2002: 45.199).

The mention of human rights can be understood as the first international orientation of the Law for the Quality of Education (LOCE). Indeed, the European and international orientation seems to lie behind the new law (as well as the law issued in 1990), as Spanish citizens seem to be very much aware of the new context in which European orientation and globalisation or internationalisation influence most Western European countries.

Citizenship education in primary and secondary education

An interesting piece of data is the fact that the Spanish phrase for 'citizenship education', *educación para la ciudadanía*, is scarcely present in the official documents. So, the question to be put is how is citizenship education dealt with in this country?

Naval *et al*. (2003: 2) distinguish three types of curriculum: the formal curriculum (which makes the knowledge, values and skills desired explicit), the informal curriculum (to be found in lessons in which students participate in school councils, community learning, etc.) and the hidden curriculum (values implicit in the interactions pupils have among themselves and with the teachers, of which few or no people are aware). Citizenship education can be considered as present in the three types of curricula, even though its value in the hidden curriculum is obviously more difficult to determine.

The informal curriculum

The informal curriculum encourages pupils' participation in the bodies that take decisions concerning the running of the school, and also their participation in other social organisations. For example, a given number of pupils, parents, administration staff and teachers constitute the school council, and most of the decisions related to school discipline, school activities and even the approval of school programmes have to be taken at the heart of the school council. The members of the school council are elected by other children, parents, administration staff or teachers respectively for a period of four years. This is required by law and creates a feeling of community in which the different groups, students, parents, teachers and administration staff have their own representatives, with a say in school policy and all the activities organised by the school.

Even though no law enumerates them, specific celebrations or activities (such as the Day of the Constitution) are an essential part of the informal curriculum and are held every year. Sometimes, the education authorities may even suggest how a particular festivity could be prepared and what it may consist of. Pupils' participation is both encouraged and required and, occasionally, the joint preparation of such activities on the part of teachers and students takes place for some days or weeks prior to the event. Obviously, the orientation of these celebrations depends on the festivity itself:

- The international or global dimension is a constitutive part of the activities carried out on the Day of the Tree or Day of Peace.

- The promotion of national identity is clear in the celebration of the Day of the Constitution (6 December). A further national celebration in Spain is the national festivity, on 12 October, but it is not generally accompanied by school activities.
- The emphasis on regional identity is evident in the Day of the 'Autonomy', 17 different days depending on the region. In Andalusia, for instance, the Day of Andalusia is 28 February.

Citizenship education in the informal curriculum is highly influenced by the young Spanish democracy. Indeed, the 'Day of the Constitution' and the 'Day of the 'Autonomy', both non-working days in Spain, appeared in the Spanish calendar after the collapse of Franco's regime. An interesting fact is that, because they are not rooted traditions in the society, they are exclusively celebrated in the school context by means of activities, sometimes suggested by the education authorities, such as: the analysis of the importance of the Constitution in the week previous to the festivity, reading aloud some extracts from the Constitution, the study of the characteristics of the 'Autonomy', colouring the regional flags, and so on. Consequently, the promotion of national and regional values and identities corresponds to political decisions to promote both the idea of Spain as a country and the diversity of its peoples.

The formal curriculum: The cross-curricular approach

Citizenship education is evident in the formal curriculum of primary and secondary education. In spite of this assertion, citizenship education is not explicitly dealt with in a specific year, subject or grade. In fact, all the considerations concerning citizenship education take place in an integrated approach from two different perspectives. On the one hand, citizenship education is closely related to courses that deal with the social and cultural environment. In primary education, citizenship education is integrated in the courses devoted to the natural, social and cultural environment (170 hours per year), whereas in secondary education it is linked to History and Geography (3 hours per week) (Kerr, 1999c: 12–15) and also to Ethics (see below in the 'Ethics' section). On the other hand, every single course offered by the school should ideally incorporate it, because citizenship education is considered in the 1990 Law (still applicable in this respect) as a cross-curricular topic, 'civic education'.

Saénz-López Buñuel explains that cross-curricular themes are introduced in the curriculum in order to incorporate values education, an aspect neglected in the Spanish education system, traditionally more knowledge-oriented, until the 1990 law (LOGSE, Law for the Regulation of the Spanish Educational System). A cross-curricular approach, then, brings to the foreground the moral and social function of education, is an excellent tool in values education and citizenship education and links the school curriculum with Human Rights (Tuvilla Rayo, 2000). They are indeed an instrument for preparing individuals for the new world of globalisation and internationalisation.

The cross-curricular themes contemplated in the 1990 law (LOGSE) are moral and civic education, education for peace, education for health, education for the equality of opportunities between sexes, environmental education, sex education, consumer education and traffic education. To this central core of themes, the different regions with education powers are able to specify further cross-curricular topics relevant for their context; for example, in Andalusia, a theme on Andalusian culture was added to this list.

Civic and moral education has been deemed to be the central cross-curricular theme, a theme around which the remaining cross-curricular topics are organised. Naval *et al*. (2003: 2) agree on civic education as a fundamental aspect for education for citizenship, even though they are not identical:

> Civic education is an essential dimension of the education imparted in schools by which young people become informed and active citizens within their society. In the context of schools, students acquire the knowledge, skills, values and dispositions to become citizens [. . .] Hopefully this means education for democratic citizenship, but not necessarily so.

Civic and moral education aims at creating individuals that become active participants in the society according to democratic values such as justice, solidarity, freedom, and so on (MEC, 1993). The goal of civic and moral education is to educate students for both critical reflection and action: the capacity to be autonomous in the formation of their own values and norms, built on a rational basis, which guide them to act and behave consistently. This, which is a good starting point, does not seem to be enough for the cosmopolitan layer of identity. Intercultural citizenship that is active – people doing things together across linguistic and cultural boundaries – presupposes some kind of intercultural communicative competence. Otherwise, there is an evident risk of maintaining it uniquely as education 'about' international citizenship.

The presence of a cross-curricular approach implies that, in order to satisfy the changing needs of Spanish society, the curriculum, as it was understood in the past, has to be revised and reconstructed, as the cognitive needs to be replaced by a holistic approach. Naval *et al*. (2003: 4) mention one of the most interesting by-products of the cross-curricular approach: the responsibility of the whole teaching community in the creation of the planning documents. Due to the balance between central and federally organised education laws, the issues concerning cross-curricular themes have only been sketched out by the Spanish Ministry of Education, conferring on the regional governments and each school the responsibility for developing and implementing them. Documents were produced to help teachers create their programmes and incorporate cross-curricular themes (MEC, 1993). The adaptation of these regulations to the context of a specific school takes place in the educational plan of the school (Proyecto Educativo de Centro), which requires the coordination of the teaching staff, among others, in the specification of the aims for each level (Naval *et al*., 2003: 5–6). This aspect has the potential for collaboration between teachers of the disciplines that deal with citizenship education, such as history and geography, with language teachers. Indeed, the intercultural side of citizenship may be reinforced by language teachers, the mediators between students' language and culture and other languages, cultures and ways of structuring and categorising reality.

Even though civic education has been part of the LOGSE (1990), its implementation has not always been successful. The flexibility of the Spanish education system and the vagueness of its proposal, with no clear goals and themes stated, have placed the responsibility of the cross-curricular approach on the teachers and the schools. As a result, scholars and teachers in present-day Spain question whether the integration of cross-curricular themes has really taken place.

If the three-dimensional model of education 'about', 'through' or 'for' citizenship is taken as a basis, Naval *et al*. (2003: 3) consider that the cross-curricular nature of citizenship education in Spain favours education 'for' citizenship. However, Kerr (1999c: 12) argues that citizenship education in Spain, in contrast with the countries in Northern Europe, the USA and New Zealand, has not yet achieved the status of education 'for' citizenship and would be somehow in between education 'about' and education 'for' citizenship. The following pages will allow us to endorse either one or the other statement.

The Formal Curriculum in Secondary Education: 'Ethics' and 'Geography and History' in the Curriculum and in Textbooks

The formulations of the LOCE (2002) have recently been specified in the two curricula for the corresponding two cycles of secondary education: the *REAL DECRETO 116/2004, de 23 de enero, por el que se desarrolla la ordenación y se establece el currículo de la Educación Secundaria Obligatoria*, for the compulsory stage of secondary education (ages 12–16) and the *REAL DECRETO 117/2004, de 23 de enero, por el que se desarrolla la ordenación y se establece el currículo de Bachillerato*, for the postcompulsory period of secondary education, *Bachillerato* (ages 17–18). The curriculum for primary education has not been issued yet. These laws detail the goals of the education cycle in question and the goals, contents and assessment criteria of each of the courses comprised in every academic year.

As an illustration of the status of citizenship education in Spain, attention will be paid to the compulsory stage of secondary education (ages 12–16). Two of the capacities that the learner has to develop during this period are within the realm of citizenship education and education for democracy:

> (a) Assume with responsibility his/her duties and exercise his/her rights in the respect for the others, practise tolerance and solidarity among people and exercise dialogue consolidating the values that are common in a participative and democratic society. [. . .]
> (j) Know the basic aspect of the culture and the history, and respect the artistic and cultural patrimony; know the diversity of the cultures and societies, with the aim of valuing them critically, and develop attitudes of respect for the own culture and for the culture of the others. (*Real Decreto* 116/2004: 5713)

A priori, the capacities of this education stage as presented by the Ministry of Education, Culture and Sport are broad and emphasise democratic values and participation. The Ministry is also similarly general in the scope of the culture to be studied, the only example of specificity being reference to the 'learner's own culture and the culture of the others'. The Ministry seems to be purposefully vague in this respect: is the learners' own culture their local culture, the regional, the national, the supranational? Does the culture of the others include other social groups within the learners' society or is it related to other national or foreign communities? The questions can only be answered by contemplating the curricula of the different disciplines, even though the preceding words reveal that a certain amount of education for intercultural citizenship is an implicit goal in secondary education, as the development of attitudes of tolerance and respect for others implies becoming aware of the existence of different groups and cultures through processes of comparison and juxtaposition.

On the basis of the *Real Decreto*, the disciplines to be studied in compulsory secondary education are: Biology and Geology, Natural Sciences, Classical Culture, Physical Education, Plastic Education, Ethics, Physics and Chemistry, Geography and History, Latin, Spanish Language and Literature, Foreign Language, Mathematics, Music, Technology, Society, Culture and Religion (*Real Decreto* 116/2004: 5713). Citizenship education is mainly developed in Geography and History, but a close analysis of the curriculum of the course on 'Ethics' reveals that values education and citizenship education are placed at the heart of the discipline.

Geography and History

Geography and History are present in the four academic years of compulsory secondary education in Spain. In their synchronic and diachronic perspective, Geography and History aim at offering a global view of the world and a system of values necessary to help the learner adopt an ethical and committed attitude (*Real Decreto* 116/2004: 5738). Values education, a characteristic of intercultural citizenship education, constitutes an explicit goal of this discipline.

Citizenship education is carried out in its different layers: global, European, Spanish and regional, with a specific interest in commonalities shared by the different peoples of Spain and the diversity of Spanish regions (*Real Decreto* 116/2004: 5738). In the supranational sphere, special attention is paid to Europe and Latin America and their different nationalities for obvious historical and/or contextual reasons.

The goals that support the four-yearly courses underscore the importance of developing a multiple citizenship (regional, national and international) from a chiefly cognitive approach. Relevant aims in this respect are: familiarising the learner with the geographic features of the Spanish territory (Goal 3), knowing the geographic diversity of the world, with particular attention to Spain and the diversity of its geography and culture (Goal 6), analysing world history and Spanish history (Goal 9), valuing and respecting natural, historical, linguistic cultural and artistic patrimony (Goal 10) and promoting the values of tolerance and solidarity through the knowledge of historical events and cultural, geographical and natural diversity (Goal 11) (*Real Decreto* 116/ 2004: 5739–5740).

In the *Real Decreto*, the contents of the first-year focus on world geography and prehistory clearly have a general view. The Western orientation takes place in the units on Greek and Roman civilisations (Units 8 and 9 respectively), with a focus on Roman Spain in Unit 10. The assessment criteria for this course are all, without exception, focused on knowledge about Geography and History. Similar contents are developed in textbooks. It is worth highlighting that the textbook by Matesanz *et al.* (2000: 106–119) incorporates, in addition, a unit (Unit 8) on the 'physical space of Andalusia', and that the textbook by Sánchez *et al.* (2002: 122–136) includes a similar unit (Unit 8), both of them with tasks 'about' citizenship. As indicated in the foregoing sections, the same curriculum applies to all regions in Spain, even though the specification of further contents specific to the region in question is a matter for the federal government.

In the second year, the European and Spanish orientation of citizenship education is evident. The contents of this course are distributed in nine units, four in the group of 'human societies' and five within the 'Middle Ages' (*Real Decreto* 116/2004: 5741):

(1) World population
(2) The economic activity of societies: with subtopics such as European and Spanish economy
(3) The organisation of societies: with subtopics such as main characteristics of European and Spanish societies
(4) The political organisation of societies: the state, democratic states, the map of the EU, the map of the world, the organisation of the United Nations
(5) The breaking-off of unity on the Mediterranean
(6) Feudal Europe
(7) Europe from the 11th to the 15th century
(8) The Iberian Peninsula in the Middle Ages: Al Andalus
(9) The Iberian Peninsula in the Middle Ages: the Christian kingdoms

The assessment criteria, also expressed in terms of education 'about' citizenship, make explicit reference to learners' geographical and historical knowledge about Europe and Spain (Criteria 3 and 4) (*Real Decreto* 116/2004: 5741). All the contents expressed above are present in textbooks. Again, in the textbooks marketed in Andalusia, such as the one designed by García and Pallol (2002), a new unit has been added, 'Andalusia in the Middle Ages' (Unit 16, pp. 240–253). However, a new way of approaching citizenship education is perceived in the activities proposed in, for instance, the unit on the political organisation of societies, in which students are asked to visit the web page of the United Nations and analyse the information it displays (García & Pallol, 2002: 94); in spite of the citizenship education 'about' approach, the use of techniques of discovery and interpretation, a highly relevant skill for the development of intercultural competence in Byram *et al.*'s model (2002), is a positive aspect in itself. In the same textbook by García and Pallol, all-important considerations concerning social conflict and change (p. 59), the inclusion of anthropological texts students have to learn how to interpret (p. 62), the presence of Spain in international organisations (p. 91) and the inclusion of the *Charter of Fundamental Rights of the European Union* (p. 103) reveal an obvious orientation towards education for intercultural citizenship.

The third year of Geography and History, even though more extensively contemplating Spanish sociopolitical aspects (Units 3–7), also reflects the supranational and European context (Units 6–7).

(1) Geographic spaces and economic activities
(2) The city as a geographic space
(3) The Spanish territory: physical and human resources
(4) The Spanish territory: population and economic activities
(5) The territorial organisation of the State and the articulation of the Spanish territory. The geographic diversity of Spain
(6) The European territory. The European Union
(7) The world; with particular attention to Europe, Ibero-America and the Magreb (*Real Decreto* 116/2004: 5742)

The national and European orientation is likewise found in the assessment criteria, again formulated in the cognitive dimension (*Real Decreto* 116/2004: 5742).

Finally, in the fourth year, devoted to the modern and contemporary ages, the European dimension appears in Units 1–6 (from the Renaissance to the Industrial Revolution), in Units 8 and 9 (the period of imperialism and the interwar period respectively) and, finally, in Units 11–13, the contemporary world (the Second World War, the Western world, the communist world). The Spanish orientation is present in Units 7, Spain in the 19th century; 10, Spain in the first third of the 20th century; 14, the Spain of the Franco's regime; and 15, democratic Spain.

To conclude, the issue of citizenship in Geography and History in Spain clearly favours an education 'about' citizenship. There is a clear balance among the different orientations: global, European, Spanish and regional (this one at the hands of the federal government) in the issues studied. However, the term 'global' or 'cosmopolitan' citizenship needs to be examined; global issues are certainly present, but there is an evident European and Western orientation in their treatment, which implies that a person from a non-European nation would possibly feel left out.

By contemplating, initially, the different layers, the hypothesis that Spanish people are nowadays very much aware of their multiple identities seems to be confirmed; the promotion of such elements on the part of the education laws and textbook designers has a bearing on the matter. Western values and a Western orientation prevail in the laws and in the pedagogic material. The European dimension becomes an integral part of the Geography and History courses, an aspect that was not so explicit in the past. The issues of globalisation and regional identity are likewise prominent. No exclusive promotion of the national identity is then fostered; raising awareness of multiple identities is, undoubtedly, in line with education for intercultural citizenship.

Ethics

Ethics is a one-year course in the fourth and final academic year of compulsory secondary education. It is a course all the students in this academic year have to take, irrespective of whether their orientation is scientific, humanistic or technological (the three paths presented by the Spanish Ministry of Education). Its presence in the official Curriculum is justified by a values education that is acknowledged as essential in the global education of young Spaniards. In a world in which science and economy constitute two of the main pillars of modern societies, the incorporation of a course on human values seems an outstanding achievement of the current curriculum.

It explicitly favours values education with the view of developing a 'moral and civic consciousness according to democratic, plural, complex and changing societies in which we live' (*Real Decreto* 116/2004: 5732). That is to say, it contributes to the development of rational, critical and tolerant citizens. The international orientation becomes obvious in some of the 10 goals of the course: human moral values, both in their individual and social dimensions, have to be based on the Declaration of Human Rights (Goal 2), cultural and moral pluralism has to be promoted, with special emphasis on Europe (Goal 3), present-day ethical projects, mainly Human Rights, have to be identified and analysed (Goal 5), together with current political organisations based on the respect for Human Rights (Goal 6); the learner is additionally encouraged to use dialogue to solve problems (Goal 8) and participate in the activities organised at school (Goal 9) (*Real Decreto* 116/2004: 5732–5733). The international and participative orientation is thus apparent.

The contents of the course are presented in 16 units ascribed to four main blocks (*Real Decreto* 116/2004: 5733): (a) current moral problems, (b) democracy as an area of contemporary ethical projects, (c) rationality and the structure of moral life and (d) theories of ethics. The international dimension of citizenship education is to be found in the second block, democracy as an area of contemporary ethical projects, in which the ethical, legal and political meaning of democracy is explicitly reflected upon. Human Rights are understood as the source of democratic life and the framework in which *ethical projects* (activities or any other types of projects that are undertaken by a person with a structured system of values and who is consistent with it in their actions) have to be placed. The four units that deliberate on democracy are listed below:

> Unit 5. Human rights
> Unit 6. Democracy and citizenship. The value of dialogue and participation. Freedom and responsibility. Justice and tolerance in democratic societies
> Unit 7. Theories of democracy
> Unit 8. Environmental protection, solidarity, active participation, other ethical projects. Education for peace as a basis for social coexistence (*Real Decreto* 116/2004: 5733)

Highly illustrative in the approach to citizenship education in Spain is the section on assessment criteria (*Real Decreto* 116/2004: 5733–5734). The majority of the assessment criteria (1–7) indicate that the type of education promoted in the course is education 'about' citizenship: the learner is to know, express and identify human morality, moral world conflicts, Human Rights, etc. In spite of that, an orientation 'through' citizenship education is discovered in assessment criteria 8 and 9, which respectively indicate that the learner has to use dialogue and argumentation (8) and participate in a democratic and cooperative way in all the activities programmed in and outside the classroom (9). Consequently, an incipient tendency to foster education 'for' citizenship can be perceived in the Ethics curriculum, although education 'about' citizenship still prevails.

As an illustration of how the issue of citizenship is tackled in current textbooks, Domingo *et al*. (2003) provide a multidimensional approach in the different units. For example, international citizenship is the focus of an activity 'about citizenship' that discusses globalisation, its advantages and disadvantages (p. 79). Local issues concerning citizenship are debated in the unit that considers immigration; in this case, the tasks are within the realm of education 'through' citizenship because the learners are asked to carry out a case study of immigrants in their city by interviewing people living in their part of the city and other pupils at school, by visiting local organisations devoted to helping groups of immigrants and by locating the place where certain objects and utensils (such as a football, chocolate, coffee, a computer, and so on) have been made (p. 111). Questions of international citizenship, nonetheless, seem to be incorporated all over the book, as is made clear in the importance given to racism and ethnocentric consciousness (p. 77); a further instance of this approach is the reproduction of the Declaration of Human Rights (pp. 124–125), again viewed in terms of education 'about' citizenship. Therefore, the tentative encouragement of an education 'for' citizenship in this textbook is similar to prerogatives in the laws. Interestingly, the textbook in question seems to favour education for intercultural citizenship in the emphasis it places on the necessity of becoming conscious of working with others (for example, in the activity carried out with immigrants) both through processes of comparison/juxtaposition and intergroup communication and also in the conscious commitment to values (texts on racism and ethnocentrism).

The intercultural orientation is also present in the book by Navarro Sustaeta and Díaz Martínez (2002). For example, some units likewise contemplate the relativity of human values and discuss ethnocentrism and universal values (pp. 28–29); the reflection on why human beings attach values to things (p. 16, with an illustrative picture of a snake accompanied by the questions 'Do you think this picture is nice? Why? How have you acquired this attitude toward snakes?'); as well as why it is so difficult to understand values that are different from ours, turns out to be a key intercultural issue. One of the most illuminating texts, 'Los sonacirema' (p. 23), presents a photograph of an 'aboriginal' from this tribe, which have as one of their main features a daily corporal ritual, including the 'repulsive' oral ritual consisting of putting a brush made of dog hair in their mouths. In the activities students are invited to analyse this tribe and the origin of their rituals and to put themselves in their shoes and look at their own reality from the point of view of an outsider; indeed, 'Los sonacirema', if read from the right to the left, are 'The

Americans', a people they know but who have been presented from a completely different angle, a provocative view for the examination of customs and norms and their social nature. Further aspects brought to the foreground are the origins of conflict in general (p. 21) and international conflict (pp. 99–103); the Declaration of the Rights of the Citizens, the Declaration of Human Rights and the Contribution of the UNESCO also occupy a relevant position (pp. 117–121). In this material, then, intercultural citizenship education is a constituent component.

In a way, both books, although particularly the first one, contain activities and passages that undoubtedly favour intercultural reflection. Specific instances are texts on socialisation, on cultural relativity or on assumed values and behaviours. The combination of cognition, affection and skills present in the laws and textbooks become key issues in education for intercultural citizenship. The course on ethics turns out to be paramount in this sense. An interdisciplinary approach would be highly beneficial because, if combined with similar tasks and discussions in the foreign language class, it is sure to help young Spaniards achieve a certain degree of intercultural competence. One of the axioms of intercultural competence, the analysis and reflection about intercultural experience necessary for 'being intercultural', constitutes an element of the ethics course and could be further developed in the foreign-language course.

Conclusion: Is the Spanish School System Oriented Towards Intercultural Citizenship Education?

Kerr (1999c: 22) says that the main challenge of citizenship education is 'how to balance global citizenship issues with national developments and with the realities of life in modern society as experienced by young people'. From the foregoing considerations, one can deduce that in Spain, either as part of the formal or informal curriculum, in the form of the cross-cultural 'moral and civic education' theme or incorporated in courses such as 'Ethics' and 'Geography and History', citizenship education is beginning to be approached from a multilayered perspective and the different identities are balanced, respected and fostered. Both in the National Curriculum and in the textbooks, regional, national, European and global identities turn out to be conjugated and presented as complementary, that is to say, 'multiple citizenships' constitute a priority in Spanish education.

As argued above, the development of 'global', 'international' or 'cosmopolitan' citizenship poses the problem that it cannot be properly achieved without a prior intercultural communicative competence. Therefore, active citizenship, mainly at this supranational level, needs intercultural competence; otherwise it will only remain education 'about' citizenship.

This study reveals that, in some specific instances, such as learners' participation in school councils, in the preparation of certain celebrations or in the sporadic realisation of fieldwork (for example, with immigrants and local organisations dealing with immigration issues), education 'through' citizenship is becoming a reality in Spain. The average methodology and assessment criteria, however, point towards the prevalence of an education 'about' citizenship approach. As a result, this study corroborates Kerr's statement (1999c: 12) concerning the fact that citizenship education in Spain has not yet achieved the status of education 'for' citizenship. This implies that there seems to be an underlying potential for political activity, even though the participative citizens the law is trying to promote would need a more action-oriented than knowledge-oriented approach because being an informed, critical and analytical citizen is only the first step towards current participation, that is to say, activity should ideally follow reflection. In this respect, the concept of 'international civil societies' (see: Kaldor, 1999) in Western countries is particularly revealing. It refers to the institutions, associations and groups of people (such as trade unions or the international business organisation), in between the individual and the state, which allow for personal participation. At this level, there is a potential for international and intercultural communication and the relevance of being aware of what 'intercultural' means and implies turns out to be paramount.

The values and knowledge orientations of citizenship education in the curriculum are implicitly Western. The National Curriculum seems to favour the development of global international citizenship to a certain extent, although the development of truly intercultural citizens seems to be a more demanding process. The main problem is not the need for further curricular development, except for the cross-curricular approach (all the aspects of the law being immediately reproduced in textbooks), but teacher training and teacher collaboration: the collaboration of language teachers with others such as ethics and geography and history teachers. If we aspire to make citizenship education a highly educating discipline for international and intercultural understanding, the problem that is still to be solved is teacher training. In Spain, most teachers have not received specific training in citizenship education. Teacher training in primary education (Zamora Fortuny, 2003: 1) is of a general nature, so teachers may not be fully prepared to deal with cross-curricular themes, which, in addition, have not been formulated in detail by the Spanish Ministry. Prospective teachers of secondary education have received a much more specific training in history, geography or religion. Citizenship education at secondary school is sometimes undertaken by teachers of Geography and History, who may be additionally in charge of the course on Ethics. It is possible that none of them have been prepared to explore the intercultural side of the discipline. Intercultural training, although scarcely present in Spain, is, at best, incorporated in foreign-language teacher training. The implication for citizenship education is that teachers have not received the appropriate training to deal with aspects of interculturality. The possibility of both professional cooperation and specific teacher training should be contemplated and promoted.

A further possibility is the combination of the objectives of citizenship education with the objectives of foreign language teaching, at present explicitly formulated in terms of international and intercultural under-standing (*Real Decreto* 116/2004: 5751–5766). As seen above, in the Ethics textbooks there are samples that demonstrate that current textbook designers are aware of the communication problem and the necessity for cultural relativity and the overcoming of ethnocentric attitudes. This idea could be better developed by language teachers, the mediators between the learner's native language and culture and foreign languages and cultures. Again, it may just be a question of professional collaboration: bringing both the historian and the language teacher together would probably result in a more complete approach to citizenship education both at its supranational levels and in the understanding of different groups within the native community that are not part of the mainstream culture, whether immigrants or not. This is an incipient tendency perceived in ethics, geography and history, and language teaching textbooks in Spain. The diversity of cultures or groups within Spain, the explicit emphasis on the immigrant community as a necessary and enriching part of Spanish society and the heterogeneity of modern Western societies seem to be a priority.

Spain is definitely moving forward in the promotion of intercultural citizenship education. The challenges the government and Ministry of Education will have to face in the future are those of developing truly international and intercultural citizens.

Notes

1. Symposium on Intercultural Competence and Education for Citizenship, Durham, 24–26 March 2003.

2. The transfer of education competences took place in 1981 in the Basque Country and Catalonia, in 1982 in Galicia, in 1983 in Andalusia, the Canaries and Valencia, in 1990 in Navarra, in 1998 in the Balearic Islands, in 1999 in Aragón, Cantabria, Madrid, Murcia and La Rioja, and, finally, in 2000 in Asturias, Castilla-León, Castilla La Mancha and Extremadura.

3. The education laws promulgated from the 1970s are:

    *   Ley 14/1970, de 4 de agosto, General de Educación y Financiamiento de la Reforma Educativa – General Law for Education and Funding of Education Reform (MEC, 1970).
    *   Ley 8/1985, de 3 de julio, Reguladora del Derecho a la Educación (Law for the Right to Education) (MEC, 1985).
    *   Ley 1/1990, de 3 de octubre, de Ordenación General del Sistema Educativo (Law for the Regulation of the Spanish Educational System) (MEC, 1990).
    *   Ley Orgánica 10/2002, de 23 de diciembre, de Calidad de la Educación (Law for the Quality of Education) (MEC, 2002).

4. All the laws in this chapter are my translation from the original source.

Chapter 11

The Intercultural Dimension of Citizenship Education in Portugal

MANUELA GUILHERME, JOSÉ MANUEL PUREZA,
RITA PAULOS da SILVA and HÉLIA SANTOS

Introduction[1]

The challenge of intercultural education within the general framework of education for democratic citizenship has been met quite differently according to the specific trajectories of states and their position within the world system.

Portugal can be located at an intermediary level of development and has for centuries been playing a role of mediation between core and peripheral countries. This means that, despite all the structural similarities with other European Union countries, both its current identity and status and the historical path to them reveal its distance from the core of the system.

Against this background, the move from a colonial dictatorship to a European democracy must be read carefully. Having been traditionally a country of emigration, Portugal has acquired, since the 1980s, a new condition of being a country of immigration, namely from former African colonies and, more recently, from Eastern Europe. Intercultural dialogue has therefore been a crucial trait of Portuguese culture for many years, but it has been assumed explicitly as a public policy only when the integration of 'different' communities (the 'peripheral danger') has been felt as a security-oriented priority (the 'core syndrome'). Two other elements must be added to this picture of the Portuguese approach to the intercultural dimension of education for democratic citizenship. On the one hand, it should be underlined that the awakening of Portuguese society as a whole to the demands of modern citizenship (and its presence at the heart of the education system) has occurred together with the dramatic intensification of transnational relations. From this point of view, the competition between traditional local identities and new experiences of citizenship (such as those coming from transnational social networks or from individual identity focuses – sex orientation, gender, race, and so on) has influenced both the difficulties and the progress of the assumption of education for citizenship as a public policy. On the other hand, all these dynamics take place against a social reality of a general lack of welfare mechanisms, and this means that socio-economic asymmetries and value differences tend to be seen as intimately related, and this creates stereotypes that influence the concrete policies in this area.

Intercultural Citizenship in Portugal in Postrevolutionary Times

In prerevolutionary times (before 25 April 1974), during what is generally called the *Estado Novo*, which lasted for 48 years (1926–1974), all of them under the rule of Salazar except for the last five, the Portuguese school system was restrictive and elitist. Compulsory education during *Estado Novo* varied between three to four years, expanded to six years in 1963 and to eight years in its last Education Reform, in 1973, just before the so-called *Carnation Revolution* in the following spring. Besides being short in its mandatory years, education in general was also limited in scope, both in terms of demography and social class. Rural areas, lower-income and illiterate social classes had very restricted access to schooling, especially that beyond mandatory education. The school population in the public system therefore became increasingly homogeneous in terms of social class the higher up the education ladder one went, in addition to displaying racial and ethnic homogeneity throughout. In ideological terms, the school curriculum was also monolithic, based on single religious, political and ethnic perspectives, such as Catholicism, conservatism (just a step below other fascisms in Europe) and nationalism. Besides political repression and economic standstill, intellectual obscurantism was a prevalent tool supporting the regime.

Another aspect of social-class segregation in the Portuguese educational system was the implementation of vocational education, which started in the late 19th century in Lisbon and expanded in the 1950s and 1960s as a result of the Marshall Plan, from which Portugal partially benefited due to its neutral status during WWII, and, in consequence, the intervention of the OEEC (later the OECD), at the request of Ministers of Education under pressure of political demands for economic development (Teodoro, 2001). However, if, on the one hand, vocational education represented a possibility of climbing the professional ladder for working-class children, on the other hand, it kept them socially segregated. Vocational education was at the time mainly focussed on the preparation of a better skilled workforce.

The long years of dictatorship and, just after the revolution, some anarchy and the attempt of a communist takeover have made the Portuguese people value an education for critical and democratic citizenship and, therefore, reference to this has remained prominent in official documents ever since 1974, despite some flaws in putting such recommendations into practice. Moreover, the transitional times just after the 1974 revolution, although somewhat anarchic, enabled creative and participatory democratic practices that still inspire political ideals and educational policies in Portugal. Furthermore, despite 'the absence of a strong, organized civil society, of social movements and citizen organizations and associations; [...] a discrepancy between the formal definition of citizens' rights and the actual access of these rights', there have been some 'movements and forms of collective action that have given rise to a number of experiences of articulating different kinds of struggles' (Santos & Nunes, 2004: 11–12) that have inspired and stimulated noticeable examples of participatory democracy in education.

Shortly after the Revolution, Portugal regained its membership of UNESCO, which had been lost due to conflict over colonial wars in Africa, and UNESCO experts came to Portugal in order to help plan educational reform. However, their Report, issued in September 1975, went unnoticed due to political upheaval and constant change of leadership at the Ministry of Education. In the 1980s, preparation for joining the European Union and deep concern with economic recovery and transformation brought back the World Bank and consequently the support of OECD expertise in educational matters. From then on, matters of democratic citizenship have had to compete with matters of professional training in the reorganisation of the Portuguese educational system and national curricula up to today. The above-mentioned transnational organisations (the World Bank, the OECD and the European Union) have, in Teodoro's view (2001), all been more concerned with political regulation and policy-making than with social emancipation. In making this point, Teodoro refers to Santos' distinction between social regulation and social emancipation. According to Santos, a state, which is mainly concerned with social regulation, is self-centred in that it does not notice colonial (de)regulation, either outside or inside itself, and it is geared towards capitalistic progress and a civilising mission. On the other hand, a state more concerned with social emancipation is more focussed on the growing awareness of its citizenry and on their capability to have and make choices (Santos, 2004). The paradigm of modernity has been based on both pillars, that of social regulation and that of social emancipation, and its fulfilment would entail the harmonisation of both, but, 'such an overreaching aim carries in itself the seeds of frustration: unfulfilled promises and irredeemable deficits' as:

> each pillar consists of independent and functionally differentiated principles, each of which tends to develop a maximalist vocation, be it, on the side of regulation, the maximization of the state, the maximization of the market, or the maximization of the community; or on the side of emancipation, aestheticization, scientificization, or juridification of the social praxis. (Santos, 1995: 2)

During the transitional period, just after April 1974, Portuguese society, and the educational context in particular, experienced an even tug of war between both forces, but gradually political and economic developments have forced stronger demands for regulation upon recent democracy. Such heavy regulation has, nevertheless, been somewhat disregarded by the population, as such an overwhelming production of legislation has caused a gap between 'advanced legislation and conservative social practices' (Santos & Nunes, 2004: 11). Intercultural and citizenship education in Portugal show this gap in that advanced legislation has provided much room for individual and collective initiative, whereas school organisation and curricula are tightly regulated, although not frequently or rigorously evaluated. This has prevented most teachers and students from daring, and supported those who do not dare, to explore these concepts. Noteworthy practices do exist but they are often made invisible while conventional routines are unquestionably predominant. Moreover, citizenship education in the Portuguese state school system, as elsewhere, has vacillated between some of the options identified by Bottery, such as educate the youth for employability, prepare workers that will contribute to fit the national workforce into the global market, educate national citizens, construct a common bond between social members or 'motivate and engage all of its citizens in the grand societal project of not only creating a more equitable and harmonious society but a more equitable and harmonious world as well' (Bottery, 2003: 116).

While between 1975 and 1985 the Portuguese state school system was the object of several official studies and the subject of innumerable creative practices at the grassroots level, the Comprehensive Law of the Education System (issued in 1986), initiated a long succession of reforms, legal acts and new national syllabi that were implemented and reviewed in the following two decades. The above-mentioned law ensures the democratisation of the Portuguese education system by providing different statements, such as the right of 'access to education by all Portuguese children',[2] and tools, such as the democratic election of all members of school boards. Notwithstanding the democratic aims of this law, it was still very Eurocentric and nationality-based, as it placed European integration and national identity at its centre, despite acknowledging 'the increasing interdependence and solidarity amongst all peoples in the world'. The regulatory legislation and documents for basic and secondary education following, in the late 1980s, the above-mentioned law, introduced one subject (Social and Personal Development) and one curricular area ('School Area'). From a regulatory point of view, these were important steps, although they did not work in the practical field. The first was mandatory for all those that were not taking an optional subject, Moral and Religious Education (Catholic or other), depending on whether the school could provide for it or not. Teachers of this subject, on a voluntary basis, could come from any academic background as long as they attended a specific short training course. Such a framework ended up in the provision of this subject in only very few schools and it happened likewise for School Area for similar reasons as it was considered a (more informal) curricular area but subject to the possibility (and will) of the school and teachers to provide for it. Similarly, for both, there were some informal and very successful experiences in some schools but they gradually died out due to other curricular pressures. School Area was put forward as an interdisciplinary curricular area that was meant to last 95–110 hours altogether and aimed to develop annual projects by each class or by the school community in order to link the school to its surrounding community (Figueiredo & Silva, 2000).

School Area and extracurricular activities played a central role in this reform as far as government documents were concerned. The fact that, one year later (in 1990), one more piece of legislation was issued by the Ministry of Education to regulate extracurricular activities, proves how central this was considered to be in this reform. However, again, they were not mandatory and depended on the initiative of schools, teachers and students, who were, at the same time, more and more pressed by curricular and bureaucratic demands. 'Special Projects' has now replaced the School Area in a different format, as it is formally inserted in the curriculum, whilst keeping its interdisciplinary approach.

Before 1974, upper secondary students were obliged to take a two-year subject called 'The Nation's Political and Administrative Organisation' and 'Catholic Religion and Morals' which was a mandatory subject for all students above primary education and it was also integrated in the primary-education curriculum. Salazar's motto 'God, Motherland and Family' extended throughout school life. After 1974, the school ethos changed radically. The subject 'The Nation's Political and Administrative Organisation' was replaced by another subject, ideologically different, called 'Introduction to Politics'. Younger students, from the seventh to the ninth form would, instead, take a new subject called 'Civic and Polytechnic Education', an interdisciplinary topic that was meant to be very practical in nature and to link the school with its community and the world of work (Figueiredo & Silva, 2000). Both disappeared from the curriculum when the new reforms started being implemented in the late 1980s. Extracurricular activities, like the so-called 'Cultural School', were given great emphasis by documents, although seldom implemented, and this gave way later to the 'School Area' mentioned above. A twelfth form was introduced, also in 1974, to precede higher education, at university or polytechnic levels, called the Student Civic Service, which was totally practical and was to be carried out in the community. This formula was given up in the 1980s and gave way to a regular twelfth year that would be introduced as the third and last year of a block that preceded higher education and is expected to be highly demanding in academic terms.

The early 1990s can be considered as the main turning point for intercultural education in Portugal. Not only foreign language education syllabi, national in scope, started approaching identity and citizenship issues and introducing related topics but also important legislation (1991) was issued by the Ministry of Education, and ratified by Parliament, creating a Board for Multicultural Education (*Entreculturas* was already its logo then, only ratified in 2001). These developments resulted, on the one hand, from the recent integration into the European Union and, on the other hand, from the acknowledgement of the decolonisation process that brought Portuguese citizens that were racially different from Asia and Africa back to Portugal or were immigrants fleeing from war in their newly independent states. Furthermore, other immigrants from Eastern Europe and also from other countries in the European Union, especially Spain, settled in Portugal, through increasing economic exchange, as a result of Portugal joining the European Union. This new development aimed to contribute to a respect for difference in the educational context by supporting projects in schools where minority students could be found. The new development also stimulated academic research support

and the inclusion of multicultural-education-related issues in initial and in-service training provided by universities. Additionally, Portugal tried to include multicultural education in other programmes that were being implemented by other departments in the Ministry of Education. Although their influence was very intense and successful in some schools and with some teachers and projects, these initiatives were generally restricted to the Lisbon area, where most minority communities are to be found.

In the same year, 1991, another piece of legislation was issued, which regulated the school exchange and twinning programmes that were completely aimed at an integrated Europe. In 1993, the Council of Ministers issued a Resolution to support immigrants and ethnic minorities of Portuguese society in various fields, including education, employment, professional training and social security. As far as education is concerned, this Resolution gave rise to another piece of legislation to introduce the Intercultural Education Project. This was supposed to be developed nationwide and aimed to influence not only school life but also teacher-development programmes. This project started by focussing on 30 schools in socially disadvantaged urban and suburban areas for a period of two years (1993–1995), after which the second phase of the project was launched for another two years (1995–1997) with 52 schools; while the final goal was to expand it nationwide. Constant change of leadership at the Ministry of Education, new legislation and structural changes from 1997 onwards have made the continuation of education policies in Portugal difficult and therefore the Intercultural Project has also gradually waned. In 2001, another piece of legislation confirmed the creation of *Secretariado Entreculturas* and revoked the 1991 law. The Board of Multicultural Education (*Entreculturas*) has, in the meantime, moved out of the Ministry of Education into the High Commissioner for Immigration and Ethnic Minorities (ACIME), which reports directly to the Prime Minister's Office. They are now more broadly involved in the integration of the ethnic minorities and in the production of materials aimed at teachers and students.

In 1997, legislation regulating preschool education had explicitly recognised the school as a site of citizenship. It advocated respect towards different cultures and demanded that teachers appreciate their pupils' identity and culture, and suggested that they interact with their families with respect to their family environment and use differentiated pedagogies, when necessary, for the success of the children at school. In 2001, the Ministry of Education introduced a new reform for basic education whose main goal is explicitly stated as 'education for all' and where 'particular attention to situations of exclusion' is specifically recommended. New subjects were also introduced, including 'Civic Education', to prepare responsible, active and critical citizens. Citizenship is the first of five topics to be covered by its syllabus, which encompasses the study of individual rights and guarantees (personal, political, social, economic and cultural), the nation's political and administrative organisation (President of Republic, Parliament, Government, courts and so on), international institutions (European Union and United Nations), citizens' duties (caring about social exclusion, different sorts of discrimination, etc.) and, finally, school democratic management. Portuguese as a second language is also required for students with another 'mother tongue' besides a second foreign language. However, foreign languages to be taught are generally English, German or French, with the possibility of taking Spanish, although this seldom happens mostly because the schools do not provide for it. This is because they have teachers of French and German ready to teach students, though English is clearly dominant. Since 2005 the teaching of English has been compulsory in primary schools. In 2004, a bill for a new Comprehensive Law of Education was introduced to Parliament and passed but it was vetoed by the President of the Republic, because it had not had the support of the opposition parties. This proposal reiterated the centrality of European and national identities but went a step further to acknowledge 'the Other' – 'their character, ideas and life projects'.

The impact of the Education for Democratic Citizenship Project (EDC) developed under the auspices of the Council of Europe between 1997 and 2000 was also impressive in the Lisbon area. The Ministry of Education created a Steering Committee, representing several branches from the Ministry, and the Board of Multicultural Education (*Entreculturas*), to supervise this project. In the Introduction of their Final Report one can read that:

> The site of Portuguese citizenship is located in the Lisbon region and involves suburban regions such as Loures, Amadora, Almada, Seixal and Barreiro. This geographic area bears evidence of the striking historical changes that have taken place in Portuguese society: formerly a country marked by a strong flow of emigration, today Portugal is facing growing immigration, with waves of immigrants coming mainly from the former African colonies. (Ministério da Educação, 2001a: 126)

The flows of immigration have since then changed and include Brazilian immigrants as well as Eastern Europeans, especially Ukrainians. These immigrants are not only competing in numbers with those coming from former Portuguese African colonies but also settling as communities throughout the country. However, Eastern European immigrants do not always bring their children with them, while Africans, and Brazilians, to a certain extent, do, and therefore these are more visible in the school context.

The EDC Project incorporated the dynamics of change in schools during the 1990s and was valuable not only in raising questions about the curricular and noncurricular dimension of citizenship education but also in stimulating projects in schools with specific ethnic characteristics. Besides working with schools, the project also dealt with city councils and associations representing, in one way or another, minority populations. The Steering Committee's mission was to articulate all activities undertaken by the various participants and eventually to write a final report. This was, according to Mendes (one of the participants), a 'bottom-up' undertaking as the schools, teachers and students volunteered to participate and set up projects originating in their own contexts (Mendes, 2004).

The EDC Project fitted well into the general project of education for democratic citizenship in the school curricula in Portugal as this is a transverse transdisciplinary area that is considered as the basis for the rest of the curriculum. The teachers are free to analyse the syllabi and decide upon which contents and methodologies they should work at each time and with each class. The teachers can work with each other across different classes with the same subject (Subject Group) or across different subjects with the same class (Class Board) or they can work independently with one subject, one level and one class. This autonomy has generated enormous creativity and initiative in some schools and by some teachers but, on the other hand, it has also allowed a great deal of avoidance of critical issues. The School Boards and heads of department have played an important role in stimulating the development of Citizenship Education transdisciplinary projects (Ministério da Educação 2001b).

The Evolution of Concepts in Citizenship Education within the Portuguese Context

In order to understand the conceptual contents and the social and political meanings of Portuguese documents that deal with democracy, citizenship, multiculturalism and interculturalism, one must know the historical background that has provided the basis for such a mindset.

Not only does the historical construction of the nation-state affect the character, the conceptualisation and the practice of citizenship, as is evident both in Europe (Preuss *et al*., 2003) and worldwide, but also the nature of the multicultural state that each nation has been building is significant. They reflect the model of citizenship that is adopted both by the state and by its national citizens. In Kymlicka's (2003: 147–148) words:

> Different models of citizenship rest upon different images of the nature of the state, and/or on different images of the nature of the individuals who belong to it. One way to explore the idea of 'multicultural' or 'intercultural' citizenship, therefore, is to try to identify its underlying images of the state and of the individual. [...] Ideally, these two levels should work together in any conception of citizenship: there should be a 'fit' between our model of the multicultural state and our model of the intercultural citizen. The sort of multicultural reforms we seek at the level of the state should help nurture and reinforce the desired forms of intercultural skills and knowledge at the level of individual citizens. Conversely, the intercultural dispositions we encourage within individual citizens should help support and reinforce the institutions of a multicultural state.

Kymlicka's division between the 'multicultural state' and the 'intercultural citizen' is most helpful, as the concepts 'multicultural' and 'intercultural' are often used indiscriminately. However, neither the 'multicultural state' nor the 'intercultural citizen' are entities that are developing harmoniously, homogeneously or gradually in a linear process. They do not always coincide synchronically or diachronically, coherently or consistently. Portugal is one of the oldest, most homogeneous and isolated nation-states in Europe that has developed since the 13th century, but one that is rapidly developing into a multicultural nation-state. The Portuguese exemplify intercultural citizens in Europe, despite their peripheral geographical position in Europe and their strong isolationism from Europe in the first half of the 20th century. Its people have many multicultural origins (Celtic, Roman, Northern European, Jewish, Moorish, and so on), but also have a tradition of travelling to many continents and establishing settlements worldwide over the centuries.

Portugal is situated in the South-western corner of Europe facing Spain to the east and the Atlantic to the west. According to historians and poets, this Janus-like geographical position determined the paradoxical features that characterise Portuguese identity(ies). Portugal was one of the first European nations to have its borders stabilised, since its political independence from Spain was established early in the 13th century. However, its national identity is itself not easy to identify, except as a 'border identity', in that it has always shown a predisposition to engage with a range of different possibilities stimulated by the open ocean to its west (Santos, 1994: 134).

As a result of their journeys, the Portuguese were the first to develop the notion of a global world (Modelski, 1987). Because their country was small, far from the centre of Europe and closed in by Spain, its adventurous people crossed the Atlantic in search of the unknown, discovering rather than conquering. Their particular way of colonising, which Maxwell describes by saying that 'the Portuguese were not conquistadors, like the Spaniards who followed them, but manoeuvrers' (Maxwell, 1995: 8), meant that Portugal was the last European power to withdraw from its colonies. This was due, to some extent, to the fact that it had 'disguised the nature of her presence behind a skilful amalgam of historical mythmaking, claims of multiracialism, and good public relations' (Maxwell, 1995: 19). In addition, the Portuguese were often immigrants rather than colonisers in their own colonies (Santos, 2001).

Portugal has been a semi-peripheral country that is far from the centre in Europe and not even central to its own colonies, not only because of its geographical position but also because Portugal has also been colonised informally, both at home and overseas. Santos plays with the relationship between Prospero and Caliban, characters in Shakespeare's play *The Tempest*, by saying that Portugal represents both Prospero, the coloniser, and Caliban, the colonised (Santos, 2001). Portugal was (and still is) represented by her informal colonisers, from Northern Europe, especially England. In the same way she represented (still represents?) those that she colonised. In the USA, Portuguese immigrants have always been ethnically identified with African and Native Americans and, more recently, with Latin Americans. Their European origin is seldom recognised in ethnic terms, even in the Harvard *Encyclopaedia of American Ethnic Groups*. The Portuguese have themselves absorbed a self-image of a 'calibanised Prospero' (Santos, 2001: 62).

Santos defines Iberian colonialism and postcolonialism as different from those of Anglo origin (Santos, 2004). As Santos points out, Portugal's subordination to other powers did not mean a colonial deficit in relation to her colonies. On the contrary, it represented an excess as they were directly colonised by Portugal and indirectly by other powers, mainly Britain. Santos has focused many of his research projects on

Mozambique, where this was (still is) particularly evident.[3] Due to her ambivalent position as both Prospero and Caliban, Portugal's colonial and postcolonial discourse has always been in the interstices between dominance and hybridisation, distance and contact. In contrast, British colonialism was constant and linear, as recognised by Santos, as their discourse was often considered to be one-sided, from a perspective of superiority, dominance, mightiness and inaccessibility, as Edward Said expounded. Portuguese and English colonialisms and postcolonialisms were/are dissimilar.

As Santos points out, although political colonialism is over, social colonialism is not, the latter being evident both in Portuguese society and in the ex-colonies, and, in the case of Portugal, both in her relation to the South (superiority) and to the North (inferiority), that is, Portugal is, at the same time, 'the north of the south and the south of the north' (Santos, 2004: 31–32). Portuguese colonialism was characterised by miscegenation and 'kaffirisation' and was more focused on commerce than on settlement (Santos, 2001). These features influenced the nature of her postcolonialist era, which oscillates between her own superiority and her inferiority, while perceiving the Other as both familiar and strange: Portugal is both inside and outside herself for she welcomes African, Latin American and Asian immigrants to Europe, because she is an integral part of Europe, and, at the same time, she introduces them to Europe, because she feels they are part of her colonial history and the essence of being Portuguese.

These colonial relationships are particularly recognisable and multicultural/intercultural education cannot avoid this element of Portuguese society. According to Santos, this relation entails the difference between 'regulatory knowledge', which understands ignorance as chaos, knowledge as order, and 'emancipatory knowledge', which conceives ignorance as colonialism and knowledge as solidarity (Santos, 2004: 16, our translation). The predominance of 'regulatory knowledge' over 'emancipatory knowledge' persists in the Portuguese educational system. This is due to the implementation of advanced legislation, with an updated discourse in terms of multiculturalism/interculturalism, by policy makers, school managers and teachers. This discourse is reflected in the mindsets of students who may only have partial understanding of the issues. The validation of different knowledge has been lagging behind as far as the understanding and appreciation of difference are concerned. Understanding and assessing the contents of Others' 'Knowledges' according to our own patterns and criteria, instead of 'understand[ing] and appreciate[ing] the fact that they *have* deeply-held views that differ from ours' (Kymlicka, 2003: 164), has still been widely prevalent in the Portuguese educational system. As we move on to reveal and highlight some of the contents of documents in force, it is also important to remain aware that there is still a gap between the ideal and the reality as well as between exceptional practices and common practices (Leite, 2002).

The use of terms such as, and related to, democracy, citizenship, multicultural, intercultural, diversity, difference and integration are naturally abundant in the post-1974 documents that focus on education, citizenship education and multicultural/intercultural education while, also naturally, absent in previous documents ruling education in Portugal. Furthermore, the use of such terms has evolved according to the development of ideology in the Portuguese education system. Based on different types of discourse about education, Correia (1999) describes the post-1974 educational ideologies in Portugal by distinguishing four phases: (a) the critical and democratising phase; (b) the democratic phase; (c) the modernisation phase; and (d) the inclusion phase. The critical and democratising discourse, which erupted with the 25 April revolution, was highly politicised and focused on local education policies, but it was more concerned with democracy and freedom than with ethnic diversity, which was almost nonexistent at the time. This discourse was intense, new and engaging. It introduced radical changes in school life like the relevance given to extracurricular activities, democratic management of schools and ideological debate about school contents. The democratic phase coincides with the late 1970s and early 1980s when changes started to be legislated, democratic stability and participation were to be the rule, spontaneity and individualism to be coordinated, collective action to be organised and prioritised. The modernisation phase started with the preparation for Portugal to join the European Union and it was justified by economic pressures and high unemployment rates amongst young people. It was translated into the reintroduction of vocational education, which had been almost totally dismantled after 1974 with the abolition of the division between *liceus* (grammar schools) and technical schools, which had been transformed into the first type of more academic schools intending to prepare all students for university. It also entailed the introduction of science and technology into the regular curriculum, the enhancement of student autonomy and the linking of schools (through their curricula) to the world of work. The modernisation discourse did not imply a rupture with the previous discourses, the democratising or the democratic, in that it stood for equality of opportunities and individual fulfilment.

Finally, the inclusion phase, from the 1990s until today, has been dominated by a concern with the failures of the educational system, both drop-outs and those that remained for many years at the same level. There were several measures taken over the years, programmes undertaken, boards created and methodologies introduced, such as alternative and flexible curricula, project work, the Board for Multicultural Education, transversal, inter- and transdisciplinary areas introduced in the curriculum that tried to prevent students from failing, in particular those of different ethnic and/or racial backgrounds as the schools' populations were visibly changing, especially in the suburban areas of the capital. Teacher-development programmes were also increased and regulated at this time while teacher training centres located in schools grew. Citizenship and intercultural education was one of the priorities, besides technology and subject methodology (Portuguese, mathematics and science). For several theorists, Correia included, this attempt at inclusion has been more apparent than real, which is proved by results, as the assessment criteria have remained the same, the curricula have in reality expanded as they have overflowed the borders of the school, by including the media, politics and the work place. Furthermore, schools and teachers are blamed and made responsible for lack of success at all levels while the ethics of difference neglects social inequality (Correia, 1999).

The phases described above determine, in our view, the choice of terms and the ideals pervading official documents perceptibly and consecutively. 'National identity', for example, is a *leitmotif* in all documents (1989, 1990, 1991, 2001, 2002). In 1986, the above-mentioned Comprehensive Law refers to 'loyalty to the historical Portuguese matrix' and the 'awareness of the cultural heritage of the Portuguese people' (Article 3). With regard to the rights and duties of students in non-higher education, it is recommended that they:

> develop national values and a culture of citizenship, able to promote the values of a human person, of democracy, of responsibility, of individual freedom and of national identity. The student has the right and duty to know and respect actively the values and fundamental principles laid down in the Constitution of the Portuguese Republic, the Flag and the Anthem as national symbols, the Universal Declaration of Human Rights and the Convention of the Rights of the Child, as a matrix of values and statement of principles of humanity. (Law 30/2002, Chapter 3, Article 12)

As can be seen from this, national identity is framed by universal documents. It is also routinely anchored in the notion of European integration, for example, 'the preservation of the values of national identity in the context of European integration' (Dispatch 142/ME/90, Article 2, h). In these legislative documents on aspects of education, European 'identity' is seldom mentioned, as the word used is 'integration'. Moreover, European integration is here described as a demand for economic advancement, that is, an attempt to build up 'a new society that is able to face the challenges of modernisation resulting from the Portuguese integration in the European Community' (Law Decree 286/89), which reminds us of Habermas' question as to 'whether there can ever be such a thing as European citizenship' meaning 'the consciousness of an obligation toward the European common weal' (Habermas, 1994: 29). However, the recurrent allusion to national identity and European integration does not prevent mentioning a 'growing interdependence and necessary solidarity among all peoples of the World' (1986 Comprehensive Law, Article 3).

Multiculturalism is also a concept used in the above-mentioned legislation regulating the creation of the Board for Multicultural Education and in launching the Intercultural Education Project, which mainly deals with minority and immigrant/emigrant populations in Portugal (Gypsy, East Timorese, Cape Verdean) or abroad (in the case of Portuguese citizens). Multicultural is here used as a general term, as a 'floating signifier', in Bhabha's words, 'whose enigma lies less in itself than in the discursive uses of it to mark social processes where differentiation and condensation seem to happen almost synchronically' (Bhabha, 1998: 31). Most of the legislation mentioned above (1991, 1993, 1997), namely that dealing with the Board for Multicultural Education, the Intercultural Education Project, Measures to Support Immigrants and Ethnic Minorities by the Council of Ministers and Monitored Study, also uses the terms 'intercultural' and 'interculturality'. The first is used in connection with 'education', 'relationship' and 'dialogue'. 'Intercultural' is however also put to vague contextual use in the legislation: for example, 'problematic intercultural relations that have been arising in modern societies and *even* in European nations' (D 63/91, our emphasis), 'provide an intercultural relationship and favour consciousness of the European space and reinforce the values of democracy' (D 28/ME/91) and 'the Intercultural Education Project, with the following aim: [. . .] c) to favour the integration of youth coming from minority ethnic groups in schools and in the community, with the aim of promoting an effective equality of opportunities' (Res. Council of Ministers 38/93, 3). These quotations give us some hints about implicit meanings. Nevertheless, theoretical studies that have expanded recently and focused on the meaning of such words as multi- and intercultural, should help us complete our conceptualisation and understanding of these terms. Particularly on the term 'intercultural', we recommend the distinction between 'intercultural experience' and 'being intercultural' as described by Alred *et al*. (2003: 3– 4), the last stage involving some awareness of the intercultural experience proper.

The Intercultural Dimension in Curriculum Guidelines and National Syllabi

Both the legislation mentioned above and others provide the framework for the curriculum guidelines and national syllabi for both basic and secondary education. These attempt to specify the principles recommended by legal acts and to give more precise orientation to the teachers. The document that provides basic education with the 'Guiding Principles for Pedagogical Action' for the First Cycle (four years of primary education) includes explicitly amongst its aims 'a vision of thought that is gradually more flexible and unifying coming out of the diversity of cultures and points of view' as well as 'cultural exchange', 'the creation of habits of mutual help' and 'solidarity'. Although the latter do not entail cross-cultural interaction, the first aims establish such a scenario. With regard to the subjects Musical Expression and Education, and Plastic Arts and Education, still within primary education, it is recommended there should be contact with local and regional arts, but cultural diversity is not mentioned in this context. As far as the Study of the Environment is concerned, primary-school pupils are expected to value their identity and roots but also to develop respect for other people and cultures, to learn about minority cultures that possibly live in the neighbourhood, and reject any type of discrimination. In Portuguese lessons, primary students are supposed to engage in situations of dialogue, cooperation and confrontation of opinions, while in Moral and Religious Catholic Education they are invited to take personal positions *vis-à-vis* different religious faiths, and to commit to universal solidarity. In the meantime, Education for Citizenship is explicitly mentioned as a transversal area to all subjects and, therefore, the basis for all the curricular organisation.

Within the 'essential competences' defined for Portuguese throughout basic education over nine years is the following aim: 'to recognise a sense of belonging to a national and trans-national community of Portuguese speakers and respect the different linguistic varieties of Portuguese and the languages spoken by linguistic minorities in the national territory' although it is also stated, in the same document that 'mother tongue is an important national and cultural identity factor'. With regard to Foreign Languages it is expected that pupils construct a 'plurilingual and pluricultural competence' and be aware of 'linguistic and cultural diversity' as well as establish and recognise affinities and differences between the culture of origin and the foreigner culture, and adopt an attitude of 'openness and tolerance' towards foreign languages and cultures. As far as Portuguese History and Geography is concerned, students are to be stimulated to feel curiosity about diverse territories and landscapes and to acknowledge the 'unequal distribution of resources among the world population' and to express 'solidarity with those who suffer from such resource scarcity'. Geography and History then split into two different subjects at the higher levels of basic education but intercultural issues remain central to them. As far as Geography is concerned, students' interest in other countries and populations and cultural diversity are explicit goals of its syllabus. With regard to History, respect and appreciation for other cultures and religions are specially noted. Artistic Education includes, amongst its aims, that of 'understanding other cultures and traditions' and of 'facilitating communication between different cultures' as well as Drama Expression and Theatre. In Music the students are expected to study 'songs and music pieces in foreign languages' and, therefore, to learn about 'international artistic musical heritage'.

Although legislation focusing on preschool and basic education is more explicit on citizenship and multicultural education, secondary education syllabi give more detail on these issues. Foreign languages national syllabi (English, German, French and Spanish) are rich in recommendations geared to education for citizenship, respect for difference, to cultural diversity, to develop competencies of intercultural communication, to question stereotypes. French and Spanish syllabi currently in force are more explicit with regard to citizenship education and human rights education. In the Spanish national syllabus for the 10th form one can read that 'transversal themes (Education for Citizenship and social and cultural aspects of countries where Spanish is spoken) should be present in all units of the programme', while the French national syllabus for the 10th, 11th and 12th forms includes amongst its aims 'to educate for citizenship' and 'to interpret aspects of French-speaking cultures in an intercultural perspective'. The English national syllabus for the 10th and the 11th forms aims to 'develop attitudes of responsibility and social and personal intervention'. The History syllabus for secondary education aims at the 'reinforcement of the ethical dimension' while Classical Literature for the 12th form also aims to contribute to citizenship education by building 'a strong cultural identity that does not exclude'. The Design syllabus for the 10th form aims to help students 'overcome stereotypes and prejudices' while the Economy syllabus aims 'to promote attitudes of nondiscrimination that are favourable to the promotion of equal opportunities for all'. The latter aims explicitly to contribute to classes on 'the education of the citizen', and teaches pupils respect for Human Rights. The Geography syllabus, at the secondary level, mentions education for citizenship as a main goal and solidarity as an important value to be developed amongst students themselves and with others. In the History syllabus, one can read that students should eventually display some openness to the 'intercultural dimension' of present societies. Students are also expected to analyse international documents like the United Nations Charter and the Universal Declaration of Human Rights. In the secondary school Philosophy curriculum there is a wide range of concepts to be studied like, racism, xenophobia, volunteer work, truth, dignity and the construction of citizenship itself.

Conclusion

The multicultural and intercultural aspects of education have not been neglected in Portuguese legislation and they have also been the object of some specific laws by the Ministry of Education, especially throughout the 1990s. From our point of view, these concepts, although under-standably vague, have been carefully used and are theoretically sound. Legal documents, and other regulatory documents following them, reflect a sudden, long expected, democratic turn in Portuguese society as well its growing multicultural/intercultural although paradoxical nature. They also express the development of this young democracy and her facing up to new challenges, mainly her new alignment with Europe and with other Portuguese-speaking countries, most of which had been until very recently her colonies and at war with her. Although peaceful, the pressing maturation process of a young democracy in the European and global context required the some stages to be rapidly stepped over (Santos, 2004), and this not only caused some turbulence but also made it more difficult for policy-makers, educators and others to keep pace with all the required changes. A great emphasis on schools being sites of democracy and citizenship has been evident both in legal documents and in real school life whereas the intercultural dimension seems to lag behind, not as far as legislation is concerned, but in most schools; despite some impressive examples of good practice being scattered all over the country, they are mostly concentrated in the suburban areas of the capital where most minority and immigrant communities are settled and more visible. Foreign-language/culture national syllabi for higher levels of basic education and for secondary education, issued in the early 1990s and redesigned in the early 2000s, have revealed particular emphasis on identity and citizenship matters, and multicultural and intercultural education. It is noticeable that interculturality and citizenship have been gradually strengthened throughout the last two decades and, with great evidence, in basic education. Although the documents mentioned above only comprise a small sample of the whole legislation, they are, we believe, illustrative of the approach taken to the intercultural dimension of citizenship in the Portuguese education system.

Notes

1. This chapter is based on work carried out under the Sixth Framework, Priority 7 Project INTERACT – Intercultural Active Citizenship Education.
2. All translations of legal documents are our own.
3. Mozambique was enclosed by British colonies and is now a member of both the Commonwealth and the CPLP (Confederation of Portuguese-speaking countries).

Education for Intercultural Citizenship

There are two purposes for this statement of 'axioms and characteristics' of education for intercultural citizenship. They act first as an approach to planning of education for intercultural citizenship in whatever form deemed desirable, and second as criteria for evaluating the degree of intercultural citizenship education already present in existing education systems.

The axioms define what being intercultural entails and the characteristics are what might be expected in education in any form that helps people to think about their experience and to determine how they should respond to it.

Axioms

- Intercultural experience takes place when people from different social groups with different cultures (values, beliefs and behaviours) meet.
- 'Being intercultural' involves analysis and reflection about intercultural experience, and acting on that reflection.
- Intercultural citizenship experience takes place when people of different social groups and cultures engage in social and political activity.
- Intercultural democratic experience take place when people of different social groups and cultures engage in democratic social and political activity – not avoiding values and judgements.
- Intercultural citizenship education involves
    - causing/facilitating intercultural citizenship experience, and analysis and reflection on it (and on the possibility of further social and/or political activity, where 'political' is taken in broad sense to mean activity which involves working with others to achieve an agreed end);
    - creating learning/change in the individual: cognitive, attitudinal, behavioural change; change in self-perception/spirituality; change in relationships with Others i.e. people of different social

groups; change which is based in the particular but is related to the universal.

Characteristics of Education for Intercultural Citizenship

- A comparative (juxtaposition) orientation in activities of teaching and learning, e.g. juxtaposition of political processes (in the classroom, school ... country ...) and a critical perspective which questions assumptions through the process of juxtaposition.
- Emphasis on becoming conscious of working with Others (of a different group and culture) through (a) processes of comparison/juxtaposition and (b) communication in a language (L1 or L2/3/...) which influences perceptions and which emphasises the importance of learners becoming conscious of multiple identities.
- Creating a community of action and communication which is supranational and/or composed of people of different beliefs values and behaviours which are potentially in conflict – without expecting conformity and easy, harmonious solutions.
- Having a focus and range of action which is different from that which is available when not working with Others, where 'Others' refers to all those of whatever social group who are initially perceived as different, members of an out-group.
- Emphasising becoming aware of one's existing identities and opening options for social identities additional to the national and regional etc. (e.g. the formation of perhaps temporary supranational group identities through interaction with Others).
- Paying equal attention to cognition/knowledge, affect/attitude, behaviours/skill.
- All of the above with a conscious commitment to values (i.e. rejecting relativism), being aware that values sometimes conflict and are differently interpreted, but being committed, as citizens in a community, to cooperation.

References

Adler, P.S. (1975) The transitional experience: An alternative view of culture shock. *Journal of Humanistic Psychology* 15 (4), 13–23.

Alred, G., Byram, M. and Fleming, M. (eds) (2003) *Intercultural Experience and Education.* Clevedon: Multilingual Matters.

Anderson, B. (1991) *Imagined Communities* (2nd edn). London: Verso.

Arthur, J. and Wright, D. (2003) *Teaching Citizenship in the Secondary School.* London: David Fulton.

Arthur, J., Davison, J. and Stow, W. (2000) *Social Literacy. Citizenship Education and the National Curriculum.* London: Routledge.

Audigier, F. (1998) *Basic Concepts and Core Competences of Education for Democratic Citizenship.* Strasbourg: Council of Europe.

Bandura, A. (1977) *Social Learning Theory.* Englewood Cliffs: Prentice-Hall.

Bandura, A. and Walters, R. (1963) *Social Learning and Personality Development.* London: Holt, Rinehart and Winston.

Banks, J.A. and Lynch, J. (eds) (1986) *Multicultural Education in Western Societies.* London: Holt, Rinehart and Winston.

Barber, B.R. (1998) *A Passion for Democracy. American Essays.* Princeton: Princeton University Press.

Barber, B.R. and Battistoni, R.M. (1999) *Education for Democracy. A Sourcebook for Students and Teachers.* Dubuque: Kendal.

Barnard, C. (2003) *Language, Ideology, and Japanese History Textbooks.* London: RoutledgeCurzon.

Barth, F. (1969) *Ethnic Groups and Boundaries: Social Organization of Culture Differences.* London: Allen & Unwin.

Bauer, R. (1984) The Hong Kong Cantonese speech community. *Language Learning and Communication* 3 (3), 289–315.

Beacco, J.C. and Byram, M. (2003) *Guide for the Development of Language Education Policies in Europe: From Linguistic Diversity to Plurilingual Education.* Council of Europe, Strasbourg: Language Policy Division.

Beck, U. (2002) The cosmopolitan society and its enemies. *Theory, Culture & Society* 19 (1–2), 17–44.

Befu, H. (2001) *The Hegemony of Homogeneity.* Melbourne: Trans Pacific Press.

Ben-Rafael, E. (1994) *Language, Identity, and Social Division: The Case of Israel.* Oxford: Clarendon Press.

Berger, P. and Luckmann, T. (1966) *The Social Construction of Reality.* Penguin: Harmondsworth.

Berlin, I. (1990) *The Cracked Timber of Humanity.* Princeton, NJ: Princeton University Press.

Beutel, W. and Fauser, P. (eds) (2001) *Erfahrene Demokratie. Wie Politik praktisch gelernt werden kann.* Opladen: Leske & Budrich.

Bhabha, H. (1998) Culture's in between. In D. Bennett (ed.) *Multicultural States: Rethinking Difference and Identity* (pp. 29–36). London: Routledge.
Billig, M. (1995) *Banal Nationalism.* London: Sage.
Black, G. and Munro, R. (1993) *Black Hands of Beijing: Lives of Defiance in China's Democratic Movement.* New York: John Wiley.
Blunkett, D. (2001) *Politic and Progress: Renewing Democracy and Civil Society.* London: Politico's Publishing.
Bolton, K. (2002) Hong Kong English: Autonomy and creativity. In K. Bolton (ed.) *Hong Kong English: Autonomy and Creativity* (pp. 1–25). Hong Kong: Hong Kong University Press.
Bottery, M. (2003) The end of citizenship? The nation-state, threats to its legitimacy, and citizenship, and citizenship education in the twenty-first century. *Cambridge Educational Journal* 33 (1), 101–122.
Bourdieu, P. (1977) The economics of linguistic exchanges. *Social Science Information* 16 (6), 645–668.
Bredella, L. (2001) *Literarisches und interkulturelles Verstehen.* Tübingen: Gunter Narr Verlag.
Bredella, L. (2003) Afterword: What does it mean to be intercultural. In G. Alred, M. Byram and M. Fleming (eds) *Intercultural Experience and Education* (pp. 225–239). Clevedon: Multilingual Matters.
Breidbach, S. (2003) *Plurilingualism, Democratic Citizenship in Europe and the Role of English.* Strasbourg: Council of Europe.
Breit, G. and Schiele, S. (eds) (2002) *Demokratie-Lernen als Aufgabe der politischen Bildung.* Schwalbach/Ts.: Wochenschau.
Brewer, M.B. (1999) Multiple identities and identity transition: implications for Hong Kong. *International Journal of Intercultural Relations* 23 (2), 187–197.
Bruno-Jofré, R. and Jover, R. (2000) Building common spaces: Citizenship and education in Canada and Spain. *Encounters on Education* 1, 1–8.
Byram, M. (1989) *Cultural Studies in Foreign Language Education.* Clevedon: Multilingual Matters.
Byram, M. (1990) Intercultural education and foreign language teaching. *World Studies Journal* 1 (7), 4–7.
Byram, M. (1997) *Teaching and Assessing Intercultural Communicative Competence.* Clevedon: Multilingual Matters.
Byram, M. (2002) Foreign language education as political and moral education: An essay. *Language Learning Journal* 26, 43–47.
Byram, M. (2003) On being 'bicultural' and 'intercultural'. In G. Alred, M. Byram and M. Fleming (eds) *Intercultural Experience and Education.* Clevedon: Multilingual Matters.
Byram, M., Gribkova, B. and Starkey, H. (2002) *Developing the Intercultural Dimension in Language Teaching. A Practical Introduction for Teachers.* Strasbourg: Council of Europe.
Byram, M., Nichols, A. and Stevens, D. (2001) *Developing Intercultural Competence in Practice.* Clevedon: Multilingual Matters.
Cansdale, J.S. (1969) Cultural problems of Chinese students in a Western-type university. In I.C. Jarvie (ed.) *Hong Kong: A Society in Transition; Contributions to the Study of Hong Kong Society* (pp. 345–360). London: Routledge & Kegan Paul.

Census and Statistics Department, Hong Kong (China) (2002) *Population Census 2001: Main Report* (Vol.I). Hong Kong: Census and Statistics Department.

Center for Civic Education, (CCE) (1991) *CIVITAS. A Framework for Civic Education.* Calabasas: Center of Civic Education.

Center for Civic Education (CCE) (1994/2003) *National Standards for Civics and Government.* Calabasas: Center of Civic Education.

Center for Information and Research on Civic Learning and Engagement (CIRCLE) (2003) *Civic Mission of Schools.* New York: CIRCLE.

Center of Civic Education (CCE) [by John J. Patrick] (2003a) *Teaching Democracy Globally, Internationally, and Comparatively: The 21st-Century Civic Mission of Schools.* Calabasas: Center of Civic Education.

Center of Civic Education (CCE) (2003b) *Res Publica. An International Framework for Education in Democracy.* Calabasas: Center of Civic Education.

Chan, B.H.S. (2003) How does Cantonese–English code-mixing work. In M.C. Pennington (ed.) *Language in Hong Kong at Century's End* (pp. 191–216). Hong Kong: Hong Kong University Press.

Chen, D.M. (2003) Duoyuan wenhua beijingxia de xuexiao gongmin daode jiaoyu tanxi [An analysis of civic moral education in schools in the milieu of multiculturalism]. *Zhaoqing Xueyuan Xuebao [Journal of Zhaoqing College]* 24 (6), 89–92.

Chew, J. (1998) Civics and moral education in Singapore: Lessons for citizenship education? *Journal of Moral Education* 27 (4), 505–524.

Choi, P.K. (1990) A search for cultural identity: The students' movement of the early seventies. In A. Sweeting (ed.) *Difference and Identities: Educational Argument in Late Twentieth Century Hong Kong* (pp. 81–107). Hong Kong: Faculty of Education, University of Hong Kong.

Chow, A.W.K. and Mok-Cheung, A.H. (2004) English language teaching in Hong Kong SAR: Tradition, transition, and transformation. In W.K. Ho and R.Y.L. Wong (eds) *English Language Teaching in East Asia Today: Changing Policies and Practices* (pp. 150–177). Singapore: Eastern Universities Press.

Chu, Y.C. (2003) *Hong Kong Cinema: Coloniser, Motherland and Self.* London; New York: Curzon.

Committee on the Promotion of Civic Education (CPCE) (2005) *Biennial Opinion Survey on Civic Education (2004).* Hong Kong: The Committee.

Corbett, J. (2003) *An Intercultural Approach to English Language Teaching.* Clevedon: Multilingual Matters.

Correia, J.A. (1999) As ideologias educativas em Portugal nos últimos 25 anos. *Revista Portuguesa de Educação* 12 (1), 81–110.

Coulmas, F. (2002) Language policy in modern Japanese education. In J. Tollefson (ed.) *Language Policies in Education: Critical Issues.* Mahwah, NJ: Lawrence Erlbaum Associates.

Crick, B. (1998) *Education for citizenship and the teaching of democracy in schools.* Final report of the Advisory Group on Citizenship. Qualifications and Curriculum Authority. Imprint London: Qualifications and Curriculum Authority.

Crick, B. (2000a) *Essays on Citizenship.* London: Continuum.

Crick, B. (2000b) The citizenship order for schools. In N. Pearce and J. Hallgarten (eds) *Tomorrow's Citizens. Critical Debates in Citizenship and Education* (pp. 77–83). London: IPPR.

Dai, R. (2002) Bangyang Jiaoyu de Youxiaoxing yu Kexuexing [Effectiveness and scientificity of education by role models]. *Jiao Yu Yan Jiu* [*Educational Research*] 23 (8), 17–23.

Dewey, J. (1916/1985) *Democracy and Education*. Carbondale: Southern Illinois University Press.

Dewey, J. (1916/2000) *Demokratie und Erziehung*. In J. Oelkers (ed.). Weinheim: Belz.

Dewey, J. (1934) *Art as Experience*. New York: Perigee Books.

Dillon, P. and Halstead, J. (2003) Multicultural education. In N. Blake, P. Smeyers, R. Smith and P. Standish (eds) *The Blackwell Guide to Philosophy of Education*. Oxford: Blackwell.

Domingo, A., Domingo, T. and Feito, L. (2003) *Ética 4 Secundaria*. Madrid: Ediciones S.M.

Donati, P. (1997) El desafío del universalismo en una sociedad multicultural. *Revista Internacional de Sociología* 17, 7–39.

Dönhoff, M. (2001) The freedom shock Eastern Europe. Between hope and concern. In J. Purchla (ed.) *From the World of Borders to the World of Horizons* (pp. 9–14). Cracow: International Cultural Centre.

Dowdle, M. (2002) Constructing citizenship: The NPC as catalyst for political participation. In M. Goldman and E.J. Perry (eds) *Changing Meanings of Citizenship in Modern China* (pp. 330–352). Cambridge, MA: Harvard University Press.

Doyé, P. (1992) Fremdsprachenunterricht als Beitrag zu tertiärer Sozialisation. In D. Buttjes, W. Butzkamm and F. Klippel (eds) *Neue Brennpunkte des Englischunterrichts*. Frankfurt a.M.: Peter Lang.

Doyé, P. (1999) *The Intercultural Dimension. Foreign Language Education in the Primary School*. Berlin: Cornelsen.

Duerr, K. (2000) *Education for Democratic Citizenship. Strategies for Learning Democratic Citizenship*. Strasbourg: Council of Europe.

Duerr, K. (2004) *The School: A Democratic Learning Community.* The All-European Study on Pupils Participation in School. Strasbourg: Council of Europe.

Dwyer, P. (2004) *Understanding Social Citizenship: Themes and Perspectives for Policy and Practice*. Bristol: The Policy Press.

Eagleton, T. (1983) *Literary Theory: An Introduction*. London: Basil Blackwell.

Eagleton, T. (2003) *After Theory*. London: Allen Lane.

Eaton, M. (2001) *Merit, Aesthetic and Ethical*. Oxford: Oxford University Press.

Edwards, J. (1995) *Multiculturalism*. London: Penguin Books.

Edwards, L., Munn, P. and Fogelman, K. (eds) (1992) *Education for Democratic Citizenship in Europe. New Challenges for Secondary Education*. Strasbourg: UNESCO.

Enslin, P. and White, P. (2003) Democratic citizenship. In N. Blake, P. Smeyers, R. Smith and P. Standish (eds) *The Blackwell Guide to the Philosophy of Education*. London: Blackwell.

European Commission (1995) *Teaching and Learning: Towards the Learning Society*. Brussels: European Commission.

Evans, R.W. (1997) Teaching social studies: Implementing an issue-centered curriculum. In E.W. Ross (ed.) *The Social Studies Curriculum* (pp. 197–212). Albany: State University of New York Press.

Evans, R.W. (2004) *The Social Studies War. What Should We Teach the Children?* New York: Teachers College Press.

Everson, M.C. and Preu, U.K. (1995) *Concepts, Foundations, and Limits of European Citizenship.* ZERP-Diskussionspapier 2/95. Bremen: Zentrum für Europäische Rechtspolitik an der Universität Bremen.

Feng, J.J. (2001) *Dangdai, Zhuti Jiaoyu Lun [On Contemporary Subjective Education].* Nanjing: Jiangshu Jiaoyu Chubanshe.

Fields, B.A. and Feinberg, W. (2001) *Education and Democratic Theory. Finding a Place for Community. Participation in Public School Reform.* Albany: State University of New York Press.

Figueiredo, C. and Silva, A.S. (2000) *Education for Citizenship in the Portuguese Education System (1974–1999).* Lisboa: Council of Europe, Ministry of Education.

Flecha, R., Puigvert, L, Santos, A. and Soler, M. (2000) Spain. In J. Holford and P. Edirisingha (eds) *Citizenship and Governance Education in Europe: A Critical Review of the Literature.* Surrey: School of Educational Studies, University of Surrey.

Fleming, M. (2003) Intercultural experience and drama. In G. Alred, M. Byram and M. Fleming (eds) *Intercultural Experience and Education.* Clevedon: Multilingual Matters.

Fogel, J.A. and Zarrow, P.G. (eds) (1997) *Imagining the People: Chinese Intellectuals and the Concept of Citizenship, 1890–1920.* Armonk, NY: M.E. Sharpe.

Educación. On WWW at http://www.uv.es/~jbeltran/ase/textos/zamora.pdf. Accessed 2.04.

Frazer, E. (2000) Citizenship education: Antipolitical culture and political education in Britain. *Political Studies* 48, 88–103.

Freire, P. (1972) *Pedagogy of the Oppressed* (M. Bergman Ramos, trans.) London: Sheed and Ward.

Gagel, W. (1994) *Geschichte der politischen Bildung in der Bundesrepublik Deutschland 1945–1989.* Opladen: Leske & Budrich.

Gagel, W. (2000) *Einführung in die Didaktik des politischen Unterrichts* (2nd edn). Opladen: Leske and Budrich.

García, M.A. and Pallol, B. (2002) *Ciencias Sociales, Geografía e Historia. Proyecto Zenit Andalucía 2 Secundaria.* Madrid: Ediciones SM.

Gibbons, J. (1987) *Code-Mixing and Code Choice: A Hong Kong Case Study.* Clevedon: Multilingual Matters.

Gilreath, J. (ed.) (1999) *Thomas Jefferson and the Education of a Citizen.* Washington: Library of Congress.

Gingell, J. (2000) Plato's ghost: How not to justify the arts. *Westminster Studies in Education* 23, 71–79.

Giroux, H.A. (1983) *Theory and Resistance in Education: A Pedagogy for the Opposition.* London: Heinemann Educational Books.

Giroux, H.A. (1988) *Schooling for Democracy.* London: Routledge.

Gliński, P. (1999) O społeczeństwie obywatelskim w Polsce: Teoria i praktyka. In D. Gawin (ed.) *Homo Eligens. Społeczeństwo świadomego wyboru. Księga jubileuszowa ku czci Andrzeja Sicińskiego* (pp. 111–129). Warszawa: Wydawnictwo IfiS PAN Warszawa.

Goh, C.T. (1996) Prime Minister Goh Chok Tong's introduction to the need for National Education in his Teacher's Day Rally Speech, 8.9.96. On WWW at http://www.moe.gov.sg/ne/keyspeeches/sep08-96.htm. Accessed 9.2.05.

Goh, C.T. (1999) Prime Minister Goh Chok Tong's speech on 'Singapore 21' in parliament, 5.5.99, entitled 'The Singapore Tribe'. On WWW at http://www.moe.gov.sg/speeches/1999/sp120599a.htm. Accessed 9.2.05.

Goh, C.T. (2003) Speech by Prime Minister Goh Chok Tong at The Remaking Singapore Report Presentation and Appreciation lunch. On WWW at http://www.contactsingapore.org.sg/nm/versea_sg/speeches/listPressRelease.jsp. Accessed 9.2.05.

Goldman, M. (1994) *Sowing the Seeds of Democracy in China*. Cambridge, MA: Harvard University Press.

Goldman, M. and Perry, E.J. (eds) (2002) *Changing Meanings of Citizenship in Modern China*. Cambridge, MA: Harvard University Press.

Gongmin Daode Jianshe Shishi Gangyao [The Implementation Guidelines to Construct Civic Morals of Citizens]. *Renmin Ribao* [*People's Daily*] 24 October 2001.

Gongmin Daode Ketizu (2002) *Zhongguo Gongmin Daode Shouce* [*A Handbook of Morals for Chinese Citizens*]. Beijing: Hong Qi Chu Ban She.

Gopinathan, S. (1997) Singapore Educational Development in a strong developmentalist state: The Singapore experience. In W.K. Cummings and N.F. McGinn (eds) *International Handbook of Education and Development: Preparing Schools, Students and Nations for the Twenty-first Century* (pp. 587–605). Oxford, England: Elsevier Science.

Görlach, M. (2002) *Still More Englishes*. Amsterdam; Philadelphia, PA: John Benjamins.

Grad, J. and Kaczmarek, U. (1999) *Organizacja i upowszechnianie kultury w Polsce. Zmiany modelu*. Poznan: Wydawnictwo Naukowe UAM.

Great Britain: Department for Education and Skills (DfES) (1999) *Citizenship. The National Curriculum for England*. London: Qualifications and Curriculum Authority.

Great Britain: Department for Education and Skills (DfES) (2000a) *PSHE and Citizenship*. London: Department for Education and Skills.

Great Britain: Department for Education and Skills (DfES) (2000b) *Schemes of Work*. London: Qualifications and Curriculum Authority.

Great Britain: Qualifications and Curriculum Authority (QCA) (1998) *Education for citizenship and the teaching of democracy in schools*. Final Report of the Advisory Group on Citizenship. 22 September (aka Crick Report). London: Qualifications and Curriculum Authority.

Gribble, J. (1983) *Literary Education: A Revaluation*. Cambridge: Cambridge University Press.

Guilherme, M. (2002) *Critical Citizens for an Intercultural World: Foreign Language Education as Cultural Politics*. Clevedon: Multilingual Matters.

Guilherme, M. (2004) English as a global language and education for cosmopolitan citizenship. In A. Osler and H. Starkey (eds) *Citizenship and Language Learning*. Stoke-on-Trent: Trentham Books.

Gutmann, A. (1999) *Democratic Education*. Princeton: Princeton University Press.

Habermas, J. (1979) *Communication and the Evolution of Society* (T. McCarthy, trans.) Boston: Beacon Press.

Habermas, J. (1994) Citizenship and national identity. In B. van Steenbergen (ed.) *The Condition of Citizenship* (pp. 20–35). London: Sage.

He, R.F. (2001) Dangdai Zhongguo Gongmin Jiazhiguan Jiaoyu de Hexin: Peiyang Geti Guannian [The core of contemporary citizenship education in China: Developing individual consciousness]. *Changbei Xuekan* 4, 59–61.

Heater, D. (2004a) *A History of Education for Citizenship*. London: Routledge.

Heater, D. (2004b) *Citizenship: The Civic Ideal in World History, Politics and Education* (3rd edn). Manchester: Manchester University Press.

Hill, M. and Lian, K.F. (1995) *The Politics of Nation Building and Citizenship in Singapore*. London and New York: Routledge.

Himmelmann, G. (2003) Zukunft, Fachidentität und Standards der politischen Bildung. Unpublished ms. Technische Universität Braunschweig.

Himmelmann, G. (2004) *Demokratie-Lernen als Lebens-, Gesellschafts- und Herrschaftsform*. Schwalbach/Ts: Wochenschau.

Hobsbawm, E.J. (1992) *Nations and Nationalism since 1780: Programme, Myth, Reality* (1st edn). Cambridge: Cambridge University Press (1st edn, 1990).

Hoffman, J. (2004) *Citizenship beyond the State*. London: Sage.

Holford, J. and Edirisingha, P. (eds) (2000) *Citizenship and Governance Education in Europe: A Critical Review of the Literature*. Surrey: School of Educational Studies, University of Surrey.

Hong Kong English School Certificate Syndicate (1952–1965) *Hong Kong English School Certificate Examinations: Regulations and Syllabuses*. Hong Kong: Government Printer.

Hong Kong Examinations and Assessment Authority (2004) *HKCEE Statistics of Entries and Results over the Years*. On WWW at http://eant01.hkeaa.edu. hk/hkea/redirector.asp?p_direction = body&p_clickurl = exam%5Freports% 2Easp%3Fp%5Fexam%3DHKCEE. Accessed 11.5.06.

Hong Kong: Curriculum Development Council, Hong Kong (China) (1999) *Syllabuses for Secondary Schools: English Language (Secondary 1–5)*. Hong Kong: Education Department.

Hong Kong: Standing Committee on Language Education and Research (2003) *Action Plan to Raise Language Standards in Hong Kong: Final Report of Language Education Review*. Hong Kong: Standing Committee on Language Education and Research.

Hospers, J. (1982) *Introductory Readings in Aesthetics*. London: Macmillan.

Huang, Z.P. (2004) Xinshiqi Xuexiao Daode de Jiben Zouxiang [Basic trends of moral education in the new era]. *Jiaoyu Kexue Yanjiu [Education Science Research]* 4, 45–47.

Ichilov, O. (1998) Conclusion: The challenge of citizenship education in a changing world. In O. Ichilov (ed.) *Citizenship and Citizenship Education in a Changing World* (pp. 267–273). London and Portland, Oregon: The Woburn Press.

Jackson, J. (2002) Cultural identity and language choice: English majors in Hong Kong. In C. Lee and W. Littlewood (eds) *Culture, Communication and Language Pedagogy* (pp. 37–50). Hong Kong: Language Centre, Hong Kong Baptist University.

Jiang Zeming (2002) *Jiang Zeming Lun You Zhongguo Tese Shihuizhuyi – Zhuanti Zaibian [Jiang Zeming on Chinese Characteristics of Socialism – Selected Topics]*. Beijing: Zhongyang Wenxian Chubanshe [Central Documents Press].

Jin, S.H. (2000) Jiaoyu de Douyuan Jiazhi Quxiang yu Gongmin de Peiyang [Multidimensions of educational approaches and development of citizens]. *Jiaoyu Lilun yu Shijian [Education Theory and Application]* 8, 2–8.

Johnson, R.K. (2003) Language and education in Hong Kong. In M.C. Pennington (ed.) *Language in Hong Kong at Century's End* (pp. 265–276). Hong Kong: Hong Kong University Press.

Joseph, J.E. (1997) English in Hong Kong: Emergence and decline. In S. Wright and H. Kelly-Holmes (eds) *One Country, Two Systems, Three Languages* (pp. 60–73). Clevedon: Multilingual Matters.

Joseph, J.E. (2004) *Language and Identity: National, Ethnic, Religious.* Basingstoke: Palgrave Macmillan.

Kaldor, M. (1999) Transnational civil society. In T. Dunne and N. Wheeler (eds) *Human Rights in Global Politics.* Cambridge: Cambridge University Press.

Kennedy, K. (ed.) (1997) *Citizenship Education and the Modern State.* London: Falmer.

Kennedy, K.J. (2004) Searching for citizenship values in an uncertain global environment. In W.O. Lee, D. Grossman, K. Kennedy and G. Fairbrother (eds) *Citizenship Education in Asia and the Pacific. Concepts and Issues.* Hong Kong: Comparative Education Research Centre and Kluwer Academic.

Kennedy, K.J. and Fairbrother, G. (2004) Asian perspectives on citizenship education: Postcolonial constructions or precolonial values? In W.O. Lee, D. Grossman, K. Kennedy and G. Fairbrother (eds) *Citizenship Education in Asia and the Pacific. Concepts and Issues.* Hong Kong: Comparative Education Research Centre and Kluwer Academic.

Kerr, D. (1999a) Changing the political culture: The Advisory Group on Education for Citizenship and the Teaching of Democracy in Schools. *Oxford Review of Education* 25 (1–2), 275–284.

Kerr, D. (1999b) Citizenship education: An international comparison. In D. Lawton, J. Cairns and R. Gardner (eds) *Education for Citizenship* (pp. 200–227). London: Continuum.

Kerr, D. (1999c) Citizenship education: An international comparison. On WWW at http://www.inca.org.uk/pdf/citizenship_no_intro.pdf. Accessed 9.2.05.

Kockel, U. and Craith, M.N. (eds) (2004) *Communicating Culture.* Münster: Litt.

Koopmann, K. (2001) Amerika, hast Du's besser? Einige (Innen-)Ansichten über schulische politische Bildung in den USA. *Politische Bildung* 2, 125–147.

Kubow, P., Grossman, D. and Ninomiya, A. (1998) Multidimensional citizenship: Educational policy for the 21st century. In J.J. Cogan and R. Derricott (eds) *Citizenship for the 21st Century* (pp. 115–134). London: Kogan Page (new edition 2000).

Kubow, P., Grossman, D. and Ninomiya, A. (2000) Multidimensional citizenship: Educational policy for the 21st century. In J.J. Cogan and R. Derricott (eds) *Citizenship for the 21st Century* (pp. 131–150). London: Kogan Page Ltd.

Kwok, K.W. (2001) Singapore as cultural crucible: Releasing Singapore's creative energy in the new century. In G.B. Lee (ed.) *Singaporeans Exposed: Navigating the Ins and Outs of Globalisation* (pp. 21–32). Singapore: Singapore International Foundation.

Kymlicka, W. (2003) Multicultural states and intercultural citizens. *Theory and Research in Education* 1 (2), 147–169.

Kymlicka, W. and Norman, W. (eds) (2000) *Citizenship in Diverse Societies*. Oxford: Oxford University Press.

Lai, A.H. (1995) *Meanings of Multiethnicity: A Case-study of Ethnicity and Ethnic Relations in Singapore*. Kuala Lumpur: Oxford University Press.

Lai, M.L. (2001) Hong Kong students' attitudes towards Cantonese, Putonghua and English after the change of sovereignty. *Journal of Multilingual and Multicultural Development* 22 (2), 112–113.

Lam, A.S.L. (1994) Language education in Hong Kong and Singapore: a comparative study of the role of English. In T. Kandiah and J. Kwan-Terry (eds) *English and Language Planning: A Southeast Asian Contribution* (pp. 182–196). Singapore: Centre for Advanced Studies, National University of Singapore.

Lam, N.M.K. (2000) Government intervention in the economy: A comparative analysis of Singapore and Hong Kong. *Public Administration and Development* 20, 397–421. On WWW at www.olemiss.edu/courses/ pol387/lam00.pdf. Accessed 9.2.05.

Lanehart, S.L. (1996) The language of identity. *Journal of English Linguistics* 24 (4), 322–331.

Lantolf, J.P. (ed.) (2000) *Sociocultural Theory and Second Language Learning*. Oxford: Oxford University Press.

Lardy, N.R. (2002) *Integrating China into the Global Economy*. Washington, D.C.: Brookings Institution Press.

Law, W.W. (2004) Globalisation and citizenship education in Hong Kong. *Comparative Education Review* 48 (3), 253–273.

Lawton, D., Cairns, J. and Gardner, R. (eds) (2000) *Education for Citizenship*. London: Continuum.

Le Page, R.B. and Tabouret-Keller, A. (1985) *Acts of Identity: Creole-Based Approaches to Language and Ethnicity*. Cambridge; New York: Cambridge University Press.

Lee, G.B. (2001) From the ground up. In G.B. Lee (ed.) *Singaporeans Exposed: Navigating the Ins and Outs of Globalisation* (pp. 152–159). Singapore: Singapore International Foundation.

Lee, H.L. (1997) The rationale for national education: Speech by Deputy Prime Minister Lee Hsien Loong at the launch of National Education, 17.5.97. On WWW at http://www.moe.gov.sg/ne/keyspeeches/may17-97.htm. Accessed 9.2.05.

Lee, H.L. (1999) *Reforming Singapore's Financial Services Sector: A Background & Progress Report*. On WWW at http://singapore.usembassy.gov/ep/1999/ finance.html. Accessed 9.2.05.

Lee, W.O. (2001) The emerging concepts of citizenship in the Asian context: Some reflections. Key note presentation at the International Forum on New Citizenship, Hong Kong: Institute of Education.

Lee, W.O. (2003) Civic education before and after 1997: Some reflections from social capital perspectives. *Journal of Youth Studies* 6 (1), 112–125. (In Chinese)

Lee, W.O. (2004) Perceptions of citizenship qualities among Asian educational leaders. In W.O. Lee, D. Grossman, K. Kennedy and G. Fairbrother (eds) *Citizenship Education in Asia and the Pacific: Concepts and Issues*. Comparative Education Research Centre, University of Hong Kong. Hong Kong: Kluwer Academic Publishers.

Lee, W.O. and Constas, M. (1996) IEA second civic education study: Case study report. Unpublished Phase One Report submitted to IEA. Amsterdam: IEA.

Lee, W.O., Grossman, D., Kennedy, K. and Fairbrother, G. (eds) (2004) *Citizenship Education in Asia and the Pacific. Concepts and Issues.* Comparative Education Research Centre, University of Hong Kong. Hong Kong: Kluwer Academic Publishers.

Leite, C.M.F. (2002) A política da diferença na reforma curricular. In *O Currículo e o Multiculturalismo no Sistema Educativo Português* (pp. 283–332). Lisboa: Fundação Calouste Gulbenkian/Fundação para a Ciência e Tecnologia.

Leung, S.W. (1995) Depoliticisation and trivialisation of civic education in secondary schools: institutional constraints on promoting civic education in transitional Hong Kong. In P.K. Siu and P.T.K. Tam (eds) *Quality in Education: Insights from Different Perspectives* (pp. 283–312). Hong Kong: Hong Kong Educational Research Association.

Leung, S.W. (1999) Social construction of Hong Kong identity: A partial account. In S.K. Lau, M.K. Lee, S.L. Wong and P.S. Wan (eds) *Indicators of Social Development: Hong Kong 1997* (pp. 111–134). Hong Kong: Hong Kong Institute of Asia-Pacific Studies, The Chinese University of Hong Kong.

Leung, Y.W. (2003) Harmony of conflict: The role of nationalistic education within civic education in Hong Kong. Unpublished Ph.D. Thesis, University of Sydney.

Levinson, S.C. (1997) From outer to inner space: Linguistic categories and non-linguistic thinking. In S. Nuyts and E. Pedersen (eds) *Language and Conceptualization.* Cambridge: Cambridge University Press.

Lewis, C. (1995) *Educating Hearts and Minds.* Cambridge: Cambridge University Press.

Li, D.C.S. (1996) *Issues in Bilingualism and Biculturalism: A Hong Kong Case Study.* New York: Peter Lang Publishing.

Li, D.C.S. (2002) Cantonese–English code-switching research in Hong Kong: A survey of recent research. In K. Bolton (ed.) *Hong Kong English: Autonomy and Creativity* (pp. 79–99). Hong Kong: Hong Kong University Press.

Li, D.H. (2001) Tan Gongmin Jiaoyu [On citizenship education]. *Kaifang Shidai* [*Open Era*] 9, 113–117.

Li, P. and Zhong, M.H. (2002) Gongmin Jiaoyu: Chuantong deyu de lishixing zhuanxing [Citizenship education: Historical transition of moral education reform]. *Jiao Yu Yan Jiu* [*Educational Research*] 23 (10), 66–69.

Li, Z.Z. (2000) Jiaoyu yu Renquan [Education and human rights]. *Jinan, Xuebao* [*Jinan Journal*] 22 (2), 9–14.

Lin, A.M.Y. (1996) Bilingualism or linguistic segregation? Symbolic domination, resistance and code switching in Hong Kong schools. *Linguistics and Education* 8, 49–84.

Lin, P. and Liu X.Q. (1998) Lun Bandula de Shehui Xuexi Lilun yu Woguo de Jiaoyu Jiaoxue Gaige [On Bandura's social learning theory and the reform of our education practice]. *Sichuan Sifan Daxue Xuebao* [*Journal of Sichuan Normal University*] 25 (3), 103–110.

Liu, J.Z. (2003) Tiyan: Daode Jiaoyu de Benti [Experience: The base of moral education]. *Jiao Yu Yan Jiu* [*Educational Research*] 24 (2), 53–59.

Lloyd, G.E.R. (2002) *The Ambitions of Curiosity. Understanding the World in Ancient Greece and China.* Cambridge: Cambridge University Press.

Lo, L. and Man, S.W. (1996) Introduction: Nurturing the moral citizen of the future. In L. Lo and S.W. Man (eds) *Research and Endeavours in Moral and Civic Education* (pp. ix–xxix). Hong Kong: HKIER.

Lockyer, A, Crick, B. and Annette, J. (eds) (2004) *Education for Democratic Citizenship. Issues of Theory and Practice*. Hants: Ashgate Publishing

Lu, J. (1999) Zouxiang shijie lishi de ren [People striding towards world history]. *Jiao Yu Yan Jiu [Educational Research]* 20 (11), 3–10.

Lu, J. (2003) Huigui Shenghuo [Returning to real life]. *Kecheng, Jiaocai, Jiaofa [Curriculum, Teaching Material, Methodology]* 9, 2–9.

Luke, K.K. (2003) Why two languages might be better than one: Motivations of language mixing in Hong Kong. In M. Pennington (ed.) *Language in Hong Kong at Century's End* (pp. 145–159). Hong Kong: Hong Kong University Press.

Lyas, C. (1997) *Aesthetics*. London: University College London Press.

Ma, E.K.W. (1999) *Culture, Politics and Television in Hong Kong*. London: Routledge.

Mach, Z. (2001) Politics, culture and identity of the Polish people after 1989. In J. Purchla (ed.) *From the World of Borders to the World of Horizons* (pp. 246–255). Cracow: International Cultural Centre.

Machiavelli, N. (1513) *The Prince*. London: Penguin.

Mao Zedong (1977) *Mao Zedong Xuanji, De We Juan [Selected works of Mao Zedong]*, Vol.5. Beijing: Renmin Chubanshi [People's Press].

Marshall, T.H. (1950) *Citizenship and Social Class, and Other Essays*. Cambridge: Cambridge University Press.

Marshall, T.H. (1977) *Class, Citizenship and Social Development*. Chicago: University of Chicago Press.

Marshall, T.H. (1981) *The Right to Welfare and other Essays*. London: Heinemann.

Massing, P. and Weißeno, G. (eds) (1995) *Politik als Kern der politischen Bildung. Wege zur Überwindung unpolitischen Unterrichts*. Opladen: Leske & Budrich.

Matesanz, J., Moralejo, P., Varela, L., Grence, T., Fernández, V. and Perales, A. (2000) *Mundos. Geografía e Historia 1er Curso ESO*. Madrid: Grazalema S.A/ Grupo Santillana de Ediciones, S.A.

Maxwell, K. (1995) *The Making of Portuguese Democracy*. Cambridge: Cambridge University Press.

McConnell, J. (2000) Language, identity and the Asian crisis: Is English causing an identity crisis? In W. Jung and X.B. Li (eds) *Asia's Crisis and New Paradigm* (pp. 139–148). Lanham, MD: University Press of America.

McDonough, K. and Feinberg, W. (2003) *Education and Citizenship in Liberal-Democratic Societies. Teaching for Cosmopolitan Values and Collective Identities*. Oxford: Oxford University Press.

McLaren, P. and Pruyn, M. (1996) Indoctrination. In J.J. Chambliss (ed.) *Philosophy of Education: An Encyclopedia*. New York and London: Garland.

McVeigh, B. (2004) *Nationalisms of Japan: Managing and Mystifying Identity*. Lanham: Rowman and Littlefield.

MEC (1970) Ley 14/1970, de 4 de agosto, Ley General de Educación y Financiamiento de la Reforma Educativa, con la modificación establecida por Ley 30/1976, de 2 de agosto.

MEC (1985) Ley 8/1985 de 3 de julio de 1985 – Ley Orgánica del Derecho a la Educación.

MEC (1990) Ley 1/1990 de 3 de Octubre de 1990 – Ley Orgánica de Ordenación General del Sistema Educativo.

MEC (1993) *Temas Transversales y Educación en Valores*. Madrid: Ministerio de Educación y Ciencia.

MEC (2002) Ley 10/2002, de 23 de diciembre, de Calidad de la Educación.

Meierkord, C. (2002) Language stripped bare' or 'linguistic *masala*'? Culture in *lingua franca* communication. In K. Knapp and C. Meierkord (eds) *Lingua Franca Communication*. Frankfurt a. M.: Peter Lang.

Mendes, M.M. (2004) As Faces de Janus: As políticas educativas em matéria de cidadania nos anos 90 em Portugal. Unpublished master's thesis. Lisboa: Universidade Lusófona de Humanidades e Tecnologias.

Meng, Z.Z. (1999) Renquan wenti shi xingshiqi sixiang zhengzhi jiaoyu de zhongyao neiyong [Human rights is a key area for ideological political education in the new era]. *Sixiang Lilun Jiaoyu Daokan [Journal of Ideological and Theoretical Education]* 8, 61–63.

Midgley, M. (2003) *The Myths we Live By*. London: Routledge.

Milroy, J. and Milroy, L. (1985) *Authority in Language: Investigating Language Prescription and Standardisation*. London, Boston and Henley: Routledge & Kegan Paul.

Ministério da Educação (2001a) *Education for Democratic Citizenship: Final Report of the Portuguese Group involved in the Council of Europe Project*. Lisboa: Council of Europe, Ministério da Educação.

Ministério da Educação (2001b) *Citizenship Education: Cursos gerais e cursos tecnológicos*. Lisboa: Council of Europe, Ministério da Educação.

Ministry of Education (2000a) Desired Outcomes of Education. Singapore. On WWW at http://www1.moe.edu.sg/desired.htm. Accessed 9.2.05.

Ministry of Education (2000b) Civics and moral education syllabus: Primary School. Singapore. On WWW at http://www.moe.gov.sg/cpdd/syllabuses.htm. Accessed 9.2.05.

Ministry of Education (2000c) Civics and moral education syllabus: Secondary school, Singapore. On WWW at http://www.moe.gov.sg/cpdd/syllabuses.htm. Accessed 9.2.05.

Ministry of Education (2000d) Civics syllabus for junior colleges and centralised institutes, Singapore. On WWW at http://www.moe.gov.sg/cpdd/syllabuses. htm. Accessed 9.2.05.

Modelski, G. (ed.) (1987) *Exploring Long Cycles*. London: Francês Pinter.

Monbukagakusho [Ministry of Education, Culture, Sports, Science and Technology] (2003a) *Shougakkou gakushuu shidou youryou (heisei 10nen 12gatsu kokuji, heisei 15nen 12gatsu ichibu kaisei)* [Curriculum guidelines for elementary school (announced in December 1998, partially amended in December 2003)]. Tokyo: Monbukagakusho.

Monbukagakusho [Ministry of Education, Culture, Sports, Science and Technology] (2003b) *Chuugakkou gakushuu shidou youryou (heisei 10nen 12gatsu kokuji, heisei 15nen 12gatsu ichibu kaisei)* [Curriculum guidelines for junior high school (announced in December 1998, partially amended in December 2003)]. Tokyo: Monbukagakusho.

Monbukagakusho [Ministry of Education, Culture, Sports, Science and Technology] (2004) *Shougakkou gakushuu shidou youryou kaisetsu: sousokuhen (heisei 11nen 5gatsu, heisei 16nen 3gatsu ichibu hotei)* [Commentary on curriculum guidelines for elementary school: general rules (announced in May 1999, partially revised in March 2004)]. Tokyo: Monbukagakusho.

Monbusho [Ministry of Education, Culture, Sports, Science and Technology] (1999) *Shougakkou gakushuu shidou youryou kaisetsu: shakaihen* [Commentary on elementary school guidelines: social studies]. Tokyo: Monbusho.

Montro, J.R., Gunther, R. and Torcal, M. (1998) Actitudes hacia la democracia en España: Legitimidad, descontento y desafección. *Reis* 83, 9–49.

Moody, A.J. (1997) The status of language change in Hong Kong English. Unpublished Doctoral Dissertation, University of Kansas.

Morán, M.L. and Benedicto, J. (1995) *La Cultura Política de los Españoles. Un Ensayo de Interpretación*. Madrid: Centro de Investigaciones Sociológicas.

Muñoz Cruz, H. (2001) *Politicas y Practicas Educativas y LingUIstica en Regiones Indigenas de Mexico*. Seminario sobre Politicas Educativas y Linguisticas en México y Latinoamericas, UNESCO, Mexico City, Mexico, 10–12 December 2001.

Murphy-Shigematsu, S. (2004) Expanding the borders of the nation: Ethnic diversity and citizenship education in Japan. In J. Banks (ed.) *Diversity and Citizenship Education: Global Perspectives*. San Francisco: Jossey-Bass.

Nai, C.X. (1995) Shehui Xuexi Lilun Guanyu Deyu Xingli de Yanjiu [A study of moral psychology in social learning theories]. *Fujian Shifan Daxue Xuebao [Journal of Fujian Normal University]* 3, 111–119.

Nathan, A.J. (1985) *Chinese Democracy*. New York: Alfred A. Knopf.

Naval, C., Print, M. and Iriarte, C. (2003) Civic education in Spain: A critical review of policy. *Online Journal of Social Science Education*. On WWW at http://www.sowi-onlinejournal.de/2003-2/spain_naval.htm. Accessed 02.04.

Navarro Sustaeta, P. and Díaz Martínez, C. (2002) *Ética 4 ESO*. Madrid: Grupo Anaya S.A.

Nikitorowicz, J. (1999) Projektowanie edukacji miedzykulturowej w perspektywie demokratyzacji i integracji europejskiej. In J. Nikitorowicz and M. Sobecki (eds) *Edukacja miedzykulturowa w wymiarze instytucjonalnym* (pp. 25–32). Bialystok: Trans Humana.

Norton, B. (1997) Language, identity, and the ownership of English. *TESOL Quarterly* 31 (3), 409–429.

Norton, B. (2000) *Identity and Language Learning: Gender, Ethnicity and Educational Change*. Harlow, England; New York: Longman.

Nussbaum, M. (1997) *Cultivating Humanity*. Cambridge, MA: Harvard University Press.

Oguma, E. (1995) Tan'itsu minzoku shinwa no kigen [*The Myth of the Homogenous Nation*]. Tokyo: Shinyousha.

Okano, K. and Tsuchiya, M. (1999) *Education in Contemporary Japan: Inequality and Diversity*. Cambridge: Cambridge University Press.

Oldfield, A. (1990) *Citizenship and Community: Civic Republicanism and the Modern World*. London: Routledge.

Ong, T.C. and Moral Education Committee (1979) *Report on Moral Education 1979*. Singapore: Singapore National Printers.

Osler, A. (ed.) (2003) *Citizenship and Democracy in Schools: Diversity, Identity, Equality*. London: Trentham.

Osler, A. and Starkey, H. (2003) Learning for cosmopolitan citizenship: Theoretical debates and young people's experiences. *Educational Review* 55 (3), 243–254.

Osler, A. and Vincent, K. (2002) *Citizenship and the Challenge of Global Education.* Stoke on Trent: Trentham.

Ota, H. (2000) *Nyuukamaa no kodomo to nihon no gakkou [Newcomer Children in Japanese Public Schools].* Tokyo: Kokusai shoin.

Pan, L.Y. (2004) Gaoxiao Zhutixing Daode Jiaoyu Moshi Tantao [An evaluation of subjective moral education models for tertiary students]. *Xiandai Daixue Jiaoyu [Contemporary University Education]* 2, 75–78.

Pan, Y.K. (2001) Yige jidai jiejue de wenti [A dilemma awaiting a solution]. *Guangxi Jiaoyu Xueyuan Xuebao [Journal of Guangxi Normal University]* 5, 44–47.

Parker, W.C. (2003) *Teaching Democracy. Unity and Diversity in Public Schools.* New York: Teachers College Press.

Parmenter, L. (1997) Becoming international in a Japanese junior high school: An ethnographic study. Unpublished PhD thesis, University of Durham, UK.

Parmenter, L. (2004) Shaping cultural identities: The roles of education and media on young Japanese people's views of themselves in the world. Presentation given at the ICRN (Intercultural Research Network) biennial conference, Florence, July 2004.

Parmenter, L., Lam, C., Seto, F. and Tomita, Y. (2000) Locating self in the world: Elementary school children in Japan, Macau and Hong Kong. *Compare* 30 (2), 133–144.

Parry, G. (2004) Two dilemmas of citizenship education in pluralist societies. In A. Lockyer, B. Crick and J. Annette (eds) *Education for Democratic Citizenship. Issues of Theory and Practice.* Hants: Ashgate Publishing.

Patrick, J.J. (2003) *Essential Elements of Education for Democracy. What are They and Why should They be at the Core of the Curriculum in Schools.* Calabasas: Center of Civic Education.

Pawełczyk, P. (2001) Polska w Europie'. In S. Wojciechowski (ed.) *Polska wobec Unii Europejskiej* (pp. 39–45). Poznan: Wydawnictwo Naukowe INPiD UAM.

Pearce, N. and Hallgarten, J. (eds) (2000) *Tomorrow's Citizens. Critical Debates in Citizenship and Education.* London: IPPR.

Pennington, M.C. (1994) *Forces Shaping a Dual Code Society: An Interpretive Review of the Literature on Language Use and Language Attitudes in Hong Kong.* Hong Kong: Department of English, City Polytechnic of Hong Kong.

Pennington, M.C. (1998a) Colonialism's aftermath in Asia: A snapshot view of bilingualism in Hong Kong. *Hong Kong Journal of Applied Linguistics* 3 (1), 1–16.

Pennington, M.C. (1998b) Introduction: Perspectives on language in Hong Kong at century's end. In M.C. Pennington (ed.) *Language in Hong Kong at Century's End* (pp. 3–40). Hong Kong: Hong Kong University Press.

Poon, S. (2003) Colonialism and English education at the University of Hong Kong, 1913–1964. Unpublished M.Phil. Dissertation, University of Hong Kong.

Potter, J. (2002) *Active Citizenship in Schools.* London: Kogan Page.

Prawelska-Skrzypek, G. (2001) Aktywność obywatelska jako reakcja na problemy społeczne w Polsce okresu transformacji. In M. Warowicki and Z. Woźniak (eds) *Aktywność obywatelska w rozwoju społeczności lokalnej: Od komunikacji do współpracy* (pp. 40–43). Warszawa: Municipium S.A.

Preuss, U.K., Everson, M., Koening-Archibugi, M. and Lefebvre, E. (2003) Traditions of citizenship in the European Union. *Citizenship Studies* 7 (1), 3–14.

Print, M. (1997) Phoenix or shooting star? Citizen education in Australia. In K. Kennedy (ed.) *Citizenship Education and the Modern State* (pp. 126–136). London: Falmer.

Quesel, C. (2003) Perspektiven politischer Bildung in England. *Zeitschrift für Politik* 50 (3), 335–348.

Rankin, M.B. (1993) Some observations on a Chinese public sphere. *Modern China* 19 (2), 158–182.

Reed, G.G. (1996) The multiple dimensions of a unidimensional role model: Lei Feng. In L. Lo and S.W. Man (eds) *Research and Endeavours in Moral and Civic Education* (pp. 245–262). Hong Kong: HKIER.

Remaking Singapore (2003) *The Report of the Remaking Singapore Committee: Changing Mindsets, Deepening Relationships*. On WWW at http://www.remakingsingapore.gov.sg/. Accessed 9.2.05.

Roberts, G. (2002) Political education in Germany. *Parliamentary Affairs* 55, 556–568.

Saénz-López Buñuel, P. Temas transversals. On WWW at http://www.uhu.es/65111/temas_transversales.htm. Accessed 2.04 and 5.06.

Sánchez, J., Santacana, J., Zaragoza, G. and Zárate, A. (2002) *Ciencias Sociales, Geografía e Historia. Milenio Andalucía 1 Secundaria*. Madrid: Ediciones SM.

Sander, W. (2001) *Politik entdecken: Freiheit leben*. Schwalbach/Ts: Wochenschau.

Sander, W. (2003) *Politik in der Schule. Kleine Geschichte der politischen Bildung*. Marburg: Schüren.

Santos, B.S. (1994) *Pela Mão de Alice: O social e o político na pós-modernidade*. Porto: Edições Afrontamento.

Santos, B.S. (1995) *Towards a New Common Sense: Law, Science and Politics in the Paradigmatic Transition*. London: Routledge.

Santos, B.S. (2001) Entre Prospero e Caliban: Colonialismo, pós-colonialismo e inter-identidade. In M.I. Ramalho and A.S. Ribeiro (orgs.) *Entre ser e estar: Raízes, percursos e discursos da identidade* (pp. 23–85). Porto: Afrontamento.

Santos, B.S. (2004) Do Pós-moderno ao Pós-colonial. E para Além de Um e Outro. Opening lecture at the VIII Luso-Afro-Brasilian Congress, Coimbra, 16 September. On WWW at http://www.ces.uc.pt/misc/Do_pos-moderno_ao_-pos-colonial.pdf. Accessed 20.9.04.

Santos, B.S. and Nunes, J.A. (2004) Introduction: Democracy, participation and grassroot movements in contemporary Portugal. *South European Society & Politics* 9 (2), 1–15.

Schiele, S. and Schneider, H. (eds) (1987) *Konsens und Dissens in der politischen Bildung*. Stuttgart: Metzler.

Sehr, D.T. (1997) *Education for Public Democracy*. Albany: State University of New York Press.

Shan, Y. (2003) Zhengzhi Jiaoyu: Cong Guanshu dao Duihua [Political education: From indoctrination to dialogue]. *Beijing Qingnian Zhengzhi Xueyuan Xuebao* [*Journal of Beijing Youth Politics College*] 12 (3), 26–29 and 57.

Shen, S.C. and Chien, S.Y.-S. (1999) Delimiting China: Discourses of Kuomin and the construction of Chinese nationality in the late Ching. Paper presented at the Conference on Nationalism: East Asia Experience on 25–27 May, ISSP Academia Sinica, Taipei.

Shu, R.J. and Tang W.J. (2003) Jianzemin dui Jiaoyu Fangzheng de Lunshu Tanxi [An analysis of Jiang Zeming's views on guiding principles of education]. *Zejiang Jiaoyu Xueyuan Xuebao [Journal of Zejiang Educational Institute]* 2, 1–5.

Singapore 21 (2003) Report of the Singapore 21 Committee: Together we make the difference. On WWW at http://www.singapore21.org.sg/menu_menu_5keys_active.html. Accessed 9.2.05.

Singapore Government Press Release (1997) Speech by Deputy Prime Minister Lee Hsien Loong at the launch of National Education. On WWW at http://stars.nhb.gov.sg/public/index.html. Accessed 9.2.05.

Singstat (2000) Vol. 2004, Singapore Department of Statistics.

Skeie, G. (2003) Nationalism, religiosity and citizenship in Norwegian majority and minority discourses. In R. Jackson (ed.) *International Perspectives on Citizenship, Education and Religious Diversity*. London: RoutledgeFalmer.

Sliwka, A. (2001) *Demokratie lernen und leben. Bd. II.: Das anglo-amerikanische Beispiel*. Weinheim: Freudenberg.

Smith, A. (2001) *Nationalism*. Cambridge: Polity Press.

Snow, D. (2004) *Cantonese as Written Language: The Growth of a Written Chinese Vernacular*. Hong Kong: Hong Kong University Press.

Soder, R., Goodlad, J.I. and McMannon, T.J. (eds) (2001) *Developing Democratic Character in the Young*. San Francisco: Jossey-Bass.

Sokolewicz, Z. (1997) Citizenship, nationality, and the civil society. In Z. Mach and D. Niedźwiedzki (ed.) *European Enlargement and Identity* (pp. 103–25). Kraków: Universitas.

Soros, G. (2000) *World Forum on Democracy*. http://www.batory.org.pl/english/events/wfd/soros.htm. Accessed 10.8.04.

Soysal, Y.N. (1996) Changing citizenship in Europe. Remarks on postnational membership and the national state. In D. Cesarani and M. Fullbrook (eds) *Citizenship, Nationality and Migration in Europe* (pp. 19–29). London; New York: Routledge.

Spiro, M.E. (1984) Some reflections on cultural determinism and relativism with special reference to emotion and reason. In R.A. Shweder and R.A. LeVine (eds) *Culture Theory. Essays on Mind, Self and Emotion*. Cambridge: Cambridge University Press.

Starkey, H. (2002) *Democratic Citizenship, Languages, Diversity and Human Rights*. Strasbourg: Council of Europe.

Stevenson, N. (2003) *Cultural Citizenship: Cosmopolitan Questions*. Maidenhead: Open University Press.

Sułek, A. (2004) Zly czas dla Judymow. *Gazeta Wyborcza* (7 September 2004), 17.

Sun, W.X. (2003) Duoyuan wenhua kechengguan xiade xingkecheng [New curricula at the influence of development of multicultural education curriculum]. *Dangdai Jiaoyu Luntan [Forum of Contemporary Education]* 7, 94–96.

Sünker, H., Szell, G. and Farnen, R.F. (eds) (2003) *Political Socialisation, Participation and Education. Change of Epoch: Processes of Democratisation*. Frankfurt: Peter Lang.

Teodoro, A. (2001) Organizações internacionais e políticas educativas nacionais: A emergência de novas formas de regulação transnacional, ou uma globalização de baixa intensidade. In S.R. Stoer, L. Cortesão and J.A. Correia (eds)

Transnacionalização da Educação: Da crise da educação à "educação" da crise (pp. 125–161). Porto: Edições Afrontamento.

The Constitution of the People's Republic of China (1982) Beijing: Foreign Languages Press.

The Education Law of the People's Republic of China (1995). On WWW at http://www.edu.cn/20050105/3125921.shtml.

Thomas, H. (2001) A European citizen – myth, sham or reality? In R. Fearey and G. Kolankiewicz (eds) *Europe 2021. Beyond Visible and Invisible Borders*. Report of a conference organised by the British Council and co-hosted by the British Council and the International Cultural Centre, Krakow, Poland, April 2001 (pp. 54–57). London: The British Council and the Slavonic and East European Studies University College London.

Thomson, D. (1995) Language, identity, and the nationalist impulse: Quebec. *The Annals of the American Academy* 538, 69–82.

Tilgham, B. (1991) *Wittgenstein, Ethics and Aesthetics*. New York State: University of New York Press.

Tsang, E. (2000) Student reflection: Fostering learning and writing. In L.Y.O. Mak and M.M.L. Keung (eds) *Changing Languages: Language Education in the Era of Transition* (pp. 128–144). Hong Kong: Language Centre, The Hong Kong University of Science and Technology; Shanghai: School of Foreign Languages, Shanghai Jiaotong University.

Tsang, W.K. (1998) Patronage, domestication or empowerment? Citizenship development and citizenship education in Hong Kong. In O. Ichilove (ed.) *Citizenship and Citizenship Education in a Changing World* (pp. 222–253). London; Portland, OR: Woburn Press.

Tsang, W.K. and Wong, M. (2004) Constructing a shared Hong Kong identity in comic discourse. *Perspectives: Working Papers in English and Communication* 16 (1), 74–100.

Tse, A. (1992) Some observations on code-switching between Cantonese and English in Hong Kong. *Working Papers in Languages and Linguistics* 4, 101–108. Department of Chinese, Translation and Linguistics, City University of Hong Kong.

T'sou, B.K. (1985) Chinese and the cultural eunuch syndrome. In R. Lord and B.K. T'sou (eds) *The Language Bomb* (pp. 15–19). Hong Kong: Longman.

Tuvilla Rayo, J. (2000) Reformas educativas, transversalidad y derechos humanos. On WWW at http://www.eip-cifedhop.org/espagnol/dosieres/tuvilla5.htm. Accessed 2.04.

United Nations Committee on the Elimination of Racial Discrimination (CERD) (2001) *Concluding Observations of the Committee on the Elimination of Racial Discrimination: Japan 27/04/2001*. On WWW at http://www.unhchr.ch/tbs/doc.nsf/(Symbol)/3e6a558a36a4639ac1256a170050a380?Opendocument. Accessed 23.4.05.

Usui, Y. and Shibata, Y. (1999) *Shakai/chireki/kouminka kyouikuhou* [*Methods of Education: Social Studies, Geography, History and Civic Education*]. Tokyo: Gakumonsha.

Wan, M.G. (2003) Lun Gongmin Jiaoyu [On citizenship education]. *Jiao Yu Yan Jiu* [*Educational Research*] 24 (9), 37–43.

Wan, M.G. and Wang, W.L. (2003) Quanqiuhua Beijingzhong de Gongmin yu Gongmin Jiaoyu [Citizenship and citizenship education in the backdrop of globalisation]. *Xibei Shida Xuebao* [*Journal of Northwest Normal University*] 40 (1), 75–79.

Wang, C.M. (2002) Lun Daode Guanshu [On moral indoctrination]. *Chuzhou Shizhuan Xuebao* [*Journal of Chuzhou Teacher's College*] 4 (4), 35–38.

Wang, G. (1987) Language policy and planning in bilingual Hong Kong. In Hong Kong University Student Union (ed.) *A Comprehensive Review of Hong Kong Educational System* (pp. 7–11). Hong Kong: Jin Lin Publisher. (in Chinese)

Wang, J. (1995) Xifan duowenhua jiaoyu yu woguo minzu jiaoyu zhi bijiao yanjiu [A comparative study on western multicultural education and minority education in our country]. *Xibei Shifan Daxue Xuebao* [*Journal of Northwest Normal University*] 32 (3), 91–94.

Wang, J. (2002). Lun Zhonghua Minzu Duoyuan Wenhua Jiaoyu [On multicultural education for China]. *Qinghai Minzu Yanjiu* [*Nationalities Research in Qinghai*] 13 (2), 52–56.

Wang, L.Y. (2003) Shilun Mao Zedong de Bangyang Jiaoyu [A discussion on Mao Zedong's role model education]. *Mao Zedong Sixiang Yanjiu* [*Mao Zedong Thought Study*] 20 (6), 28–30.

Wang, X. (1998) Daode Jiaoyuzhong Guanshu de Shizhi Jiqi Gengyuan [Fundamental nature and origin of indoctrination in moral education]. *Jiaoyu Pinglun* [*Education Commentary*] 2, 28–29.

Wang, X.F. (2002) Xuexiao Gongmin Jiaoyu: Suozao Gongmin Daode de Bixiuke [Citizenship education: The obligatory subject for constructing civic morals]. *Sixiang, Lilun, Jiaoyu* [*Ideology, Theory and Education*] 3, 3–6.

Ward, I. (1999) Shakespeare and the Politics of Community. *Early Modern Literary Studies* 43 (2), 1–45.

Wardhaugh, R. (1987) *Languages in Competition: Dominance, Diversity, and Decline.* Oxford, New York: B. Blackwell; London: A. Deutsch.

White, J. (1996) Education and nationality. *Journal of Philosophy of Education* 30 (3), 327–344.

Williams, K. (2002) The limits of aesthetic separatism. *Westminster Studies in Education* 25 (2), 163–173.

Winch, P. (1964) Understanding a primitive society. *American Philosophical Quarterly* 1 (4), 307–324.

Wittgenstein, L. (1953) *Philosophical Investigations.* Oxford: Basil Blackwell.

Wong, R.B. (1999) Citizenship in Chinese history. In M. Hanagan and C. Tilly (eds) *Extending Citizenship, Reconfiguring States* (pp. 97–122). Lanham, MD: Rowman and Littlefield.

Wong, T.H. (2002) *Hegemonies Compared: State Formation and Chinese School Politics in Postwar Singapore and Hong Kong.* New York: RoutledgeFalmer.

Wringe, C. (1992) The ambiguities of education for active citizenship. *Journal of Philosophy of Education* 26 (1), 29–38.

Wu, FH. (2003) A study of written Cantonese and Hong Kong culture: The development of Cantonese dialect literature before and after the change of sovereignty. Unpublished MA Dissertation, University of Hong Kong.

Xiang, J.Y. (2003) Lun Shixiang Daode Jiaoyu Jiazhi de Shixian Tujing [On the means to realise the value of moral education]. *Jiao Yu Yan Jiu* [*Educational Research*] 24 (10), 46–51.

Xiao, C. (1999) Zhutixing Daode Renge Jiaoyu: Gainian yu Tezheng [Moral and character education with students as subject: Concepts and features]. *Beijing Shifan Daxue Xuebao* [*Journal of Beijing Normal University*] 3, 23–28.

Xing, Z.Y. (2002) Guanyu woguo duowenhua jiaoyu yanjiu cunzai de wenti yu sikao [A reflection on the problems of multicultural education in our country]. *Guizhou Shifan Daxue Xuebao* [*Journal of Guizhou Normal University*] 3, 94–97.

Yang, C.M. (2001) Gongmin daode jianshe de jichu – Yide zhijiao [The foundation of citizenship construction – Teaching with morals]. *Renmin Jiaoyu* 12: 8–9.

Yao, X. (2000) *An Introduction to Confucianism.* Cambridge: Cambridge University Press.

Yau, S.C. (1992) Language policies in post-1997 Hong Kong. In K.K. Luke (ed.) *Into the Twenty-First Century: Issues of Language and Education in Hong Kong* (pp. 15–29). Hong Kong: Linguistic Society of Hong Kong.

Yip, S.K., Eng, S.P. and Yap, Y.C. (1997) 25 years of educational reform. In J. Tan, S. Gopinathan and W.K. Ho (eds) *Education in Singapore: A Book of Readings* (pp. 3–32). Singapore: Prentice Hall.

Yiu, W.O. (March, 2002) Anti-intellectual culture in Hong Kong media. *Media Digest.* Hong Kong: Radio Television Hong Kong. On WWW at http://www.rthk.org.hk/mediadigest. Accessed 11.5.06.

Yoder, R.S. (2004) *Youth Deviance in Japan.* Melbourne: Trans Pacific Press.

Yu, X.Z. (2002) Citizenship, ideology, and the PRC constitution. In M. Goldman and E.J. Perry (eds) *Changing Meanings of Citizenship in Modern China* (pp. 288–307). Cambridge, MA: Harvard University Press.

Zamora Fortuny, B. (2003) Andando no siempre se hace el camino. La paradoja entre la formación y el rol del profesorado en la legislación educativa en España. X Conferencia de Sociología de la Educación. On WWW at http://www.uv.es/~jbeltran/ase/textos/zamora.pdf. Accessed 02.04.

Zarate, G. (2003) Identités et plurilinguisme: conditions préalables à la reconnaissance des compétences interculturelles. In M. Byram (ed.) *La Compétence interculturelle.* Strasbourg: Conseil de l'Europe.

Zarate, G. and Gohard-Radenkovic, A. (eds) (2004) *La Reconnaissance des competences interculturelles: De la grille à la carte.* Paris: Didier.

Zarrow, P. (1997) Citizenship in China and the West. In J.A. Fogel and P. Zarrow (eds) *Imagining the People* (pp. 3–38). Armonk, NY: M.E. Sharpe.

Zhan, W.S. and Xu, J.Z. (2002) Shehui zhuanxin shiqi xuexiao deyu de fansi yu goujian [Rethink about the structure of moral education in the period of social transition]. *Jiao Yu Yan Jiu* [*Educational Research*] 23 (9), 3–8.

Zhang, P. (2002) Aiguo zhuyi jiaoyu de sixiang chuangxing [Ideological innovation for education in patriotism]. *Jiao Yu Yan Jiu* [*Educational Research*] 23 (12), 11–15, 32.

Zhang, X. (2003) Gongzhong canyu yu mingzhu jiaoyu [Public participation and democratic education]. *Jiaoyu Kexue Yanjiu* [*Education Science Research*] 5, 20–22.

Zhang, X.Y. (2003) Cong qianrang yu chengshi tanqi: Fansi dangdai zhongxiaoxue deyu jiaoyu [Forbearance and honesty: A reflection on moral education in primary and secondary schools]. *Jiaoyu Kexue Yanjiu* [*Educational Science Research*] 4, 40–42.

Zhao, H. (2003) Dangdai shijie gongmin jiaoyu linian de kaocha [A general review of the conceptions of citizenship education in the world]. *Waiguo Jiaoyu Yanjiu* [*Studies in Foreign Education*] 30 (9), 25–30.

Zhonggong Jiaoyubu Dangzu Guanyu Jiaoyuzhanxian Xuexi Guanzhe 'Gongmin Daode Jianshe Shishi Gangyao' de Tongzhi [Memorandum to all educational institutions on studying and implementing 'The Implementation Guidelines to Construct Civic Virtues of Citizens' by the Party Branch of the Ministry of Education] (15 November 2001) On WWW at www.moe.edu.cn. Accessed 20.2.03.